The Apocalypse:

The Revelation of the Redeemer

The Apocalypse:
The Revelation of the Redeemer

Expository Messages from Revelation

By
Dr. C. Randy White

E-BookTime, LLC
Montgomery, Alabama

The Apocalypse: The Revelation of the Redeemer
Expository Messages from Revelation

Copyright © 2007 by Dr. C. Randy White

All rights reserved. No part of this book may be reproduced or transmitted in any form or by any means, electronic or mechanical, including photocopying, recording, or by any information storage and retrieval system, without permission in writing from the copyright owner.

ISBN: 978-1-59824-425-0

First Edition
Published February 2007
E-BookTime, LLC
6598 Pumpkin Road
Montgomery, AL 36108
www.e-booktime.com

*This book is fondly dedicated to Margaret.
She has been not only my companion but also my
completer and the lady of my life.*

Contents

Preface ix

Introduction xi

The Revelation of the Redeemer 1:1-3 1
A Delightful Doxology 1:4-8 6
The Preacher and His Power 1:9-11 15
The Vision of the Victor 1:12-20 21
The Cooling Church 2:1-7 34
The Committed Church 2:8-11 39
The Compromising Church 2:12-17 45
The Corrupt Church 2:18-29 50
The Corpse-Like Church 3:1-6 55
The Conquering Church 3:7-13 59
The Counterfeit Church 3:14-23 63
Come…Up 4:1-3 and 10-11 68
Beholding the Throne 4:4-9 73
When the Search Concludes 5:1-14 80
The Horsemen Are Coming 6:1-8 91
The Price of Commitment and the Failure to Do So 6:9-17 100
Who will Be Saved in the Tribulation 7:1-17 109
Why Heaven was Silent 8:1-13 119
Something Like Hell on Earth 9:1-12 125
Just when You Think it Can't Get Any Worse 9:12-21 131
The Angels' Announcement and Assignment 10:1-11 138
God's Last Call 11:1-19 146
The Woman, War and Woe 12:1-17 156
The Beast 13:1-10 168
The Second Beast…The False Prophet 13:11-18 177
A Preview of Victory 14:1-11 183
The Winepress of God's Wrath 14:12-20 193
The Next Step is Judgment 15:1-8 200
God's Final Fury 16:1-21 207
Mystery, Babylon 17:1-18 217
The Destruction of Babylon 18:1-24 226

Contents

Christ Coming for His Church 19:1-8 239
The Marriage Supper 19:7-10 244
The Revelation of the Redeemer 19:11-21 247
Reigning with the Redeemer 20:1-10 252
The Great White Throne Judgment 20:11-15 258
What is New 21:1-22:5 263
What to do Till Jesus Comes 22:6-21 273

Bibliography 283

Preface

The contents of these pages are not intended as a scholarly theological treatment of the text; they were originally messages delivered to the congregation of Trinity Baptist Church. For this reason you will encounter the words "I" and "you" as well as "I believe" throughout the pages. They have been revised somewhat and I have sought to give due credit to those from whom I have gleaned. In an article by Becky Badry in *Facts and Trends* the story is told that the governor of North Carolina once complimented Thomas Edison on his inventive genius, but Edison denied that he was a great inventor. "But you have over a thousand patents to your credit, haven't you?" asked the governor. "Yes," replied Edison, "but my only original invention is the phonograph. I guess I'm an awfully good sponge. I absorb ideas from every source I can, put them to practical use, and improve on them until they become of some value. The ideas are mostly those of others who don't develop them themselves." Edison would be described as "adaptively creative." This is what I have sought to do in putting these messages in print. They are the product of 40 years of study; research and I hope personal growth in understanding.

Dr. C. Randy White, Executive Director of Missions
New South River Baptist Association

Introduction

The book of Revelation is one of the most *neglected* and *controversial* in the entire Word of God. Many have *abandoned* it while others have *abused* it by making playground for their religious imaginations. The various viewpoints of different writers make this book one of the most difficult to interpret. One said of this book, *"This study finds a mad man or leaves him mad."* Luther would have denied it a place in the N.T. He declared that it contained only images and visions that are found nowhere else in the Bible. He said, *"Christ is neither taught nor acknowledged."* Zwingli said, *"We have no concern for it, it is not a Biblical book."* Due to the vast difference of opinion man has attempted to do with this book the very thing that God, in the book, told him not to do, namely, *"Seal not the sayings of the prophecy of this book for the time is at hand"* (Rev. 22:10).

There are four things we should consider in the introduction of this book that will assist us as we seek to understand its meaning and message.

First we will observe the:

I: BACKGOUND! A good understanding of the background is essential as well as helping us appreciate and apply the message of Revelation to our individual hearts in an hour of darkness and despair. There are two things we should note in this regard. First,

A: IT'S LOCATION! Revelation is the union station of the Bible. All the trains come into the station in Revelation. There is no reason why we should not be able to pull all our thinking about the Bible together here in this book. *This is the book of consummation*; thus it is fitting that it should have been assigned the last place in the Bible. One careful reading of the Bible will convince anyone that this volume forms a complete cycle. For a

Introduction

moment we will compare the book of Genesis and the book of Revelation.

Genesis is the book of commencement; Revelation is the book of consummation. Revelation is an excellent finish to the Divine library. Dr. Lehman Strauss has it this way:

In Genesis we have the commencement of heaven and earth. (1:1)
In Revelation we have the consummation of heaven and earth. (21:1)
In Genesis we have the entrance of sin and the curse. (3:1-19)
In Revelation we have the end of sin and the curse. (21:27)
In Genesis we have the dawn of Satan and his activities. (3:1-7)
In Revelation we have the doom of Satan and his activities. (20:10)
In Genesis the tree of life is relinquished. (2:9 and 3:24)
In Revelation the tree of life is regained. (22:2)
In Genesis death makes its entrance. (2:17)
In Revelation death makes its exit. (21:4)
In Genesis sorrow begins. (3:16)
In Revelation sorrow is banished. (21:4)

Revelation brings to a close all things that were begun or prophesied in the other 65 books of the Bible. Without the book of Revelation we would be left in doubt about the outcome of all the things prophesied. Its location is last, but not last in importance. Secondly we have:

B: IT'S LANGUAGE! Judging by the way many people read this book; one could easily be lead to believe that it had never been translated from its original Greek language. Note carefully two things about its language. First, its language is:

1. Symbolic! That means that this book has in it symbols that have another meaning. That raises the issue as to why? At least a partial answer is that when this book was written the Christians were suffering severe persecution at the hands of the Roman emperor Domitian (A.D. 81-96). If the message had been

Introduction

written in a simple, easy to understand language, the Christians would have suffered all the more. Many things were yet to come to pass. In addition, suppose someone had tried to tell you about a nuclear explosion 200 years ago. The symbols remain the same. Words change in their meaning but not symbols.

We should not allow this to disturb us, when another meaning is called for the book itself will tell us. For example read chapter 1:10, *"A great voice, as of a trumpet,"* it was not a trumpet but as a trumpet. Another is chapter 4:1, *"After this I look and, behold, a door was opened in heaven and the first voice when I heard was as it were of a trumpet talking with me."* We know that a trumpet does not talk that it is symbolic. When you read, *"As it were"* take note that it is symbolic. Usually the symbolic interpretation is given in the book itself, if it is not there it will be found in the book of Daniel or one of the other prophetic books of the Old Testament. Second, the language is:

2. Simple! There is a simple, sound rule of Biblical interpretation, let the Bible mean what it says, and unless it indicates that something else is implied. Further, there is the rule of *"first use."* When a problem arises go to the first use of the word in the Bible. Be sure it is the first use in Greek. When you read the Gospels you do not come away with doubts about what has been said, neither should we leave this book with doubts as to its meaning and message. Secondly, let us consider the:

II: BOOK! The Revelation is a book, written by in large in symbolic language, but a book for this present generation. There are two thoughts we should keep in mind about this book. First, I will mention its:

A: INSPIRATION! If this book is in fact a book for us, and if it is a book that we should understand, then it must have the same inspiration as the other 65 books of the Bible. Does it? There are degrees of inspiration but not in the Bible. This book is a part of the divinely inspired Word of God as chapter 1:10-11 reveals. John was in the Spirit and heard behind him a great voice saying, *"Write."* In addition each of the letters to the churches ends by saying *"Let him hear what the Spirit saith unto the churches."* Thus this book has the same human author as does the

Introduction

Gospel of John, 1,11, and 111 John. You do not read a section of the Gospel and wonder what the message and meaning is normally, neither should you with this book that has the same human author. It is inspired, and the One that inspired it is capable of giving to us its meaning as easy as any other section of Scripture. In the face of this fact this book is almost ignored in many circles. Secondly we mention its:

B: INTERPRETATION! Can this book be interpreted? The book can be understood if a person does not seek to make it say something that it does not say. Another problem with many is they simply do not know some basic rules of interpretation. In order to help us I will present several schools of interpretation. The first school is:

1. The Preterits! There are people chiefly concerned with the past. In the strict meaning of the term these say that the prophecies in the book have all been fulfilled in the past. They do not see any prophecies in the book having to do with the Second Coming of Jesus Christ. Secondly,

2. The Presentests! This is one who views the events in Revelation, not as actual events, but rather as an expression of those principles and forces active in any age. Thus, according to them their fulfillment may be repeated over and over in history. The third school is:

3. The Prophetic! These hold that the largest portion of the book is prophetic, and it applies to a period still future. Everything from the 4th chapter to the end of the book is still future, and will follow the removal of he church from the earth at the coming of Christ in the air (1Thess. 4:16-17).

There are three schools of interpretation based upon the 20th chapter of the book. These three schools deal with the millennium. The millennium is the thousand-year reign referred to six times in this chapter. The first of these schools is the:

(a) Present Millennialism! Or Amillennialism. This group holds to the literal coming of Christ, but it spiritualizes the thousand years. This group says that we are now living in the reign of Christ by His Spirit. There is some merit in that in the hearts of individuals that are submitted to Him, but His enemies are not under His feet at this time. These also declare that Satan is

Introduction

bound; yet the Bible says that he is the god of this world. The second school of interpretation is:

(b) Postmillennialism! This group does not deny the literal coming of Christ nor the thousand years reign. But they say that the kingdom is going to be ushered in by the preaching of the gospel. This group holds that man will bring in the kingdom through his own efforts. The third school is the:

(c) Premillennialism! This school takes the position that Revelation 20 must be interpreted literally. The thousand years are treated as a thousand years. This group believes that Christ will come back to the earth at the close of Daniel's 70th week, before the millennium. There can be no kingdom on earth until Christ, the King, returns and Satan is removed from the earth. This, I believe to be the true Biblical position. Thirdly we now note the:

III: BEATITUDES! No book in the entire Bible has an introduction and conclusion quite like this one. It commences with a promised blessing, and closes with a promised blessing. The word *"Blessed"* has the same meaning here as it does in the Sermon on the Mount. It really means "Happy." We will briefly mention the beatitudes of this book. First we have:

A: THE BLESSED CHALLENGE! Chapter 1:3, *"Blessed is he that readeth."* This is contrary to everything that most people know or believe about the book. It means to have the book taught, to have an understanding of what the book teaches. Thus we are challenged to study this book, to grasp its meaning, to seek to comprehend those things that are set forth therein. Secondly we have:

B: THE BLESSED COMFORT! Chapter 14:13, *"Blessed are the dead."* That does not make a great deal of sense does it? But there is more. *"That die in the Lord."* That one little word, "In" makes all the difference in the earth. This is one of the greatest means of comfort to be found in the entire Bible. We know that one gets *"In"* the Lord only by the new birth. Thirdly we have:

C: THE BLESSED CAUTIOUSNESS! Chapter 16:15, *"Blessed is he that watcheth and keepeth his garments."* The

Introduction

keeping of the garments clean is based upon watching with caution. Why should we be cautious? It is so easy to get our garments dirty in this world. We must be on guard against Satan and his plots to contaminate us with the filth of this earth. This can only be done as we watch with our spiritual eyes opened to the leadership of the Lord. Fourth we have:

D: THE BLESSED CALLING! Chapter 19:9, *"Blessed are they which are called unto the marriage supper."* The called are the Old Testament Saints, those that died before the church was founded. Jesus said of John the Baptist (Matthew 11:11) that there has never been a greater than John. But He added that the least in the kingdom was greater than him. Is this a contradiction? No! John died before the church was established; therefore, all those that are privileged to be a part of the church are greater than he is. But John will be among those called to the marriage supper of the Lamb. Fifth we have:

E: THE BLESSED CONQUEST! Chapter 20:6, *"Blessed... shall reign with Him a thousand years."* These are reigning with Him because He ruled over them in this life. In this connection please study the story given by our Lord in the Gospel of Luke chapter 19. There Jesus said to the faithful servant, *"Have authority over ten cities."* This is, I believe, a reference to His reigning over the earth. However, the citizens that refused to have Him reign over them were cast out. Sixth we have:

F: THE BLESSED CHERISHING! Chapter 22:7, *"Blessed is he that keepeth the sayings of this book."* This is surely a reference to our hiding His Words in our hearts, and living them in our lives. Before we can keep the sayings of this Book, we must have an understanding of what those saying are. We must inform ourselves by prayerful study of His Word. How much time do we devote to real Bible study each day? We will never experience a real revival in our day until there is a return to His Word. Seventh we have:

G: THE BLESSED CONFORMITY! Chapter 22:14, *"Blessed are they that do His commandments...right to the tree of life."* Keeping His commandments is a reference to conforming to His likeness. This is just the opposite of being conformed to this world. When we are conformed to His likeness it means that He is

Introduction

being formed in us, that we are allowing Him to guide and govern our lives to the extent that He is being seen by the world. The fourth area of help is the:

IV: BREAKDOWN! Chapter 1:19 This verse is the key to this book, it gives us God's order of the events. The breakdown involves three areas. But before we consider the breakdown note an outline of dispensations that is necessary. **First,** *there is the age of the Gentiles.* This age covers two thousand years, from Adam to Abraham. This is recorded in Genesis chapters 1-11. Here we have one nationality, one race, and one language. **Second,** *there is the age of the Jews or Israel.* This also covers two thousand years, from Abraham to Christ. Here we have many races, languages and nationalities. **Third,** *there is the age of the Church.* This age will last until the Church is completed. The length of this age is not known. At the end of this age Jesus will come for His completed Church, then the age will turn again to the Jews. God promised them 490 years, but that was cut short by the cross, they only received 483 years. These seven years will be given to the nation of Israel, this is called the tribulation and it will be the last seven years of the 490 years. It is with these seven years that the book of Revelation devotes most of its space. Now we come to the breakdown. First, we have the:

    A: PAST! *"The things which thou hast seen"* these words refer to the vision of the Glorified Christ, which was just given to John; this is chapter one. It is of the uppermost importance that we do not place things that belong in the past in the future. Second, we have the:

    B: PRESENT! *"The things which are"* these words refer to the letters to the seven churches in chapters 2 and 3. Here we have the history of the church pre-written from Pentecost to the rapture. These were literal churches, but they are also representative of church history. These were not the only churches in Asia Minor at this time. There were churches at Colossae, Hierapolis, and Troas. These churches were selected because they hand in them problems that would be representative of the history of the church age. Third we have the:

Introduction

C: PROPHETIC! *"The things which shall be hereafter"* this comprises chapters 4-22. Chapter 4 begins with our Lord's words, *"Come up hither, and I will shew thee things which must be hereafter."* Everything in the book from chapter 4 to the end will occur after the church is taken out of the earth. The church does not appear again until she comes with Christ in chapter 19. This does not mean that the world has not experienced some of these things on a much smaller scale, but those things were only a type of the actual events that are forthcoming to the earth during the time of Jacob's trouble.

This breakdown is clear, it does not overlap, hold to it, and you will not go astray. Do not at any time lift events from one division to another. It will only confuse the events.

The Revelation of the Redeemer
Revelation 1:1-3

We are embarking upon a very exciting journey. It will be essential that we allow the Holy Spirit to be our Instructor. Our responsibility is to have opened yet hungry hearts in order that the Spirit of God may interpret to us His Word. One thing is or should be clear to us; namely, that the Lord is seeking to enable us to make a difference in our world and in the world to come for the vast host that do not know Jesus. This is or will be done, as we better understand the Person of Jesus Christ as He is presented to us in the pages of the Revelation. This book will reveal to us the urgency of our sharing our faith as we behold the events that will transpire after He comes for His church.

There are three thoughts that we want to observe in the first three verses. This is foundational to understanding the first three chapters and an understanding of these chapters is essential to understanding the remainder of the book. First, we note:

I: THE REVELATION! Verse 1 declares, *"The Revelation of Jesus Christ."* Note that it is singular, not plural. There is one Revelation of which there are many scenes. The word, *"Revelation"* in the Greek is *"Apokalupis,"* from which we get our English word, *"Apocalypse."* The meaning is to unveil, present, to uncover, and a manifestation. Thus the Revelation is a presentation, a manifestation and an uncovering. This is in contrast to the apocryphal or something hidden, concealed or not authentic. In the Catholic Bible there are 14 books between Malachi and Matthew. These are called the apocryphal. All one need do is read these and it will be evident that they are not on the same spiritual level as Scripture. They are what are called, *"Spurious."* There are several things to consider in verse one. First,

A: THE PERSON! Verse 1 states this clearly in the words *"The Revelation of Jesus Christ."* This is the *title* of the book. And as such it is one of the primary keys of the book. This is true because the book is a revelation of a Person and not a program. This is also the *theme* of the entire book. The Person of Jesus Christ is presented to us in the Revelation in ways that we have not encountered in any book. We are reading and studying about the Person of Jesus Christ especially as it relates to that day of His future administration in the earth. There are many subordinate themes (the tribulation, the antichrist, and countless others) but each of these themes reveals an aspect of the Person of Christ and His dealing with mankind in the future. The Revelation is the presentation of the Lord Jesus Christ to mortal view in all His glory. Secondly,

B: THE PRESENTER! Verse 1, *"Which God gave unto Him."* The presenter is God the Father. The Revelation is a gift given by God the Father to His Son. It can be said that this is a full and final revelation; there is nothing to add to what is given by the Father to the Son. This was done because the Lord Jesus voluntarily accepted the mediatorial office of sacrifice. He willingly took upon Himself the form of man, poured out His life, paid the ultimate price for sin with His blood and the Father is giving Him this full and final revelation. Thirdly,

C: THE PURPOSE! Verse 1, *"To show unto His servant."* If we did not have the Revelation we would have a very limited conception of how our Lord is going to deal with the earth. The purpose of the Revelation is to, *"Show unto His servants things which must shortly come to pass."* He is going to show His servants. The Greek word is *"dulos,"* those that are bondservants of God. Perhaps the problem in understanding the Revelation lies in the fact that He reveals it to those that are His surrendered servants.

Observe that the word, *"Must"* is used. This indicates that it is a necessity. We believe in the, "Must of the new birth," i.e., it is not an optional matter if one is going to have a relationship with God. The same is true of Revelation 1:1, *"These things must"* we know that it is necessary. Further, God will do all that is necessary for this to come to pass. There is another word in verse

The Apocalypse: The Revelation of the Redeemer

1 that calls for our examination. That is, *"Shortly."* The Greek word is *en tachei,* which is an adjective denoting swiftness. We have developed our word, *"Tachometer"* from this word. This is an instrument for measuring velocity. The argument of many is that this was written about 96 A. D. and we are living in the 21st century; therefore it cannot be literal. The word means *"speedily"* and declares that when these things begin to come to pass they will come to pass speedily. The purpose is to show to us beforehand those things that when they start to happen will happen speedily. We should be challenged to do all within our power to rescue the fallen for when these things begin to come to pass our opportunity will have expired. Fourthly,

D: THE PLAN! Verse 1, *"And signified it by His angel."* We are not interested in seeking to discover who this angel was. What we do know is that the things that were going to come to pass were passed before John's sight and hearing. We also know that John was a personal witness of those things that he penned. How that happened we do not know. It could have been in a similar fashion as that of the temptation of our Lord when He was shown the kingdoms of this world.

The word, *"Signified"* can be spelled with a hyphen so it reads as *sign-ified.* This is what we have in the book. Some of the things sign-ified are people and some are places. The antichrist is symbolized as a beast and both a religious and political movement. We can understand something of this plan by looking at one verse. Chapter 4 verse 3 is very helpful. The *jasper* is our diamond. It speaks to us of the *clearness, purity,* and the *holiness of God.* The *sardine* stone is our ruby. This reveals to us the *atonement in the cross* by its color. The *rainbow* represents our *covenant keeping God.* The *emerald* is green, which speaks of our *every living hope.* All of this is sign-ified. The plan of the Revelation is to present the Person and purpose of the Revelation in such a manner that its message and meaning will not be lost. Fifthly,

E: PENMAN! Verse 1, *"Unto His servant John."* This is the one that heard John the Baptist say, *"Behold the Lamb of God"* and followed Jesus. He was a fisherman until he was called to be a follower; he was of the inner circle of Peter, James and John. He was designated as a, *"Servant;"* one that was surrendered to the Lord. The point is that the Lord uses those individuals that will allow the Holy Spirit to use them. John was such a person. Secondly,

II: THE RECORD! Verse 2, *"Who bare record."* This word can also be translated as *witness*. He bears record of three things. First,

    A: THE SCRIPTURE! Verse 2, *"...record of the Word of God."* This expression is used five times in the book, and it underlines the uniqueness of the communication that John received from the Lord Jesus. I am also told that it stands for a prophetic message. This is a message that is yet to happen. I further believe that John is declaring that he stands upon the Scripture as being true, trustworthy and tried. Where do we stand? When we stand upon the Scripture we are standing on a solid foundation. Secondly,

    B: THE SAVIOR! Verse 2, *"And of the testimony of Jesus Christ."* These two things (Scripture and Savior) are in agreement. There is no contradiction. It would be marvelous if that were true of His people, i.e., our testimony and the Scripture were in accord. Thirdly,

    C: THE SIGHT! Verse 2, *"Of all things that he saw."* What is being recorded is what he saw and heard and it is recorded for our benefit. His imagination does not replace inspiration. The record is one that we can depend upon. Thirdly,

III: THE REWARD! Verse 3, This is the most unusual book in the entire Bible in that it commences and concludes with a promise. The reward referred to in this verse is three-fold. First, it is for:

    A: THE READER! Verse 3, *"Blessed is he that readeth."* This indicates the one reading in the synagogue, or better the one that studies and seeks to apply the message of the Revelation to his heart. I have known individuals that would drive a hundred miles to hear a "name brand preacher" but would not walk across the room, pick up the book and read for themselves what the Lord has to say to them. Why is there a blessing to the reader? It

The Apocalypse: The Revelation of the Redeemer

presents Christ in all His purity and power. Moreover, when we see Him, as He is our life will be enriched. Secondly, it is for:

B: THE RECIPIENT! Verse 3, *"And they that hear the words of this prophecy."* The recipient's responsibility is to hear and to keep. Keeping is based upon hearing. We will not keep what we do not hear. Note that it does not say, "And they that understand all things that are written therein." But they that hear and keep, that is guard and watch those things. There is a tremendous responsibility that rest upon the hearer. Eight times in this book we are admonished in this book to hear. Hearing refers to spiritual ears to hear in order to heed those things that are written in the prophecy. Thirdly, there must be:

C: THE READINESS! Verse 3, *"The time is at hand."* This is more accurately translated as, *"The season is near."* When the season draws near we will be able to see those things that are leading up to the coming of the Lord. We do not know if the coming of Christ is immediate but it is imminent. His coming may be this evening or five years but the fact is that He is coming and we are challenged to be about His business now.

Conclusion:
There are some key words used in these three verses that should be applied to us. One of those words is *"Servant."* That indicates surrender to the Savior that has priority over everything else. Does that designate you? Another word is *"Keepeth."* That indicates that we are acting upon what we know. Is that true of you? A final word is *"The season is near."* Jesus is coming and it may be today or tomorrow, but He is coming. Our challenge is to be prepared to meet Him should He come now.

A Delightful Doxology
Revelation 1:4-8

The Revelation ushers us promptly into the presence of God. The opening chapter is all about God and particularly about God the Son. We are brought face to face with deity. We are not dealing with the opinion of man. The course, character and the consummation of the age are seen in relationship to Him. God has no plan and no purpose for this planet that is not centered ultimately in His Son.

In verses 4-6 we are presented the first paean of praise. This is John's doxology; this is his dedication. It is to and for the Person of Jesus Christ. There are two thoughts in these verses that present a delightful doxology. First,

I: THE COMFORT OF THE SAINTS! Verses 4-6 In considering comfort it will be helpful to remember why comfort was needed by these saints. The saints of God were being persecuted and punished for their faith and faithfulness to the Father. Times were indeed difficult, yet in the midst of their trials John seeks to comfort these saints in a two-fold manner. First,

A: THE BLESSING TO THE SAINTS! Verses 4-5a The blessing to the saints is stated in the words, *"Grace be unto you and peace."* Some might suggest that theses are merely words of greeting, much like we would say, "Hello" or, "How are you." But there is more involved. John was writing during severe persecution, after his death there would come the Judaizers that would mix law and grace. These would say that the believers must go back to the Law of Moses. John uses these words to help establish them in the truth. Note two things. First,

1. The Substance of this Blessing! Verse 4, *"Grace be unto you and peace."* The entire fullness of the gospel, in its

The Apocalypse: The Revelation of the Redeemer

length, height, breath and debt are ours in His grace. This book deals primarily with judgment, yet God begins it with grace. In this book wicked men get richly deserved judgment from God, yet He begins it by telling men that they can have what they do not deserve; grace. Grace has been defined as God's Riches At Christ's Expense! This is grace that lifts, liberates and loves. This is grace that saves, sustains and satisfies. This is grace that enables you and me to be a part of the family of God. This is grace that takes something that is broken and of no real value, takes it to Calvary and makes something worthwhile out of it. I read the story of a little fellow that when to the milk store with a pitcher to buy milk. On his way home he fell and broke the pitcher. Mr. Morehouse tried to console the crying boy. After many attempts to fix the pitcher he picked the boy up, went to a crockery store, bought a new pitcher, went to the milk store; carried the boy and the pitcher to the steps of the boy's home and ask him if he thought his mother would whip him now. The little fellow said to the big preacher, "No sir, this is a better pitcher than the other one." That is what God's grace does for each one of us.

In the substance of the blessing there is also peace. Remember that the book deals with the opposite of peace; it deals with bloodshed, war, conflict and carnage. This book tells of the fall of empires, oppression and terror. But at the outset it mentions peace. What kind of peace is this referred to by John? It is peace founded upon the forgiveness of sins and the reconciliation of our souls unto God. It does not say, "Grace and happiness," but, "*Grace and peace.*" This is peace with God that was made possible at Calvary and the peace of God made possible by the indwelling of His Spirit. The child of God's peace is not determined by events from without, but his peace flows from within because it is based upon a relationship.

John knew that after his death the saints of God would face greater persecutions, therefore, they must know that His grace and peace are constantly with them, that they are a part of their very lives. A second thing to note about the blessing of the saints is:

    2. The Source of this Blessing! Verses 4b-5a This is a blessing that has as its source heaven. The source is actually three-fold. First, **it is from a Sovereign God!** Verse 4a, *"From His which is, and which was, and which is to come."* From the context this can be none other than God the Father. He is presented as the One that transcends all time. This reveals His Eternalness. He is the everlasting *"I Am."* He lives in the past, present and in the prospective tenses of time. He never changes, and He is not dependent upon time or place to be all that He is. It is possible that someone might argue that they could understand how He could be in the present and future but that He cannot be in the past. When we look up at the stars we are not seeing things as they are but as they were. If you were on the star Sirius, you could see what you were doing nine years ago. Thus, with God, every sin and evil thought we have had we are still doing and will continue to do apart from God's forgiveness. Second, it is from the **Spirit of God**. Verse 4, *"From the Seven Spirits which are before His throne."* This does not refer to angelic beings; this is from the Holy Spirit. The expression seven Spirits refers to the perfection of the Spirit's Person and plenitude of His power. He is before the throne. One cannot have a closer relationship or fellowship than His being in you. He is the executor of God's purpose. Isaiah 11:2 may be helpful to us here. He is the Spirit of the Lord, and wisdom, understanding, counsel, might, knowledge, and of the fear of the Lord. Thirdly, this blessing is from the **Son of God**. Verse 5 states it clearly, *"And from Jesus Christ."* There are descriptive notes given about Jesus that reveal His relationship with the present age. Note that **He is a Prophet**. Verse 5 declares that He is, *"Faithful witness."* He came to be a witness to a dark, degenerate world. As The Prophet He witnesses to the Name of God. The names of God reveal something of His character. Jesus, as the Prophet revealed a new name that we can know God by. That name is Father. In addition He reveals something of the nature of sin. There are fifteen words used in the New Testament to describe something of sin. If you desire to see sin at its height go to the cross. As a prophet He revealed sin for what it is and He brought the good news of salvation. Secondly, **He is a Priest**. Verse 5 states, *"First begotten from the dead."* The word *"First"* is used to inform us of the priority of the order of things. The firstborn received a double portion. Verse six shares with us what that double portion was in the words, *"Glory and dominion."* He is the leader of all who will rise through Him to everlasting life. He rose to the position of priest. He is our only priest after the order of Melchisedec. He intercedes for us at the right hand of the Father. We do not need another to mediate for us with God. Thirdly, **He is a Potentate**; verse 5, *"Prince of the kings of the earth."* Prince informs us that He is the ruler. His humiliation is forever in the past. He is not a baby in a barn, but the soon ruler of the universe.

Secondly, in the comfort of the saints we have:

B: THE BENEDICTION TO THE SAVIOR! Verses 5b-6 The blessing has hardly been uttered when the saints respond with a grateful benediction to the Savior. Why? There are two answers. First,

1. Because of What He has Wrought! Verses 5-6 Some might ask what has Christ wrought, however the real question is what has He not wrought? These verses reveal three things He has wrought for us. First, **He has Loved us**, verse 5, *"Unto Him that loved us."* This is not to be understood as something in the past. It is in the present tense. It could be said, *"Loveth us."* We are prone to think of the love of God as reaching its height at Calvary and descending after that but that is not the case. We might be able to think of One having pity on us, but He loved us before we ever thought of loving Him. He loved us before we were ever washed, while we were foul and unclean. I heard about a missionary walking into a village that had been decimated by fire. As he walked around the chard ruins he saw the remains of a hen. He kicked the chard body and to his surprise from under the burned body of the mother hen came out her chicks. The love that Jesus has for us is like that mother hens only greater. It is saving love, as the mother hen gave her life to save her chicks even so Jesus gave His life to save us. It is also sheltering love. The mother hen sheltered the chicks from the fire and Jesus shelters us from the fires of this world. It is also sacrificing love. That mother hen sacrificed her life for that of her chicks. That is what Jesus did and continues to do for us. Secondly, **He has Liberated us**. Verse 5; *"Unto Him that washed us form our sins in His own blood."* This is a past action completed action with present results. The word, *"Washed"* is better translated as *"Loosed."* Observe a thrilling truth. It is His blood and it is He that does the washing. The blessing is that it is all Christ work. What can wash away my sin? Modern theology says a good life, or good works, no. It is His blood. Thirdly, **He has Lifted us**. Verse 6, *"And hath made us kings and priest unto God and His Father."* We have been lifted to the ministry of the priest. We are to represent God to man and man to God. The tragedy is that we glory in the doctrine but fail in the practice. If you have not been lifted, He has paid the price for you to experience liberation through His blood. Secondly,

    2. Because He is Worthy! Verse 6; *"To Him be glory and dominion for ever and ever."* This is the glory that He had before He came into this world and mankind will acknowledge His glory that one day. The dominion shall be His as well. He shall reign from the east to the west, to the ends of the earth. The dominion placed into the hands of Adam, lost by sin, shall be reigned over by Christ. He is worthy of the saints' benediction.

    We move from the Comfort to the Saints to:

II: COMING OF THE SAVIOR! Verses 7-8 When men write books of action and intrigue they build toward a dramatic conclusion. Men must keep the reader in suspense. The author must build up the tension, the mystery, the sense of impending doom, and he must prolong the suspense as long as possible. This is not the case with John. He is going to receive enough tension, mystery, and drama to write a dozen books and keep the readers in suspense to the last page, but that is not God's plan. The end is so wonderfully good that he cannot wait to tell it. He does so in the words of verse 7, *"Behold, He cometh."*

    The prophets looked forward to His first coming. Some of them saw His first coming while others saw His Second Coming and some were privileged to see them both. So marvelous is this message that one out of every twenty verses in the New Testament concerns the Second Coming of the Savior. That means that if all preaching were balanced that one message in six would deal with the Second Coming of the Savior.

The Apocalypse: The Revelation of the Redeemer

The coming of the Savior is the **challenge for our service**. Jesus said in Luke 19 that we are to *"Occupy till He comes."* The coming of the Savior is the **comfort of the saints**. Jesus said in John 14, *"If I go I will come again."* If this promise is removed from our faith all we have is a mutilated fragment and a maimed relic. There is no Christianity of this book apart from the exalted hope of the return of our Lord.

There are two thoughts presented to us about the coming of the Savior. First,

A: THE EVENTUAL TRIUMPH OF JESUS! Verse 7 Because I am using the word eventual triumph does not mean that He is not presently triumph. He has all the power now that He will ever have, but the day is coming when it will be demonstrated. The day is coming when this earth shall be His footstool. Before we consider this verse we should understand with clearness and certainty the Coming of Christ. His coming is in two parts. The first part of His Second Coming is private and it is called the rapture. This is His coming for His saints, and they rise to meet Him in the air. This is His thief like coming and it is shared in Revelation 3:3 and 16:15. The second part of His Second Coming is public. This is His coming with His saints and John says, *"That every eye shall see Him."* This is called the revelation. These two events are separated by seven years and prophecy must be kept in line or confusion will about. There are two truths shared in verse 7 that relate to the eventual triumph of Jesus at His coming. First,

1. It will be Visible! John says, *"Every eye shall see Him."* However, it does not say that everyone will see Him at the same time, in the same place, in the same manner, and with the same feeling. There will be some who see Him when He comes as a thief to steal away His jewels and others will see Him upon a throne in judgment. The visible return of the Savior speaks to us about *His personal appearance* in the words, *"He cometh."* Doesn't that remind you of the words in Acts 1:11, *"This same Jesus will come in like manner?"* We are told that every eye shall see Him, not every mind shall see Him. The reality is that we shall look upon Him with your eyes. Consider Job's words in chapter 19:25-27, *"I shall see God."* His visible coming also shares *His prophetic apparel* in the words, *"Behold He cometh with clouds."* The word, *"behold"* is used to secure attention, it indicates that something special is about to either be said or transpire. The clouds are the clothing of His glory; when He ascended clouds accompanied Him. When He comes for His saints and to battle beast He will be clothed with clouds.

There is an interesting phrase used in verse 7 that we should consider. Note that John says, *"Those that pierced Him."* Those that drove the nails in His hands, thrust the spear in His side, those that shared in that shameful scene, those that cried, "Crucify Him" shall one day confront Him face to face. John selected this group because he was there, he saw their fierce looks, beheld their hard, impenitent hearts, he saw their cruel hands, and witnessed their blasphemy and unbelief. These shall one-day look upon His face.

The eventual visible coming of the Savior reminds me of the historical account concerning Richard I, the Lionhearted. He was a respected and revered king of England. His nation was engaged in a war that took him away and in his absence England fell on bad times. A part of that was because his brother John decided that he would occupy the throne in the absence of Richard. He ruled to the ruin of England. The people prayed for soon return of their beloved king. In time Richard returned. Upon his arrival, without fear of reprisal he marched into the city and deposed his brother and resumed his rightful position as king. England was glad and rejoiced. This world has a usurper on the throne. It is the devil and he presently rules but when Jesus comes He will the enemy will be deposed and Jesus will reign over the world He created.

The question is not if you will see Jesus, but where will you see Him? Will it be in joy or judgment? Secondly, we note:

2. It will be Victorious! Verse 7, *"And all kindred of the earth shall wail because of Him, amen."* The word for kindred is tribe and many scholars believe that this refers to the fulfillment of Zechariah 12:10 when those of Israel wailed because of Him Whom they pierced. It also includes all the families of the earth, those that are impenitent because God's people have been removed.

The Apocalypse: The Revelation of the Redeemer

The word, *"wail"* in Greek means to *"cut."* Do you recall the account of Elijah and the false prophets of Baal? When their god did not answer they cut themselves. This is the scene presented to us in Revelation 6:14-17. In a moment how the earth changes from it's sinning into awful despair because of the horror of the judgment of God. I recall hearing that just before the Titanic hit that iceberg that the band was playing and the people were enjoying activities that were foreign to God, but soon the band was playing, "Nearer My God to Thee." How quickly devastation can come, the sad tragedy is that unless Jesus is your lifeboat you will be eternally lost!

Secondly we observe,

B: THE EVERLASTING TRIUMPH OF JESUS! Verse 8 His triumph will be complete and everlasting. Hitler said that his third Reich would last a thousand years. It lasted 148 months that is 12 and 1/3 years. Jesus will establish His kingdom and it will last a thousand years. Then it will be dissolved, not by decline or decay but because He wills it to be so. The everlasting triumph of Jesus is based upon three attributes of deity. First,

1. He is Omniscient! Verse 8, *"I am Alpha and Omega."* These are the first and last letters of the Greek alphabet. Letters are the means by which we store history. He is God's alphabet, the first and final source of knowledge, understanding, and wisdom. He is all knowing; He knows the end from the beginning. There is no hindsight with Him. Humankind has never surprised Him. I am sure that He has been disappointed and even embarrassed but never surprised. Secondly,

2. He is Omnipresent! Verse 8, *"I am the beginning and ending."* This is stated in terms of time. He was there when it started and He will be there when it ends. But there is more, He is there all the way through it! He is ever present. Matthew 28:20 assure us that He is among every company of believers. Thirdly,

3. He is Omnipotent! Verse 8, *"I am the Lord ...which is, was and is to come, the almighty."* This expression has already been used once in this chapter where it referred to God the Father; here it refers to God the Son. The word, *"almighty"* is used ten times in the New Testament and nine of those times is in

Revelation. God is sovereign. He does what He pleases. He does not need our permission to accomplish His purpose.

Conclusion:
The question is not "When is Jesus going to come again" but, "Am I prepared to meet Him should this be the time of His private coming for His saints?" Every one of us will see the Lord Jesus. It will be either in joy or in judgment. We make that decision now.

The Preacher and His Power
Revelation 1:9-11

We are approaching the first of many visions given in the Revelation. It is only fitting that the first vision be of the glorified Christ. We are about to see Christ as He is in all His glory. Yet, before we enter this portion of John's vision of the living Lord, it is appropriate that we sit with him on the isle of Patmos and hopefully enter into this wonderful experience with him. If we can join with John in these verses we shall be more excited when we enter into the vision of the Victor that John was being prepared to receive.

There are two thoughts given to us in these three verses that should challenge us to a closer more meaningful commitment to Christ. First we will note:

I: THE PREACHER! Verse 9 begins by stating simply, *"I John."* This is not intended as an introduction; twice already the writer has been identified (verse 1 and 4). Therefore, there must be more, and there is in the remaining portion of the verse. There are two things shared with us about John, the preacher. First we have:

A: HIS RELATIONSLHIP WITH THE SAINTS! Verse 9 states, *"Who also am your brother."* At this time John is the only living apostle. Yet, he did not feel that this gave him any special privilege. He did not view himself as a "super-saint." He simply refers to himself as *"Your brother."* Note that this word *"Brother"* signifies a relationship that is sure and not superficial. Remember the account in Acts 9 where Ananias said, *"Brother Saul;"* when one says *"Brother"* he is declaring that he is part of the same family. This is what John had already declared in his gospel that "As many as received Him, to them gave He power to become the sons of God." If we are sons of the same father we are brothers. This is biblical brotherhood and it is based solely upon one knowing Jesus as Lord. However, John goes further in describing his relationship with the saints. He tells us of two things that intensify this relationship. **First** in verse 9 he shares that he is a *companion in tribulation.* During the time of Johns writing the Christians were experiencing one of their most severe times of testing. The man responsible was Domitian. He was bloodthirsty and cruel. He was the first Roman Caesar to demand that all his subjects address him as "our lord and god." He was the first to make images of himself and place them in all places of worship and demand to be worshipped. In this respect he is a type of the anti-Christ. When John says that he is their companion in tribulation he is saying that he is a fellow sufferer of the same tribulation. He does not have sympathy but empathy. He is not in a high tower isolated from reality. The reference to tribulation is not to be understood as "The tribulation" that will be experienced by the ungodly masses of mankind that reject Christ. This tribulation will be a time of vengeance and the outpouring of the wrath of God.

Yet, the Bible states in John 16:33 that, *"In the world ye shall have tribulation."* Have you found that to be true? Acts 14:22 says *"We must through much tribulation enter the kingdom of God."* Then Romans 5:3 declares, *"Tribulation worketh patience."* Paul asks in Romans 8:35, *"Who shall separate us from the love of Christ? Shall tribulation?"*

Someone said that in the furnace of tribulation the holiness of our Lord is revealed to and through us. The believer shall not be present when "The tribulation" is experienced upon the earth but he is not exempt from severe times of testing. These as well as untold and unknown believers have and do suffer for their faith. It would have been easy for them to believe that they were suffering "The tribulation." As bad as their plight may be it is nothing to be compared with the outpouring of God's wrath recorded in the Revelation.

Secondly we have the *coming triumph* presented in the words, *"And in the Kingdom and patience of Jesus Christ."* The readers were aware that the prophets had made it clear that the

The Apocalypse: The Revelation of the Redeemer

Messiah would sit on the throne of David as King of the world. John is declaring that Kingdom is coming, be patient even in the midst of your present trials.

The present kingdom is spiritual, we are told in Romans 14:17 that *"The Kingdom of God is not meat and drink, but righteousness and peace and joy in the Holy Spirit."* However, when the church age is over He shall reign as King of kings and Lord of lords. Further, Revelation 11:15 tells us that the *"Kingdom of this world are become the Kingdom of our Lord and His Christ."*

When John referred to *"The kingdom and patience of Jesus Christ"* they would be assured of the coming triumph that they would be privileged to participate in with the Savior and all His saints.

Not only does the preacher share his relationship with the saints, he also tells us:

B: THE REASONS FOR HIS SENTENCE! Verse 9 John is now an aged apostle but he grows stronger under the persecution he experienced. The heathen leaders were aware of his tremendous influence. Their dilemma was in how to handle him so as to lessen and not expand that influence. Their decision was to exile him to the isle of Patmos rather than make him a martyr. But why; what was his crime? Was he a murderer, gangster, a drunkard, or traitor? No! He is sentenced because he is a faithful follower of Jesus. In this verse he shares two reasons for his sentence. The **first** was his *stand for the scriptures*. Listen to it in his words and hear what might appear to be a strange reason; he shares it was *"For the Word of God."* This is the Word of God in its larger context. John was wielding the sword of the scripture, and rather than compromise what the scripture said he was willing to give his life. We don't use the word "compromise" that much; rather we use the word "negotiate" to soothe our consciousness. We have negotiated our stand on the scripture. Some will argue but when we are selective in what we act upon have we not compromised that truth of the Word of God.

The **second** reason for his sentence was his *steadfastness for the Savior*. Verse 9 reveals this in the words, *"And for the testimony of Jesus Christ."* Stated simply John refused to bow to the images. He knew that Jesus had purchased him and that to bow to any image would mean that He was not sufficient for salvation or that he did not feel it necessary to worship only the Lord. Do you recall the three Hebrew men? They declared that they would not bow even if it meant their lives. For John to bow would have meant disaster for the Christian assembly. His shadow was indeed lengthy but so is yours. We are being observed by the world and I can assure us that the enemy has his images set up and the world is looking to see if we will bow. We must be steadfast for the Savior because what we do will influence what others do.

We move from the preacher to:

II: THE POWER! Verses 10-11 The power for any work that is going to succeed is that of the Savior transmitted through His saints by His Spirit. This is what is presented in verse 10. If the modern church and Christian could only grasp this dynamic truth that is stated in the Word that it is not *"By power or might, but by My Spirit saith the Lord"* we will be closer to recognizing our dependence upon God. There are two thoughts presented to us in these verses that can literally change our lives. First, John was:

A: ENGULFED BY THE SPIRIT! In verse 10 it is stated in these words, *"I was in the Spirit."* John is banished to the isle of Patmos yet the Spirit of God was present. This reveals to us that even though God was not the direct cause of John's circumstances that He uses them for His glory. This was true with Joseph and Daniel as well. In these cases the enemy hoped for one result but God changed their personal disappointments into an appointment with Him. If John had not been exiled to Patmos he probably would not have received the Revelation! Moses wrote the Pentateuch while in the wilderness; and David wrote many of the Psalms while fleeing from Saul. Scholars share that the Greek word for "was" is a word that means, "Came to be." There are those that believe that while John is on the isle of Patmos that he started feeling sorry for himself and got out of the will of God; that he said something like this, "God I have been faithful; I have stood in the gap and now I am forsaken;" and that he confessed and rebounded and was placed again in the will of God. Things

The Apocalypse: The Revelation of the Redeemer

like that do happen, however, I do not believe that was John's attitude. I feel that he was mediating upon His Lord; possibly even thinking of others that had faced greater crises and how mightily they were delivered. There are three things to note about his being engulfed by the Spirit. **First** we have *the testimony*. We are told that he was *"In the Spirit."* Is this a reference to being "Filled with the Spirit?" I think not, the filling of the Spirit is Him filling hearts that are obedient. John had been filled with the Spirit. A side note, Spirit-filled people are faithful, fruitful and followers. Here John declares, *"He was in the Spirit."* That is, the Spirit was in John and John was in the Spirit. The Spirit engulfed him! This is total control; his mind, heart, will and emotions were captured by Christ and enabled to receive the visions that followed. John was as close to being infallible in what he saw, heard and received as anyone could be and remain a mortal man. If you think I am going to far simply consider that this is what happened to Ezekiel (Ezekiel 2:2; 3:12, 14), and to Peter in Acts 10:10. This was the preparation necessary for him to receive the revelation that was forthcoming.

Secondly there is *the time*. John informs us that his transpired *"On the Lord's day."* This expression was commonly used to indicate the first day of the week; that is Sunday. It is my conviction that on the first day of the week John was engaged in worship, reflecting upon the Lord, and then he was transported to the "day of the Lord" that is recorded in the Revelation. Permit this query, would it make any difference in our services if we gathered "In the Spirit on the Lord's Day?" Surely it would impact how we live during the other days of the week.

Thirdly we have *the trumpet*. John declares that he heard *"A great voice as of a trumpet."* In order for John to hear he had to have spiritual ears. Only spiritual people have spiritual ears and thus are able to hear spiritual truth. He does not say it was a trumpet but it sounded like one to him. It was (verse 12) the voice of the Lord, but John does not realize that as yet. How many times is this true of you and me? The sounding of the trumpet had been important in the history of Israel. It was used to call an assembly, to announce the giving of the law and the year of jubilee. Temple worship began with the sounding of the trumpet.

It was used to make special announcements. It will be so when Jesus comes. It will be a piercing and penetrating sound, so much so that every person that has died in the faith will come forth when it sounds.

Secondly John was:

B: ENCOURAGED BY THE SPEAKER! Verse 11 The voice belongs to the Savior; it is a voice that John has not heard in about 50 years. The speaker encouraged John in a twofold manner. **First** *by what He says*, *"I am alpha and Omega, the first and last."* To whom is this referring? Simply trace it back and begin with verse 8, then 7, 6 and 5 and you will discover that it is the Lord Jesus. He was hearing from the eternal *"I Am."* He still speaks by His Spirit through the scriptures to our hearts.

Secondly the Speaker encourages John *by where He sends*, *"Unto the seven churches."* If these churches were to receive this Revelation then John would be encouraged that the church was going to be triumphant. These churches when followed form a candlestick or lampstand. The Speaker was encouraging John by assuring him that His church would continue until He came; that her light might grow dim but it would not go out.

Conclusion:
John was a man that yielded to the control of God in the Person of the Holy Spirit. He was not a super human; he experienced sufferings and disappointments. Yet, John was so yielded to God that he was useable. Suppose you came to the Lord's house next Sunday with a heart hungry to hear and heed His word to you…!

The Vision of the Victor
Revelation 1:12-20

John has identified himself as one with those that are suffering. He further states *"He was in the Spirit on the Lord's day."* At this time he was privileged to hear a voice speaking to him. The voice said, *"I am Alpha and Omega."* John is instructed to write what he has seen and send it to the seven churches. Naturally John wanted to see the One speaking, wouldn't you? This leads us to the first vision in the Revelation and it is only fitting that it be of the glorified Christ.

We must be careful in our generation when we speak of visions. This is a very subtle approach to leading individuals in a manner that ultimately results in them walking by sight and not by faith. Please do not misread that statement. I did not say that God cannot give visions for He is God and can do anything He chooses to do. It must be remembered that the enemy can duplicate many things that God does and he can give a vision if it will result in leading people astray from the Word of God.

I am not an Einstein but I can with absolute certainty assure you of this fact, no one will ever receive a vision from the Lord that contradicts His word.

Someone asked Charles Spurgeon what he would do if an angel appeared to him and told him something that was not in harmony with the character of God? Mr. Spurgeon said, "I would tell the angel 'I have a higher authority...the Word of God.'" There are two thoughts in these verses that can bless the heart. First,

I: THE VISION! Verses 12-16 Using the experience of John as our precedent it is safe to say that for any individual to have a vision from the Lord he must *"Be in the Spirit."* An aged pastor once shared that he encountered a man that talked about his vision from the Lord and how it had changed his life. The pastor then asks, "Where do you attend church?" The man replied, "I don't believe in going to church, I worship at all times and in all places." This same man was not a practicing steward; he never shared his faith with the lost and was critical of the people of God. It is my studied opinion that anyone that has a vision from the Lord will love the things that He loves and the Book shares that Jesus loved the church and gave Himself for her. In these verses John had a vision of two things. First, he had a vision of:

A: THE CHURCH! Verse 12 Does that strike you as odd? It should not, John says in verse 12, *"I saw seven golden candlesticks."* The word *"candlesticks"* is better translated as *"Lamp-stands."* We are told in verse 20 that the *"Lamp-stands are the churches."*

What is a (the) church? The Greek word is *"ekklesia."* It means the "called out." The church is that group of people whom the Spirit of God has called out of the world to be a witness to the world. What did John see in his vision about the church that we need to see? He saw two things. **First** he saw *the preciousness of the church.* This is revealed in verse 12. Observe the word *"Golden."* Gold is precious material. He saw gold, not tin, iron, bronze or scrape, but the most precious of all materials. This reveals how Christ values His people. They are valued as such because His blood has redeemed them, His Spirit indwells them, and they comprise His body. Further, they are His future bride. Yes, they are golden, precious. The church is a living organism established for the on going of the work of His kingdom in the earth. There is not a man made organization that can replace the ministry of His church.

The church is so precious to Him that she cannot be violated without the person touching His heart. You cannot love one and neglect the other, and you cannot support one and starve the other; you cannot cling to one and criticize the other. If you desire to be a part of the most exciting, precious thing in all the earth then be a part of the church of the Living Lord.

If the church is that precious to Jesus, she ought to be precious to us, and our membership ought to be more meaningful

The Apocalypse: The Revelation of the Redeemer

than having our name on a piece of paper. Since Christ shed His blood to purchase the church, she ought to be precious enough to you and me to live and support by our service.

Secondly we witness *the purpose of the church*. What is the primary purpose of the church? There are a number of secondary purposes of the church and each of them is important and will be fulfilled if the primary purpose is indeed primary. The primary purpose of the church can be seen in the word *"Lamp-stand."* The purpose of the lamp stand is simple, yet profound; it is to give light. The illustration of the lamp-stand comes from the tabernacle and the temple. There the priest trimmed the wick and supplied the oil to the seven pronged lamp-stand. Neither of these would have had any light if it had not been for the lamp-stand.

The church has no natural light of her own; the oil of the Spirit and the scriptures supplies her light. The light of the church is the reflected light of Jesus. Perhaps you remember having a "glow-in-the-dark" toy. If so you remember that the only way it could give light was for it to receive or absorb light. The same is true of us; we cannot reflect and radiate the light of the Lord until we have received His light. The purpose of the church is to reflect the light of her Lord. If she does this properly every other purpose will be successfully accomplished.

This is not the purpose of a selected group or a church here and one there. John saw *"Seven golden lamp-stands"* which indicates that this is the purpose of every church, the number seven being the number for completion. Therefore, any group that claims to be a church and does not reflect the light of the Lord is not a true church of Jesus Christ.

If the Lord is lifted His light will be seen and it will lead men from their darkness to His light; that is evangelism. If He is lighted He will lead men out of their ignorance; that is education. If the Lord is lifted His light will lead men from their despondency; that is edification.

In order to have adequate light the priest had to frequently trim the wick. The trimming of the wick did not lessen the light but it made it possible for more light to be produced. Perhaps the Lord by His Spirit and through His scriptures is seeking to trim away all that is charred and hindering His light from burning brightly in and through our lives. May our prayer be that He will trim away all that is unnecessary and useless from our lives that His light might be better reflected through us.

Secondly he had a vision of:

B: THE CHRIST! Verses 13-16 The Christ that John saw in these verses is not the same in appearance as when he laid his head on his breast. That was the Christ of humiliation; that was the man Christ Jesus. The Christ of these verses is the Christ of the present, of the now! If you desire an up-to-date picture of the Lord Jesus do not go to the cradle; we like the baby Jesus because we can control a baby! Neither go to the cross, rather go to Revelation chapter one and behold Him as He is in the present.

This vision of Christ exceeds the vocabulary of the most learned; it goes beyond the comprehension of the mind of man; it surpasses the painters brush. This is the Christ of glory. The shame, rejection, ridicule, humiliation and mockery of man are forever in the past.

In John's vision of Christ he witnessed several things that the Christian of this hour needs to see anew and afresh. **First** note in verses 13-14 *His presentation.* How do you present the eternal *"I Am?"* In the vision of Christ He is presented in a most unusual fashion. It is so unusual that you will not find anything with which to compare it; it stands alone. There are four things that arrest our attention in His presentation. **(a)** We have in verse 13 *His position.* His position is presented in a very clear and concise manner. He is *"In the midst."* His very position should inform us that He is intimately interested in everything the church does as well as what happens to her. Learn: He is no absent Lord! He was not then nor is He now; rather He is active *"In the midst"* doing what only He can do, ministering to the lamps; trimming and supplying oil so the lamps will not go out. Do you recall the many times in the gospels where we are told that Jesus was in the midst? That was and is His present position in His church today. He said, *"Where two or three are gathered together in My name, I'll be in the midst."* There are those that say, "Isn't it nice that He is in our midst;" is it? Do you think that it is nice that He is in the midst of the shallow, sensuous conversations between professed Christians? Is it nice that He is in the midst of our secret

The Apocalypse: The Revelation of the Redeemer

thoughts? If we are not careful we will seek to isolate Him to certain areas of our life and labor. Is He in the midst of the activity of my hands; of the attitude of my heart; of the ambitions of my head? If we would allow His Spirit to burn the reality of His position in our hearts it would surely affect the way we live, love and labor. We would not; we could not be as indifferent to eternal matters as we are. **(b)** In His presentation we also have *His person* stated in the words of verse 13 *"One like unto the Son of man."* This title is a clear reference to His humanity. This is His favorite title for Himself. It is used 81 times in the gospels referring to Him. I would like to ask a question of our hearts…what was there about the glorified Christ that would cause John to say "One like unto the Son of man?" It is possible that John saw the scares that were placed there by wicked men when He was crucified. Some will object but He did show those scares to His disciples after His resurrection. Further in Zechariah 12:10 the Word declares, *"They shall look upon Me, whom they pierced."* The point is that John was beholding a different Christ in appearance than the One that walked the shores of Galilee and yet He was recognizable.

As John is looking at His person he calls our attention to the *garment* of the Lord Jesus. In passing, do you remember that His robe on earth was gambled away? However, the robe that Jesus is wearing at this time has deep significance. The Greek word is *poderes*. It is the robe of a *priest*; it is the robe he wore when officiating in his office. This robe came all the way to the feet. The responsibility of the priest was that of mediating, caring, interceding, and ministering as he cared for the lamps by trimming and supplying the oil. All of this reveals the priestly character of the risen Lord. All that the Old Testament priest did the Lord Jesus does today as He moves and ministers to and in His churches, and we are to do on behalf of the lost. This is also the robe of a *prince*. This is the dress of dignity. The same word that is used to describe the priest robe is used of the robe of Saul and Jonathan. This was the robe of royalty that tells us that He is not a criminal on a cross but the ruler of this entire universe. Further, this is the robe of the *prophet*. The messenger that came to tell Daniel the truth of God was dressed in this manner (Daniel

10:5). When these are placed together we have a picture of the three-fold present ministry of Jesus. He is prophet; He is the very truth of God. He is priest; He is our mediator, and intercedes with the Father. He is potentate; that is King of kings and Lord of lords.

It is interesting to note that the robe is held to the waist with a golden *girdle*. The robe was pulled between the legs and secured to the waist. This was to enable free movement. It indicates that our Lord is not inhibited in any area of His ministry; that it is not a cumbersome burden for Him. We should gather from this that the girdle that the Lord provides does not bind or burden but it enables us to meet our responsibilities with joy and freedom. **(c)** Thirdly we have in His presentation *His purity*; verse 14 declares *"His head and His hairs were white like wool, as white as snow."* White is a reference to His purity and the added reference to wool and snow tells us of His complete purity. While He lived among men even His enemies marveled and said there was no fault to be found in Him. The reference to His head gives the added thought of total wisdom. The head represents the intelligence of man, and he sees the Lord as purely wise. So wise that He never makes a mistake. The hair is a symbol of His glory. In the Old Testament it was a sign of wisdom and glory. Here it is this as well as authority and antiquity, wisdom, maturity but it is all summed up in His purity. He was and is the lamb without spot and blemish. The use of the word snow reminds me of what the Lord said about our sins, *"Though they be as scarlet they shall be as white as snow."* That is purity. We become pure in Him as we receive His forgiveness. **(d)** Fourthly in His presentation we have *His penetration*. Verse 14 shares this in the words, "His eyes were as a flame of fire." These are piercing, penetrating, and searching eyes. This is the eyes that see straight through the make-up to the real you. There is nothing anymore discomforting than to have a pure person look steadfast at you, especially if you are trying to conceal something. Do you recall His look at Peter? Listen to these words of Jeremiah in chapter 23:23-24, *"Am I a God at hand, saith the Lord, and not a God afar off? Can any hide himself in secret places that I shall not see him? Do I not fill earth and heaven? Saith the Lord."*

The Apocalypse: The Revelation of the Redeemer

Not only does the Lord see but He also sees accurately. He sees it all just the way it is, not like we tell it or wish it was but as it is. In this connection notice the words of Hebrews 4:13, *"Neither is there any creature that is not manifest in His sight; but all things are naked and open unto the eyes of Him with whom we have to do."*

What impact does this truth have upon our hearts? Does it strike terror to know that He sees and knows all things? If this is the case it is due to one of two reasons; one you are afraid of judgment because you do not know Jesus or two you are a Christian harboring sin. Do we like what He sees and knows?

In the vision of Christ we move from His presentation to **secondly** *His performance*. Verse 15 shares *"And His feet like unto fine brass, as if they burned in a furnace."* The word "Brass" is literally "Bronze." This is a picture of while, glowing bronze. In the tabernacle and temple the fixtures that had to do with the sin offering were made of bronze. This is true because they had to do with judgment; therefore bronze became symbol of judgment. Why does it say feet and not a fist? A fist raised high to heaven would seem to be more appropriate symbol of judgment. It is feet because the king sat on an elevated throne; his subjects approached him and bowed, when they looked up the first thing the saw were his feet. Anyone being condemned would fall at the feet of the king and plead for mercy. His feet like bronze burned in a furnace speaks of two important things. **First**, it speaks *of the judgment He bore*. For the believer seeing those feet already burned is a blessing because they tell him that the judgment against his sin has been borne by Jesus. He not only bore our sins in His body on the tree; He became the sin of the world. His performance accomplished for man what no other could do. He paid the debt of sin in full. His feet burned in the furnace of the judgment of God in order that we might walk with Him in white. **Secondly**, they speak *of the judgment He brings*. Paul said in Second Thessalonians 1:1-10 that He is coming in judgment, and soon He will crush sin and receive His glory. This should strike terror in the heart of all lost men as well as stir His saints to surrendered service.

In the vision of Christ we now move to *His pronouncement*. Verse 15 shares this in the words, "*His voice was as the sound of many waters.*" Ezekiel heard this same voice in 43:2. This is a thundering voice; it reveals the majesty, power and over all authority of Christ. When the thundering voice of Christ speaks at this time everybody in the universe listens. When He speaks in judgment it is going to be like thunder.

Previously it had not been so. When the sea was raging He spoke in a *comforting* voice, and said "*Peace be still,*" and it was. How many times has He said those words to our storm tossed soul? At the grace of Lazarus He spoke in a *commanding* voice, "*Come forth,*" and he did. One day that voice is going to thunder like a million oceans and it's going to call the ungodly to judgment.

At the *present* it is a voice that calls *sinners to salvation* and *saints to service*. It is the voice that *convicts of sin, controls the surrendered, and commissions to service*. It is the voice that *cries over society*. This is the voice that the pretender will hear say, "*Depart from Me, I never knew you.*" Wisdom says, hear Him now and respond to His voice.

In addition, we have **fourthly** *His power*; verse 16 says it clearly, "*And in His right hand were seven stars: and out of His mouth went a sharp two-edged sword.*" His power is demonstrated in a two-fold manner in this verse. *First* in the *messengers He holds*. Verse 16 says it clearly, "*And in His right hand were seven stars.*" This prompts at least two questions. First, "Why the right hand?" The right hand is the position of power, peace and protection. He is at the right hand of the Father. The second question is "Who are the stars?" verse 20 provides the answer, "*The seven stars are the angels of the seven churches.*" The angels are the ministers, messengers, leaders or pastors of these churches. Someone might suggest that I am only saying this because I am a pastor! No, I'm saying this because it is the Word. There are members that wonder why the pastor is the spiritual authority in the church. He is because of his position but and as importantly because of his responsibility and accountability to the One that holds him in His right hand. The pastor of the church is the one that God is holding accountable for the church. **Secondly**

The Apocalypse: The Revelation of the Redeemer

in *the message he heralds*, verse 16 presents the heralding of the message in the words *"Out of His mouth went a sharp two-edged sword."* This is a reference to the Word of God. It is the delivered Word of God that has power to transform lives. One man said; "A Bible in hand is worth a dozen on the shelf," and that may be true. However, one in the head and heart is worth a dozen on the shelf. I want to make a comparison with Hebrews 4:12, *"for the Word of God is quick and powerful than a two-edged sword."* I am told that the word for "sword" in Hebrews implies a small sword. The word in Revelation 1:16 is for a large sword, one that would require both arms in the swinging of it. The difference is that the one in Hebrews 4:12 cuts open and convicts, the one in Revelation is a weapon wielded in judgment; both however, are the Word of God.

The message that man will face in the Day of Judgment is the message of the Word of God. In the vision of the glorified Christ there is **fifthly** *His projection*; verse 16, *"And His countenance was as the sun shineth in his strength."* There is a glimpse of this in the gospels and in the book of Acts. When Jesus was on the Mount of Transfiguration a portion of His countenance projected through, as much as the disciples were able to bear. When Saul was on his way to Damascus a light struck him and then he heard the voice of Jesus. It is possible that the light was indeed the Lord shinning in His strength.

Further, we are told that in the city of God that there will not be a need of light for the Son will provide all the light needed. This is Jesus in His full deity; He is no longer veiled, no longer contained in human form but revealed as He truly is: the glorified Son of God!

We move from the vision to:

II: THE VICTOR! Verses 17-18 The victor is the Lord Jesus and in His victory we can enjoy present tense triumph. This statement does not imply that this will always be so. It is not automatic; the Bible states, *"This is the victory that overcometh the world even our faith."* It also declares, *"Greater is He that is in you than he that is in the world."* Yes, victory has been won but the Christian must decide if he will live in the Savior's victory or as Satan's victim. Moreover, it is not a one time decision, it is not even a daily decision; it is a moment-by-moment decision. We are constantly confronted with the issue of who or what will be in charge of our lives.

John has shared what he has already witnessed. He saw Christ in the brilliance of His full deity and glory. One might think that he will be filled with joy after all he is seeing the Lord Jesus for the first time in about 50 years. This is not the case; *John fell at His feet as dead.* I personally think that if he had not been *"In the Spirit"* (verse 10) that he would have died because mortal man cannot behold Christ in His full deity and live. In so doing he reveals the desired position of the believer, at the feet of the Lord Jesus. There are those that resent and even rebel against this truth because of pride. Yet, this is the position that declares that He is Lord and I submit myself totally to Him. I am His servant. Have you been to this position lately? No one ever graduates from this position. If your fellowship is stale, if your friendship is stagnated it is time to check your position. When we are at His feet His presence is new and refreshing as the morning dew.

John is privileged to gaze upon things never or since witnessed by man. He will see the throne of God, the judgment of God upon a rebellious world and he will see heaven and hell without a response but he could not look upon Christ in His unveiled glory and remain unmoved. This is sufficient to inform us of the fact that the closer we are to the Lord Jesus the more we recognize His holiness. This will also enhance our reverence for Him and respect for the things of God. Further, when we are in His presence the desire of our heart will be to worship as His subject. As we behold the victor there are two truths that should grip our hearts. First there is:

A: HIS COMFORT! Verse 17, *"And He laid His right hand upon me."* It is His right hand, the hand of favor and power. That is the hand strong enough to uphold the universe yet gentle enough to wipe tears from a baby's eye. There is a surface truth in this for each of us. To be strong in the Lord and in the power of His might does not lessen the necessity of our being an extension of His loving hands of Jesus. True power in the Lord will

The Apocalypse: The Revelation of the Redeemer

manifest itself in selfless service, like wiping tears from the heart of the despondent. There are a couple of things worthy of note in the comfort of the Victor. **First** we observe *His action* as stated in verse 16 in the words, *"He laid His right hand upon me."* This was not done in judgment or in anger; rather this was a touch of love. It is true that He is about to judge a godless world but He has time to minister a comforting touch of love. Can we learn a lesson from this? Surely there is or there should always be time for the Master to minister through us to others. In the 1989 *Church Administration* magazine an article appeared that suggest that high tech might give us more time to touch. I do not know about your experience but it hasn't proved that way for most people. **Secondly** we have *His attitude* revealed in the fact that it was not necessary for Him to touch; He could have simply said, "Get up." There is something about a comforting touch of love that is indescribable. It goes beyond words it is its own communication. The touch of Jesus exceeds empathy. It is His heart touching your heart.

There is an amazing truth revealed in the experience of John. He is the same Lord; His heart has not changed. His outward glory has changed but the love of His heart is as it has always been. It is a touching, tender and comforting heart; a heart that yearns to minister to the needs of His people.

While He was in the flesh this was His practice. He ministered by touching. He touched blinded eyes and they were open to the beauty of God. He still touches eyes that are blinded by sin and through His Spirit they are opened to the reality of sin and then to salvation in Christ. He touched deaf ears and they were opened to the music of the Master. He, through His Spirit, touches ears hardened by sin and they are opened to the music of heaven. He laid that comforting had upon the sick and they were restored. He lays His hand upon the spiritually sick and they are restored and revived. He refused no one, not even the defiled leper. He willingly touched him and cleansed him. Only He could do that, only He can do that for man today.

Can you imagine how John must have felt when he experienced the comforting touch of the warm hand of Jesus? The Lord Jesus still touches, and He does it personally, never by proxy. This touch informs us that He is not afraid to be identified with us. He touched me in my blind, deaf state and gave me sight and hearing. He touched me when I was spiritually sick. He has comforted me in my journey and there is no reason to think that He is about to change.

In addition we have:

B: HIS COMMAND! Verses 17-18; *"Fear not."* The very fact that Jesus said, *"Fear not"* tells us that John was filled with fear. One can easily understand why John was so fearful if he will read again the vision John has just seen. His fear is not the fear of fright; it is recognition of the holiness of the person of the Lord Jesus. There are those times when we should be fearful. We should be filled with fear if we are living lives that are loose and that lead to sin and separation from the Savior's fellowship. This is the primary reason fear fills our hearts the majority of the time.

Because the Lord has vanquished fear He can say with meaning, *"fear not."* We need to hear those words often because it is a part of the enemy's strategy to cause fear in our hearts.

It is important that we notice the order of these events. First, John received the comforting touch of the glorified Christ then he heard Him say to him, *"Fear not."* The command followed the comfort. These are words easy to say and anyone with the vocabulary of a three year old can say them but the Lord Jesus tells John why he, as well as we, should not fear. **First** John *"Fear not'* because *I have conquered*; verse 18, *"I am He that was dead."* I cannot read those words without remembering that He is the eternal *"I Am."* He said to John, *"I am He that was dead."* John was eyewitness to many of the events that transpired during Passion Week. He was there, he saw Him hanging on the cross, and he heard Him speak to him about His earthly mother. He probably beheld the blood and water flow from his side. Yes, John knew He was dead but he also knew he was alive.

It is important that we note that the Lord Jesus spoke in the past tense. He *"was dead"* that is an action completed in the past but He moves into the present when He sates, *"Am alive for evermore."* There is no crucifix, no dead Christ, no bowing before a Jesus still on the cross. It was and is the atonement that we remember. He is alive, the tomb is empty, He lives, and we serve a risen Savior. He is alive for *"evermore."* The suffering and humiliation is forever finished.

The Lord Jesus could command John to *"Fear not"* because he had conquered every foe, including the last enemy death. He conquered and He will conquer my fears as well. Before we leave this thought notice that the Lord Jesus says, *"Amen."* It means *"Truly."* He is reaffirming what He has said, *"John it is true, you can trust this, build your life upon it, rest in this as an established fac*t." **Secondly**, He could command John to *"Fear not"* because of *His conquest*; verse 18 shares His conquest in the words, *"And have the keys of hell and of death."* It is His conquest because he conquered. We are familiar with the expression, "to the victor goes the spoils." The keys are a symbol of ownership, authority, control and possession of government. These keys being the property and not merely in the possession of the Lord Jesus informs us of His universal Lordship. We say and sing often, *"He is Lord"* but the biblical fact is *"He is Lord of all."* There is not a single area of this universe that is not under the authority of the Lord Jesus and that He will not one day reign over.

The conquest includes Hades; that is, the region of the unseen world. It also includes hell, which is the realm of the damned.

However, as we gaze upon our world with all its evil, perverseness, vileness, profanity and blasphemy we might be persuaded to think that the Lord has removed Himself from where the action is transpiring. As corrupt as death and hell are they are not allowed to run loose without authority and control. Because of the Lordship of Jesus John was commanded to *"Fear not."* It was as if the Lord Jesus said to John, *"Do not be afraid, I have conquered and it is My conquest, I am in control."*

Conclusion:
Jesus Christ is the Victor! I can be a victor in Him or I can be a victim, I must decide for myself. If one will think he will realize the folly of his being a victim when the Lord Jesus has done everything for him to be a victor.

The Cooling Church
Revelation 2:1-7

The two chapters that share the history of the church are located between two visions. In the first chapter we have the vision of the *Glorified Christ*, this is the Christ of the present. And in chapters 4 and 5 we have the *Glorified Church*, this is the prospective church. These two chapters deal with *"The things which are."* They serve as a yardstick by which the church can measure her standing in the sight of God.

Paul founded the church at Ephesus on his third missionary journey. They had been blessed with great leaders; including both Paul and John. Ephesus was the metropolis of Asia; it had a population of over 200 thousand and was the economic and religious center of its day. It boasted of one of the seven wonders of the ancient world, the temple of Diana.

Each of the letters has a three-fold application. The first is **primary**; that is, it deals with a real local church and shares its progress and problems. Two, it is **personal**; *"He that hath an ear"* applies to them and us. Third, it is **prophetic**; it is giving the history of the church since her conception to her completion. The actual time period for the Church at Ephesus is 33-100 A.D.

There are three thoughts for us to consider. First,

I: THE COMMENDATION! Verses 2-3 and 6 It is clear that our Lord observes all, and if there is good He will commend it. There are four things worthy of our Lord's commendation. First,

A: THEIR SERVICE! Verse 2, *"I know thy works."* This is better shared in saying; "I know the difference your presence has made in that place." The Lord declares something like this, "I know the hearts, homes and human relationships you have helped to mend and keep."

The Apocalypse: The Revelation of the Redeemer

The church whose presence fails to make a community a better place to live is dead. What is there that would not be here except for our presence? Here there were those things being accomplished that could not be recorded. *The church not only remakes lives but it keeps them from being broken.* This is true because she is to be both salt and light.

Second He commended,

B: THEIR SACRIFICE! Verse 2, *"Labor."* Here the word indicates toil and pressure. *"I know the sacrifice that has been necessary for you to do these things."* This church had not been dreamed into existence. They were blessed because they bleed. They could say with David, *"I will not offer the Lord a sacrifice that cost me nothing."*

Most of us take our church membership to lightly, it cost us nothing and that it what it is worth. Jesus said, *"I know the deeds that are there that would not be there except for your willingness to sacrifice to bring them to pass."* He commended thirdly,

C: THEIR STAND! Verses 3 and 6, *"Can't bear them which are evil; tried those that say they are apostles."* They knew what and why they believed what they did. If one came into their midst speaking things that were not true they had nothing to do with them. That is what is meant by the expression, *"Can't bear them that are evil."* The test was what did these believe and teach about the person of Jesus Christ. Today the reverse is true, the bigger the heretic the larger the audience.

In verse 6 the expression, *"The deeds of the Nicolaitanes"* is used. There has been much controversy over exactly who and what the Nicolaitanes were. Some declare that it was the evil practice of having a division between the "clergy and the laity." God is a God of order and when that order is violated, His blessing will cease. This came into being through Nicolas the proselyte of Antioch. This was the heresy that declared that the flesh had nothing to do with the spirit. These taught that one could sin all he wanted to in the flesh because it did not really affect the spirit. These took a stand against evil in the church. Those that stand are ridiculed more than the evil that they stand against. He commended fourthly,

D: THEIR STEADFASTNESS! In verse 3 it is said of them that they, *"Had not fainted."* In addition the word *"Patience"* is used twice to describe them. They were patience in the face of opposition. They could be counted on when things were well and when they were going bad. These had a steadfastness that enables them to continue the course. I heard about a bulldog, new to the area, and exploring. He encounters two Irish Setters. The two Setters had a field day with him. He went home, licked his wounds and the next day at the same time he appeared again. They whipped him again. This process continued for several days until finally when the Bulldog came in the yard the two Setters would run away whining. These people were something like that. They did not give up but continued in their faith.

What a church and record. How wonderful to realize that Jesus knows all. What does He know about us? Is it pleasing to Him? Secondly we have:

II: THE CRITIQUE! Verses 4-5, *"I have this against you that you have left off loving Me as you did at first."* Or, *"You don't love one another as you did."* It could be a mixture of both because one affects the other. The former is reflected in the latter and the latter is revealed in the former. There are two things we will note about this criticism. First,

A: THE REASON! Verse 4, *"Left their first love."* Observe that they left, not lost. This indicates a deliberate action on their part. It was not stolen from them, but surrendered. Jesus looked deeper than their works and observed their motives. He saw the flaw that lay within their hearts. The love referred to is that of honeymoon or first love. It is a love that should be increasing. It had been said, *"My how those Christians love one another."* When the pagans cast out their own the Christians would take them in. Love begets love. They were still going on the momentum of the past. They were coasting, like a car out of gas. They were orthodox, but they had left loving Him. Is this the critique that our Lord would bring against us? Lets' asks a simple question and see if there is an answer. What are the reasons that cause this to happen in this church? It is not stated in the text but the reasons

The Apocalypse: The Revelation of the Redeemer

for this happen can not be that different from why it happens today. **First**, there had been a *shift in priorities*. Doubtless the secular became more important than the spiritual and duty replaced devotion. **Secondly**, they became *selfish in their pursuits*. Self and not the Spirit controlled their hearts. **Third**, they were *soulish in purpose*. Their desires are now to satisfy the carnal man. **Forth**, they had become *shallow in their praise*. The problem was not in their works but in their worship. Secondly,

    B: THE RESULTS! Verse 5, *"Remove their candlestick."* This does not refer to their salvation but to their testimony for Him. This was fulfilled in 252 A.D. when the Goths destroyed the city. It never returned to its glory. The glory had departed and they were never the same. *"Ichabod"* had been written over the church at Ephesus. This is a sad result of failing to love the Lord as we ought. Thirdly,

III: THE COUNSEL! Verses 5 and 7 Is there any hope? Yes! Hope is why the letter was written; to give counsel to get back where they should be. There are four parts to this counsel. First,

    A: REMEMBER! Verse 5; *"Remember from whence thou hast fallen."* Remember where you were, the joy, and the gladness of going into God's house, of the delight that filled your hearts, and take note of how you have drifted in your devotion. They were not to live there but remember and comparing would challenge them to continue in their growth. Secondly,

    B: REPENT! Verse 5, *"And repent."* This shares that the purpose of remembering is to lead to repentance. Of what are they to repent; of their lack of love, of leaving the Lord. The lack precedes the leaving. Do you recall Demas? He left Paul because of the desire for this world. Thirdly,

    C: RETURN! Verse 5 *"Do the first works."* The first work is loving Him. True repentance leads to a return to Him, and unless there is a return there has been not repentance. Repentance is a change of mind that is manifested in ones will. When the Prodigal repented he returned to his father's house ready to serve. Fourth,

    D: REWARD! Verse 7, *"He that overcometh."* Who is the overcomer? 1 John 5:4 answers when it tells us that they are the ones that are born of God. The tree of life was lost due to sin; it is restored in Gods paradise.

Conclusion:
Are you an overcomer or are you being overcome? Jesus says, *"He that hath an ear?"* Do you? Can you hear Him calling you back to Him in love?

They were cooling not cold; doing never replaces devotion. Does He have anything against you? He counsels us to return, to our first love. Would you hear a commendation or counsel to return to Him? You cannot return where you have never been.

The Committed Church*
Revelation 2:8-11

Many people have made the mistake of thinking that becoming a Christian eliminates their troubles, trials, problems and pressures. It does not take long for that thought to take flight, does it? Being a Christian does not mean that life is a bowl of cherries. Life may be a bowl but often it is filled with pits.

The church at Smyrna was on the verge of giving up. They had experienced suffering and scorn so severely that they were not merely weary in but growing weary of the way. These suffering saints needed to hear a word of hope. Most of us can identify, at least in some respects with this desire. It was at this dark hour that they received this letter from the Lord.

If you use your imagination you can see them as they gather to hear what the Lord has to say to them. However, I am not sure they were ready for what they were about to hear. The main thought running through this letter is that if you are committed to Christ there is cost. There are three thoughts shared in this letter. First,

I: THE REVELATION OF THE COST! Verse 9 The Lord seems to be saying to them that things are bad, but before they get better they will get worse. However, they are not kept in the dark about the cost of commitment. There are three cost presented. The first of these is:

A: PRESSURE! Verse 9, *"I know thy tribulation."* The Greek word is *"Thlipsis."* It literally means *"Pressure."* This pressure was not verbal or mental abuse. It was not the threat of being excommunicated. It was not being tied to a pole and beaten with the whip. This pressure has a dual meaning. It presents a picture of a winepress in which the juice was squeezed out of the grapes. The other is of a huge boulder on the shoulders of a man. The weight gradually is pressing the life out of him. In both of these the process is not sudden but prolonged.

A reasonable question is "Why are they experiencing the cost of this pressure?" The basic cause is their refusal to compromise with the world in their relationship with Christ and His church. All that was necessary for them to be removed from this pressure was forsake Christ and His church. If we were facing pressure like that how many of us would be a part of the gatherings in the Lord's house? The second revealed cost is:

B: POVERTY! Verse 9, "*...and poverty.*" There are two Greek words used for poverty. The first is "*Penia*" which is a word used to eke out a living. The word here is "*Ptocheia*" which means beggarly or destitute. These were not living in total poverty because they were lazy. Nor was it because of a wicked lifestyle or that they were not thrifty. They were living as beggars because they would not deny Christ. When one of them sought employment he was asked if he was a Christian. If he said, "Yes" he would not be hired. Suppose you were applying for a job that you had to have to feed your family and the first question was, "Are you a Christian?" and you knew that your answer would determine if you were employed or not; how would you respond? These responded, "Yes!" But there is more the soldiers came to their homes and if they refused to recant their faith their crops and buildings were burned. The choice was presented Christ or Caesar. If they said "Caesar" the pressure and poverty would cease but if they said Christ is Lord and I will serve Him it meant more of the same. There are things worse than death and they experienced many of them because of their relationship with Christ. The third cost revealed was:

C: PERSECUTION! Verse 9, "*I know the blasphemy.*" This is not blaspheming against the Holy Spirit but slandering the people of God. Yet, when one slanders the people of God he is slandering the Person of God. Verse 9 continues, "*Of them which say they are Jews but are of the synagogue of Satan.*" It had been the synagogue of God but they denied the Messiahship of Christ and now it is the synagogue of Satan. It is still true that religion

The Apocalypse: The Revelation of the Redeemer

that denies the Person of Christ and the power of God is the greatest hindrance to the growth of the Gospel.

Why are they suffering this persecution? They were accused of being cannibals because of the symbols of His body and blood used during the Lord's Supper. They were accused of having sexual orgies because of their Agape feast. They were accused of being atheist because they did not have images or idols. They were accused of damaging family relationships because Christianity often divided homes. They were accused of being disloyal because they would not say Caesar is lord. They were persecuted because they preached the end of the world in flaming fire.

These saints knew the cost of pressure, poverty and persecution. If we thought there was even a remote possibility that we might face the same cost would we be here? Our second thought is:

II: THE REALIZATION OF COMFORT! Verses 8-10 Is there any solace for these suffering saints at Smyrna? These verses reveal five rays of comfort that shine as brightly as the noonday sun. Where will they find comfort in all they are experiencing? First in His,

A: PERMANENCY! Verse 8, *"First and last."* Jesus is saying to these committed Christians, "Before your pressure, poverty and persecution I was and I will be when it is no more." I preceded it and I will succeed it. I am permanent. These words would reveal to them that He never changes. When you consider the permanency of Christ think about this fact. He is the only man born of woman who was older than His mother, as old as His Father, and His birthday was not His beginning. They would receive comfort secondly in His,

B: POWER! Verse 8, *"He that was dead and alive forever more."* I am glad that is not reversed. That is what the followers of Joseph Smith, Mary Baker Eddy, and Mohammed must say, but not the saints. The saints can stand in the graveyard and shout with Paul, *"O, death where is thy sting? O, grave where is thy victory?"* It is true He was dead, but not now, He is alive. Yes, He was nailed to a cross and placed in a borrowed tomb. They probably sang very gladly, "Lo in the grave He lays, Jesus the prophet, He's dead. He has been defeated!" But on that third morning, "Up from the grave He arose with a mighty triumphant ore His foes, He arose a victor from the dark domain and He lives forever..." Because of this He has power to comfort the Christians when they are facing times of persecution. Thirdly, we have His comfort in His:

C: PERCEPTION! Verse 9, *"I know."* The Greek word is *"Oida."* It does not mean to know by observation but by experience. They would be comforted in the fact that Jesus had already faced everything they were experiencing. What does He not know? He never does research on any subject. He knows everything in heaven, earth and hell. There are times when that blesses me. Especially when I am pushed in a corner by the devil. There are times when that burdens me. When I have evil thoughts, when my tongue is loose, when I fail to spend time in the Word and prayer, or when I fail to witness or withhold His tithe, He knows and that burdens me. The forth ray of comfort is in His:

D: PRONOUNCEMENT! Verse 9, *"There are rich."* This is the only rich church in the New Testament. This seems like a contradiction after saying, "I know your poverty." The world says they are paupers, but He says they are rich. The world says they are fools, but He says they are rich. We must understand that poor here does not mean rich there. If you have lost your goods, home, for your stand for Christ, you will be rich over there. Yet, we can be rich here in the things that really matter. You can be rich in grace, mercy and peace with God and man. The fifth revelation of comfort is in His:

E: PROMISE! Verse 10, *"ten days shalt thou suffer."* That does not seem to be much of a promise does it? Who wants to hear that they are going to have more of the same? You are going to suffer; however, it is only for a season. The expression *"ten days"* indicates a definite period of time and that there is an eleventh day on God's calendar. Moreover, the second death will have no power. The third major thought is:

III: THE RECOMMENDATIONS FOR CONSISTENCY!

Verses 10-11 Haven't these saints already experienced enough? They are being challenged to consistency, and this is the pattern for you and me. Please note two truths in this recommendation for consistency. First,

A: THE CALL! Verse 10; *"Be faithful unto death."* The reality is that things are going to continue only worse. It is important to note that they are being called upon to be *"faithful unto"* not *"till"* death. They are called upon to be faithful to Christ and His church even if it cost them their life. We have great problems with faithfulness costing us a portion of our time, talent or treasure. Secondly,

B: THE COMPENSATION! Verse 10, *"I will give thee a crown of life."* This is the victors' crown. The Lord Himself gives this crown. These saints suffered because of their commitment to Christ. They were not afraid of the cost because they knew they had been purchased and were not their own.

Conclusion:

Polycarp was the pastor of the church at Smyrna. He was called upon to deny Christ in the stadium before the throng of people and the proconsul. His response was something like this: *"Eighty and six years have I served Him and He has never did me an injury: how then can I blaspheme my King and Savior?"* They threatened to destroy him with beast and he said, *"Bring on the beast."* When that did not cause him to recant, they said they would burn him. He said, *"Bring on the fire."* His hands were bound behind him, and the fire was set, but it formed an arch. One was called upon to thrust him with a dagger, and the record reveals that a dove flew from the fire and enough blood flowed forth to put out the flame. He died with a prayer upon his lips for those that had taken his life. The witnesses said that there was an aroma from the fire like frankincense. Polycarp was faithful unto death. He was not afraid of the second death because for him it did not exist. Could you measure your commitment to Christ? Are you faithful?

*Thirty years ago I heard Kenneth Ridings, now president of Fruitland Baptist Bible Institute share a message on this text. A portion of the outline is his.

The Compromising Church
Revelation 2:12-17

Compromise is a word that has become more and more a way of life both in and out of the church. The tragedy is that when the church begins to compromise she has great difficulty in knowing how and when to stop the process. The sad truth is that compromise is a never-ending road that leads to destruction and damnation.

The word *"Pergamos"* means marriage. And the prefix indicates that it is a mixed marriage. This is what has transpired in this church. They have so compromised the standard that they have joined with the world in that they have adopted the practices of the world.

Pergamos prophetically represents that period of time from about 312 to 590 A.D. The one person most responsible for this mixed marriage was Constantine. Constantine was engaged in war trying to regain the Roman Empire. It is said that the night before he was to enter into a great battle that he supposedly had been at prayer. As far as I know he was not a Christian at this time. In a vision he saw a flaming cross in the sky and was told, *"In this sign conquer."* He is reportedly to have said to the Lord, *"If I win the battle tomorrow, I will see to it that the entire empire becomes Christian."* On the surface that sounds wonderful doesn't it? However, Christianity is and always has been an individual matter. He won that battle, he marched the entire army into the river and they were baptized. It is easy to see something of the strategy of Satan. Up to this point he had opposed Christianity from without, but now he is joining the ranks to weaken the church from within. Constantine was responsible for the church becoming popular with the world. This resulted in the church compromising the teachings of Christ to the point that the world realized that she had nothing of spiritual significance to offer and thus despised the church because of her powerlessness. In these verses there are three thoughts that are worthy of observation. First,

I: THE FAITHFULNESS OF THIS CHURCH! Verse 13 Their faithfulness should *challenge us to serve, give us courage to stand* and *convict us of our slothfulness*. There are three things presented to us about the faithfulness of this church. First,

A: THEIR LOCATION! Verse 13 reveals this in the expression *"Where Satan's (seat) throne is."* How would you like to be located right next door to Satan's throne? This was a difficult location but they were there because the need was so great! The city of Pergamos was noted for its idolatry. There was an altar built to Zeus. It was 90 feet square and 40 feet high. There were three different temples built for emperor worship. This city was the place of sin but God had placed a band of individuals there in spite of the location that had been faithful to Christ. This is the story of many. The work place does not have environments that are Christian in their make-up, and many want to quite because of the difficulty in working there. It is possible that you are there for that very reason. It is in the dark place that light is needed. Any church that is not causing the enemy some trouble is so useless that the enemy is ignoring it. This is an internal issue that must be dealt with by the Spirit of God. Secondly,

B: THEIR LOYALTY! Verse 13, *"Hast not denied my name, and hast not denied My faith."* These were loyal in spite of their location in two specific areas. First, *"You have not denied My name."* They were called upon every year to go to one of the temples and say, "Caesar is Lord." They were to make this public declaration once a year and then they were free to worship whom they pleased. They knew that to do such a thing was to deny His name. If we applied the rational today to this we would say, "I can say this with my lips but the Lord knows what is in my heart and it will be all right." These were not cowards nor ashamed that they belonged to Christ. Secondly, *"You have not denied My faith or your faith in Me."* These individuals had not turned their backs

The Apocalypse: The Revelation of the Redeemer

on Him. They did not say that the price was too high, rather they declared that they stood firm upon their convictions. Thirdly,

C: THEIR LANGUISH! Verse 13, *"In those days wherein Antipas was My faithful martyr, who was slain among you, where Satan dwelleth."* They were called upon to suffer. The name, *"Antipas"* is the same word used by the Lord in chapter 1 as martyr. We do not know anything about him; tradition says that when he was called upon to offer that pinch of incense that he refused to do so. The ruler of Pergamos said, "The whole kingdom is against you." His response was, "Then I am against the entire kingdom." His name therefore means, "Against all," but in a positive manner. He was one that not only stood for His Lord; he witnessed for Him as well. A real test of whether or not you and I believe a matter is to answer this question, "Am I willing to die for it?" The second major thought is:

II: THE FAILURES OF THIS CHURCH! Verses 14-15 There are two things being either practiced or tolerated by them that the Lord quickly pointed out to them. First,

A: THE DOCTRINE OF BALAAM OR THE LACK OF SEPARATION! Verses 14 Before we deal with this simply allow this word about doctrine. Doctrine is body of what is taught. You can not sing a song, teach a lesson or share your heart without conveying doctrine. Jesus placed a high value upon doctrine and so should we. I can not take the time to develop the account of this from the Old Testament in this message so you will need to read in the book of Numbers chapter 22 for the account of this incident that is referred to in verse 14. Summarized it is this: King Balak wanted to stop the advancing Israelites. He sent for a hireling of a prophet named Balaan and offered him a huge sum of money to come and curse Israel. However, God would not permit this. This happened three times until finally he told the king what to do. He was to have a party, get everyone together, and have his women entice their men. This would result in their intermarriage and would bring the wrath of God upon his own people. This was successful and in the church at Pergamos this is what was transpiring. When these people offered their sacrifice they were keeping a part of it and having a communal meal and these Christians were participating with the knowledge that this is what it was. Thus Baalism is worldliness. The manner that is presented today is something like this, the standards of the church are too high, if we are going to reach the world we must adopt the ways of the world. It is interesting to note that this does not generate from the world but from "worldly Christians." We must be willing to compromise with the world in order to reach the world. Secondly,

B: THE DOCTRINE OF THE NICOLAITANES OR THE LACK OF SPIRITUALITY! Verse 15 Remember that this was called deeds in Ephesus but it has progressed to the point of being called *"doctrine."* This was a misunderstanding about what Nicholas had taught about the flesh and its involvement in sin. The accepted practice of many was that they could sin all they desired in the flesh that it did not effect the spiritual part of man. Yet, we all know that it does. The spiritual man does not participate but he is definitely affected by sin. The third major thought is:

III: THE FUTURE OF THIS CHURCH! Verses 16-17 It is interesting to note that He calls upon the entire church to repent. There might be someone that would argue and say but I am not guilty. The entire church was to repent of their tolerance of evil. There are two things we observe about the future of this church. First,

A: THE PURPOSE OF THE SWORD! Verse 16, *"I will fight against you with the sword of My mouth."* The purpose of this sword is twofold. Its **first** purpose is that of *protection*. There are two groups referred to in this verse. *"I will come to thee."* This refers to the faithful Christians. He is going to protect them from the dangers and persecutions they were facing. The **second** purpose is that of *punishment*. Verse 16, *"And fight against them with the sword of My mouth."* The *"them"* are those that sought to lead the church astray and into either of the practices that were at hand. The sword of His mouth is the Word of God. Secondly,

B: THE PROMISE TO THE SAINTS! Verse 17 The promise is to those that overcome rather than being overcome. It is a twofold promise. First, it is a promise of *spiritual sustenance*.

The Apocalypse: The Revelation of the Redeemer

Verse 17, *"He that hath an ear let him hear...I will give him to eat of the hidden manna."* These saints were not allowed to eat the forbidden things offered to idols but He is going to be the manna to and for them. The Psalmist called this *"Angel's food."* It is a type of Christ. Here it refers an intimate relationship with Him. Second it is a promise of *spiritual security*. Verse 17, *"And will give him a white stone, and a new name written therein."* This white stone had several meanings. It could mean *acquittal*. After a trial the jurors would vote by either a black or white stone. Jesus is saying all your sins have been removed, the blood has cleansed them. Further, the white stone could mean *abundance*. It was something like credit card. The man with the white stone was entitled to hospitality in certain places. Jesus is saying that He is all that is needed and our abundance is in Him. Thirdly, this white stone could mean *acceptance*. It was cut in half and given to another person. At a future date he could claim shelter and protection by showing the person the other half of the stone. In the Lord Jesus we are accepted. In this stone there is a *"New name written."* What is that name? I don't know but it must be closer than that of son or child of God. We will know in that day.

Conclusion:
This was a compromising church. Are you a compromising Christian? Some compromises started with individuals when you decided to lessen your involvement in church. Our future is like this church it depends upon our response to the call to repentance.

The Corrupt Church
Revelation 2:18-29

The city of Thyatira is the most insignificant of the ones that received letters from the Lord. Its only distinction is that it served as an outpost to the capital city of Pergamos. Their purpose was to hold the enemy forces off until word could reach Pergamos. This would allow them the time to prepare to defend themselves. This city is noted for two products that it produced. One of those purple dye, the dye came from a Madder root. This root was crushed and it produced the color purple. It is also known for producing bronze. They were so insignificant that they did not have their own god. They worshipped the gods that were popular at that time. While they are the most insignificant of these cities they receive the longest letter.

Lydia probably founded this church. Paul meet (Acts 16) with a group of women and preached the gospel and the record informs us that God opened her heart and she was saved. She must have been something like Andrew in that she carried the gospel back to her home. This church probably started in her home. It was not long until problems arose in the church. This is or should not be a surprise to us. As early as Acts 5 we read of sin making its way into the fellowship. The church at Thyatira is continuing stronger in the sin that was present in Pergamos. So much so that the best description one can offer is to call her the corrupt church.

The situation in this church was something like this. There was an evil personality that so influenced the people that they were afraid to do anything without the consent of this personality. There are several truths to observe about this corrupt church. First,

The Apocalypse: The Revelation of the Redeemer

I: THE CHURCH! Verses 18-19 It is essential that we understand that the dearest thing to the heart of the Lord Jesus is the church for which He shed His blood on the cross of Calvary to purchase. Christ and His church are inseparable. There are two truths that arrest our attention. First,

A: THE DESCRIPTION OF DEITY! Verse 18 shares a unique description of the Head of the church that is entirely different from the other six and that is omitted in chapter one in the vision of the Victor. Note them carefully; *"These saith the Son of God."* They are dealing with deity. This is not a prophet that is sharing what he thinks but the Head of the church, Jesus Christ. Sinners forget that they must face Him and saints forget that they are accountable to Him. There are two fascinating things shared about the description of deity in this verse. First He has *"eyes like unto a flame of Fire."* This refers to His divine knowledge and piercing vision. It informs us that He searches the hearts of men like no other. When I was a child one of my favorite TV shows was Superman. He was able to do superhuman things like jump over a building with a single bound; he could be shot and the bullets would bounce off him. One of the most amazing things was his ability to see through objects. This was merely a show but The Son of God is the One that possesses the ability to see not merely through lead but into the human heart. I read about a photographer who had taken pictures of children and one of the mothers was viewing the proofs. As she looked she saw spots on the face of her daughter. The mother protested saying that her child did not have spots on her face. The photographer replied that he was using a super sensitive lens and that the camera merely takes a picture of what is in front of it. The mother stomped out but the next day her daughter broke out with the measles. The Son of God has piercing, penetrating and purging eyes that are like *"a flame of fire."* The second thing we note in this description is *"His feet are like fine brass."* Brass symbolizes judgment. This is a church that has sin powerfully present. God will not be silent in the face of sin. His actions may not be today or even tomorrow but it will certainly come to pass. Secondly we consider the:

B: DECLARATION OF DELIGHT! Verse 19 reveals that there are six things in which the Lord takes delight. This church was standing for some good things, but they were not involved in the best things. They were engaged in social ministry and omitting spiritual ministry. Note that this is the only church that the Lord commends their love. However, the love that they are noted for was something of the type that is manifested among many Christians today and that is a saccharin tolerance for any and everything under the sun. Love does not condone what God has condemned. If the Lord Jesus were talking with us would He share a similar declaration a delight as it related to or about us?

The second major thought is:

II: THE COMPLAINT! Verses 20-23 I must confess that if I received a letter like this from the Lord that I would be thrilled. However, the Lord looks deeper than mortal man does and He does not generalize rather He particularized. The complaint is threefold. First, we have the:

A: SIN! Verse 20 states *"Nevertheless I have a few things against thee."* The sin was that Jezebel was doing the work of the devil and they were permitting her to continue. Note that she is called *"Jezebel."* In all likelihood this is not her real name. There has been all sorts of speculation as to the real identity of this person including Lydia. If you read the record in 1 Kings 16:28 and 11 Kings 9:30-37 you will discover some interesting facts about her. She is the daughter of F Baal and the wife of Ahab. She is a woman whose loyalty to false faith manifested itself in an evil character. If you desire to describe a truly wicked woman you call her *"Jezebel."* I would not even name a cat *"Jezebel."* She was a woman that was highly placed. She was the wife of the king of Israel. Further, she was a woman of vast ability. She possessed a zeal for spreading her false faith.

Verse 20 informs us that she was teaching them to *commit fornication and to eat things sacrificed to idols*. One scholar said that her priest were sexual perverts. She was teaching what she called, *"The deep things of God."* The reality is that, according to verse 24; they were the deep things of Satan. She claimed to have a new revelation from God that would make her followers more spiritual. Her teaching is the development in the church of the system of replacing the word of God with the words of man. A serious warning is to be learned from this: One should never go outside the word of God for truths about God. The second thing involved in the complaint is the:

B: SORROW! Verse 21, *"I gave her space to repent but she repented not."* Grace was extended even to this evil woman that was leading many into damnation. The sorrow is that she refused to repent. She loved her sin and power more than she feared God. When this is true there is only one thing for God to do and that is to pronounce judgment. The literal Jezebel was killed and the dogs ate her body. Paul declared in Romans 6:23 that *"The wages of sin is death."* The third thing is the:

C: SEPARATION! Verse 23, *"And I will kill her children death; and all the churches shall know that I am He which searcheth the reins and hearts."* It is important to note that others will experience suffering as a result of her actions. Moreover, He will judge everyone *according to his or her works*. The church must know that He will not long be tolerant of sin. Also, He placed all those that followed her teaching in the same category as her. There is a verse given in 1 Peter 4:17 that must be noted in this context. The verse declares, *"That judgment must begin at the house of God."* This helps us understand the words, *"That all the churches may know"* and what must they know; that their tolerance of sin will be judged by Him.

There is a third truth we note about this corrupt church. That is:

III: THE COMFORT! Verses 24-29 What was His word to those that were following His way rather than the way of Jezebel? There are three recorded for our consideration. First,

A: THE PRONOUNCEMENT! Verse 25; *"Hold fast till I come."* The pronouncement is that He is coming. In light of this they are to hold fast! To what are they to hold fast? They are to hold fast to their *faith* in Christ. In verse 19 He said that He knew their faith, now they are called upon to hold to it. That is do not deny your faith in Christ even in the midst of pressure to do so by Jezebel and her followers. They are to hold fast and be *faithful* to

Christ. The incentive to do so is the reality stated in verse 23, *"I will give unto you according to your works."* They are to hold on and *follow* Christ. They are to follow *"Till He comes."* They are to hold fast because He is coming. Secondly,

B: THE PROMISE! Verse 26 reveals this in the words *"To him will I give power over the nations."* These knew almost nothing about power. But He promises them power to rule with Him. This refers to His future reign over the earth. Thirdly,

C: THE PERSON! Verse 28 shares this in the words *"I will give him the Morning Star."* Who or what is the Morning Star? Revelation 22:16 assures us that this is Jesus Christ. I am told that the morning star appears at its brightest when it is darkest, and that it is just before dawn. He is the light and they shall have Him to guide them, He is truth and He shall grant liberty to those that know and walk with Him in His light. However, there is something better than the gift; there is something better than the blessing. What? The Giver exceeds the gift, and the Blessor exceeds the blessing!

Conclusion:
This corrupt church was going to have to deal with the Son of God but so are we! He knew them and He knows us as well. He has given us this time to repent and renew our hearts to and with Him.

The Corpse-Like Church
Revelation 3:1-6

The city of Sardis is somewhat a *"riches to rags"* story. This was true both secularly and spiritually. The wealth of Sardis is perhaps one of the things that resulted in its name becoming a common word for a slack and effeminate lifestyle. There is an unwanted distinction about the church in the city of Sardis. There is no mention either in sacred or social history that this church was experiencing any sort of persecution because of their faithfulness, commitment, or their stand for the Savior or the Scriptures. Someone said this church is at peace, but they are at peace with the dead!

This church is like the *"Whited sepulchres"* that Jesus spoke about when talking about the religious activity of his day. The church at Sardis was one that doubtless externally looked fantastic, and they were probably extremely active. I think they were program oriented. However, they were housing the dead; there was no spiritual vitality, concern or compassion for souls.

There is nothing more exciting than a church that is bubbling with enthusiasm for the Savior and souls. When an assembly like this comes together it is indeed a time of celebration. May I inquire, which of these churches would you prefer to be a member of; the living, vibrant, excited for and about the Savior church or the depressed, dead church? **The reality is our church is what we are and it will never become what we are not!** There are three thoughts in these verses that will challenge our hearts. First,

I: THE CONDITION OF THE CHURCH! Verse 1 We are not talking about the physical aspects of the building, although this often is a reflection of the hearts of the people. This is true because we will desire the place of worship to reflect the One worshipped. There are two things worthy of note. First,

A: THE REPUTATION OF THE CHURCH! Verse 1 declares *"A name to live."* This *"name"* had to be earned. This probably came about because in some circles they were known as a *"church on the go,"* that is, they were progressive and active in those things that did not require any spiritual involvement. I must insert that we too have a reputation, a name. In your opinion what is the reputation of your church? It would be easy to say, "Well, I don't care what others think about our church." That would be a moronic statement. We should care as much about the reputation of our church as we do our own. Is our reputation cold, indifferent, or spiritual? Our reputation will either draw or drive individuals to the heart of Jesus. Secondly,

B: THE RUIN OF THE CHURCH! Verse 1 states it simply *"Thou are dead."* The reputation is what the members thought of themselves, the ruin is what the Savior knows about them. This church was still going through the motions of service. They probably enjoyed sitting around talking about things were in "The good old-days." They still had their *"form of worship"* but it was without the Spirit and lifeless. I am told that when Spurgeon's Tabernacle was built that it was filled with both worshippers and seekers. Today it is a museum filled with reminders of what use-to-be. This is not only true of churches but Christians as well. Our second thought is:

II: THE COUNSEL OF CHRIST! Verses 1-3 reveal that the Lord Jesus is not idle nor isolated but involved. He is definitely interested in what takes place in the assembly. There are two aspects of His counsel that they and we need to hear and heed. First, we have:

A: THE REVELATION OF CHRIST! Verse 1 When we write letters we sign at the conclusion. Jesus does not want this church to spend a second wondering who this message is from. He reveals Himself in two rather unusual ways but they are extremely apropos. First, *"He has the seven Spirits."* There has been a great deal of discussion about this expression however; it is my opinion that this is simply a reference to the fullness of

The Apocalypse: The Revelation of the Redeemer

power that Christ possesses. It is used to inform us of the Holy Spirits completeness, fullness, and the diversity of His ministries. This indicates that He has all the power necessary to do either for or among them what needs to be done. Secondly, *"He holds the seven stars."* This is a reference to the awesome fact of the position and protection and He provides. Note please that if anything is in your hand it is, for that moment within your control. You may cast it aside or creases it; it depends upon you. Secondly, we have:

B: THE REMEDY OF CHRIST! Verses 2-3 The remedy in the counsel is such that if it is heard and heeded it will produce a radical change in the individuals and in the assembly that will be manifested to the world. It is a three-fold remedy. First, they are to **ready**. Observe the words; *"be watchful."* The Greek word is *"agrupneo."* It means *to chase sleep*. That is they are not to act as if they are sleepy but they are to be prepared to go, stay and do His will. Secondly, they are to **remember**. Verse 3, *"remember and hold fast."* They are to remember how they have received and heard. This would involve remembering how lost they were before they received Jesus; they are to remember the love that drew them and that has sustained them. Thirdly, they are to **repent**. Verse 3, *"And repent."* This is the heart of the issue because it is an issue of and with their hearts. As wonderful as their past may have been it is not sufficient to sustain them in the present. Thirdly we have:

III: THE CHRISTIANS COMPENSATION! Verses 4-6 There are blessings untold waiting for the child of God. There are two thoughts that I would like for us to consider. First, we have:

A: THE REMNANT! Verse 4, *"A few names even in Sardis."* There are a couple of key words in this statement. The first is *"few."* They are not in the majority; their numbers are not enough to brag about. The second is, *"even."* The remnant was serving in difficult circumstances. I have never encountered a single individual that was experiencing a difficult time that did not consider their circumstances as being "difficult." *"Even in Sardis"* a city filled with love for the material. The question for each of us to answer is, "Am I one of His little flock?" Secondly, we have:

B: THE REWARD! Verse 5 He is aware of your faithfulness and service. He has a reward for those that overcome. The reward includes three things. First, it includes **apparel**; they shall *"Walk with Him in while."* One can choose to walk with the world, to walk indifferently, or to walk with the Savior. Those that walk with Him in a worthy fashion will, one day, walk with Him in white. Secondly, it involves **assurance**; *"I will not blot His name out of the book of life."* This expression means that the name would be found there on the great day of final account, and would be found there forever. It is stated in the negative to emphasize the absolute certainty that it will not happen. Thirdly, it includes acknowledgment, *"But I will confess his name before My Father."* One must confess Him now before men and He will then confess them before His Father.

Conclusion:
What is your present condition? Does it glorify Christ? What is your reputation? Christ calls each of us to hear and heed His counsel.

The Conquering Church
Revelation 3:7-13

Attalus Philadelphus founded the city of Philadelphia. He, not being a modest man had the city named after himself. The name means, *"Brotherly love."* It is the true church within the professing church. The time period covered by the church at Philadelphia is from about 1750 to around 1950. This was the time of *"The open door,"* of great spiritual opportunity and advances. W.A. Criswell states, "This was the time of the missionaries; of the evangelists; of the Bible societies; it is the church of the soul winners;" it is the church that took advantage of the open door of opportunity. One of the old writers said, "If I had the privilege of attending any of these seven churches, I would have chosen this one; and if I could have chosen the service I would have chosen this one for the reading of this letter from the Lord."

Here, as in the letter to the church at Smyrna, there is no word of complaint. There is a letter of praise and encouragement! How wonderful! Surely this stirs within us a desire to know something not only about the church that thrilled the heart of Jesus but how we can bring the same joy to His heart.

There are three thoughts presented to us about this conquering church. First,

I: THE PERFECTION OF THE SAVIOR! Verse 7 This word can not be used about any other. There are those that propagate the thought that it is possible for a person to arrive at what is called *"sinless perfection."* In a rather lighthearted sort of way I have asked some of these proponents just what or how many sins a person must commit to no longer have a relationship with Jesus. The Lord Jesus is the only Perfect One. There are two things for us to consider about the perfection of the Savior. First,

A: THE MANIFESTATION OF PERFECTION! Verse 7a The reality is that perfection (in and of the person of Jesus Christ) is manifested at all times and in every way, but there are two very specific manifestations for us to consider. **First**, it is manifested in His *Character*. Note the description in verse 7, *"He that is holy."* Character flows from within and is manifested without. It is revealed in attitude; is the real you shinning through in public. **Second**, it is manifested in His *Conduct*. Again note the expression, *"He that is true."* There are two Greek words that are used for *"true."* Let me try to illustrate. If I say, "the sky is blue" that is a true statement, but I may turn around and say, "and I am 39 years old." Because I tell you the truth does not mean that I am truth. The word here indicates **truth itself**. He is the reality; if you know Him you will know truth. Secondly,

B: THE MIGHT OF HIS PERFECTION! Verse 7b, *"He that hath the keys of David, He opens and no man shuts; He shuts and no man opens."* The expression, *"He has the keys of David,"* reveals His position as being the One in authority and control. A reasonable question would be "Who has the key to your heart?" The keys are His and further there is a strong inference to His sovereignty when He says, *"I open...I close...what I open is open...what I close is closed."* This tells us that He not only has the right to rule but that He does rule. May I suggest that the key that locks and unlocks is secure! Further He delights to unlock heavenly treasures for those that love and seek Him with all their hearts? A good study in this regard would be Isaiah 22, especially verse 22.

Our second major thought is:

II: THE PORTRAIT OF SUCCESS! Verse 8 The Lord said that He has *"set before them an open door."* He did this because *"He knew their works."* However, He knew more than their work, He knew their **wills** and their **willingness**. He set before them this open door for two reasons. First,

A: THEIR FAITHFULNESS! Verse 8, *"You have kept My Word and not denied My name."* Their faithfulness shines through in that they were faithful to the *Scripture*; *"You have kept My Word."* We are not to worship the Word of God, but we are to be

The Apocalypse: The Revelation of the Redeemer

students of the Word. It is so easy for the physical or social concerns to replace the study and application of the Word of God to our lives. Not so at this church, they were faithful to the Scriptures. They were also faithful to the *Savior*; *"Not denied My name."* His name represents all that He is. These are in this order because for one to walk faithfully with the Savior he must have some knowledge of what the Scriptures teach.

There is little wonder that He set before them this *"open door"* of opportunity. He knew they were willing to take advantage of it. Secondly this door was opened to them because of:

B: THEIR FRAILTY! Verse 8 is revealed in the words *"Thou hast a little strength."* They knew that they did not possess, in and of themselves, those things needed to walk through this door. They knew they must depend upon Him. I remember a man that often talked about how things were when "we were in the old building." Finally I ask him to share this journey with me. It seems that moving into the "new building" gave them a sense of independence, that they could do what they wanted…that they were capable of doing whatever needed to be done. The issue was simply one of who had moved? It was clear that the Lord had not changed, therefore, the ones that literally moved had also spiritually moved. Remember Paul's words, *"When I am weak, then I am strong."* It is never a question of numbers and nickels but of our dependence upon Him.

Our third major thought is:

III: THE PROMISE TO THE SAINTS! Verses 10-12 The promises wait for glory for their ultimate fulfillment, however all of them are in some measure fulfilled in the here and now. There are three tremendous promises made to these saints. First,

A: SHARING WITH CHRIST! Verse 12, *"I will write upon him the name of My God, and the name of the city of My God, and My new name."* Since *"name"* signifies all that He is this indicates our identity with Him. In Old Testament times slaves were branded thus signifying that they were purchased as well as the one that purchased them. This name declares that we share His identity because He purchased us. Further, to have His name is to have His likeness. The reference to the *"city of My*

God" helps us understand something of our citizenship. We are citizens of heaven. Our words, walk and work should reflect this. Have you observed that you can tell where some people are from by their accent? The Christians accent should be heavenly. We now, even though not in the measure we will, share in these things. Secondly,

    B: SECURITY IN CHRIST! Verse 10, "*...I will keep you.*" This is a positive statement. From what are they and we secure; the "*temptation.*" This word is translated better as *trial* or *ordeal*. It is my conviction that there is nothing that touches you that does not touch Him. This does not mean that you will not have times of trial and testing, but the redeemed will not be here to experience the final hour of testing that comes to try the earth. Thirdly,

    C: SERVICE FOR CHRIST! Verse 12, "*Him that overcometh will I make a pillar.*" The word is "*pillar*" and not "*pillow.*" There were huge pillars in the temples and inscribed in them was a name of some one that had distinguished himself in battle or government. Being a pillar meant *support*. It was holding something up. There are at least two groups of individuals in the church. These are *lifters* and *learners*. It also indicates *steadfastness*. The pillar is in place. These would go no more out; this was the practice because of earthquakes in the city. But these will be settled. The pillar was not only a thing of strength; it was also a thing of *splendor*. The people of this church reflected the splendor of Christ because He was seen in their lives.

Conclusion:

Note verse 9. How was this going to come to pass? These Christians were to so live for Jesus that these would desire what they possessed. Note verse 11. We can win a crown, and we can loose a crown. How? We can allow sin to dominate our lives and thus rob us of our reward. 11 John 8, "*Look to yourself that ye loose not your reward.*" What has the Lord placed before and what are you doing with it?

The Counterfeit Church
Revelation 3:14-23

The city of Laodicea was noted as being a city of means. Their location was very strategic. They were on the main thoroughfare where three of the most traveled roads intersected. This enhanced their commercial appeal. Due to these and other factors Laodicea became the banking center of that time. History reveals that when it was destroyed by an earthquake they did not request or want any government assistance in rebuilding an even more beautiful city. Another factor that contributed to their material means was that they were the producers of the best wool to be purchased. The city was also noted as being a city of medicine. They were noted for making and exporting *"eye salve"* that was purported to be able to cool, cleanse and even cure problems with the eyes. In addition, at Laodicea were the springs that were purported to possess healing qualities for those that indulged themselves in them. However, it is not the city that we are examining; it is the church in the city that warrants some investigation.

To say the least this is a very *sad* picture; sad because it reveals a people without a real knowledge of their need and no awareness of their spiritual condition. Sad because it reveals something of what the professing church will look like just prior to the coming of Christ.

It is a *solemn* picture. It is solemn because it reveals the position of Christ. He is excluded.

It is a *strange* picture; strange because they were spiritually destitute and more than content to remain so. It is really difficult to even call them a church. It is called a church because even in this *"lukewarm"* assembly there were those that knew Jesus as Lord.

There are three thoughts for us to seriously note. First, we observe:

I: THE CHALLENGING CHRIST! Verses 14-16 present us with the powerful person of the challenging Christ. Does Christ challenge you? There are two things in these verses that should challenge us. First,

A: HIS DESCRIPTION! Verse 14 There are three distinct attributes in this one verse that can be applied to none but Christ. He is the *"Amen." "Amen"* is a word that is used at the end of a statement to guarantee its truth. In Isaiah 65:16 God is called the God of truth or the *"Amen!"* Often Jesus began His teaching with a double *"Amen."* The word He used was *"Verily, verily"* or *"Amen and Amen!"* This informs us that all that He said was and is absolutely reliable and trustworthy. We can not fathom the depth of what He says, but this we should know: **It is absolute truth**! A second aspect of His description is that He is *"The faithful and true witness."* When He speaks He states things exactly the way they are. There is no wavering, nor embellishment. He speaks out of concern and compassion because He cares. It is not said harshly or with hate; it is not even said in haste. If He ever said something was sin, guess what it still is. Note this statement: If anything ever was truth, it still is truth. A third attribute that can only be attributed to Him is, *"He is the beginning of the creation of God."* The Greek word for beginning is *arche*, which means *"source"* and *"origin."* One thing that this does **not** indicate is that He was the first of the creation...the first made by God. I read this expression that applies only to Jesus, *"He is the uncreated Son of God."* Jesus Christ is the creative agent, the One responsible for all things being created. Secondly we have:

B: HE DIAGNOSES! Verses 15-16, *"You are neither cold nor hot."* This was what Christ knew to be true of this church. It is no complement to say that a group is neither *"cold nor hot."* Being *"cold"* would indicate that they were without Christ. The word for "cold" is *nekros* and it does not mean something that was once hot and now cold. It means *"dead."* If this had been the case there was the hope of them coming to Him in faith and repentance. If they had been "*hot*" (Greek *zestos* which means to boil) they would have had hearts filled with love and commitment for Him. Verse 16 uses the term that not only describes them but multitudes in the church. That word is, "*Lukewarm.*" These people had no enthusiasm, no sense of urgency; they lacked compassion. They were halfhearted and indifferent to spiritual realities. This diagnoses produced from the Lord what many might call a strange word, "*I wish you were one or the other.*" It is time to move from the middle of the road and allow the Spirit of God to do a work or a fresh work in your heart.

What does Christ see as He observes our hearts and the heart of our church? What is filling our hearts? Is it love for Him and a desire to see souls saved or is it temporal things that easily cloud the mind and lead us into a life of "*lukewarmness?*" Our second thought is:

II: THE CONDITIONS OF THE CHURCH! Verse 17 The real condition of the church was nauseating to Christ. He said in verse 16 that He would *spue them out of His mouth*. There are two truths that we must consider. First we have:

A: THE MEMBER'S OPINION OF THE CHURCH! Verse 17 reveals this in the words "*Thou sayest.*" These thought a lot of their church and for this they are to be commended. However, they were merely looking at the externals. They said,

"*We are rich and increased with goods and have need of nothing.*" They were self-deceived. Usually if a person only looks at the outward they will base their relationship with Jesus upon their ability to do something that in their eyes will make an impression with God. Look around you, everything you see and what you cannot see He made. What can man possibly do that will in any wise impress the One that created it? By the way what is your opinion of your church? Secondly,

B: THE MASTER'S OBSERVATION OF THE CHURCH! Verse 17 While they were dealing with the externals Christ was dealing with the eternal, their hearts and relationship with Him. One of the most revealing indications of the decay in this church was the fact that they spoke only of themselves. They boast of their material resources but never offer praise to the One responsible for their blessings. He observed at least five things that He shared. First, they were *"wretched."* This indicates that they were oppressed with a burden. The burden was their wealth that produced an attitude of self-sufficiency. Second, they were *"miserable."* This means to be pitied and not to be praised. Third, they were *"poor."* This means extreme beggarly. This is a reference to their spiritual condition. Forth, they were *"blind."* That is they were blind to their own spiritual need. This was the center of exporting *"eye-salve"* but it did not affect the spiritual. Fifth, they were *"naked."* This was a clothing center, but Christ speaks of their spiritual state. What does He observe as He looks into the heart of our church? Our third thought is:

III: THE COUNSEL OF CHIRST! Verses 18-21 It is important of note that it is counsel and not commands that He gives. His counsel if heard and heeded will change their eternal destinies. He gives counsel in three areas. First concerning:

A: RIGHTEOUSNESS! Verse 18 contains two expression of righteousness that was sadly lacking. The first is *positional* righteousness. This is revealed in the words, *"buy of Me gold."* This represents a righteousness that will stand the test. The word *"buy"* does not indicate that it is possible for one to buy positional righteousness. Isaiah 55:1 clears this up for us, *"Ho, every one that thirsteth, come ye to the water, and he that hath no money; come, ye, and eat."* The price is faith. This is the only righteousness that exceeds the scribes and Pharisees. Secondly there is *practical* righteousness. Note the words *"and white raiment, that thou may be clothed."* Clothing is outward; others observe what is outward. This was a clothing center famous for making "black wool." This is the condition of the heart until it comes to faith in Christ; once Christ is received we are to demonstrate that He lives in us. Others will observe this. Secondly,

B: REPENTANCE! Verse 19, *"As many as I love, I rebuke and chasten: be zealous therefore, and repent."* This counsel to repent is one of the greatest indicates of His love for them. This was the only way to recover any of their former usefulness. They could go on with their form that was devoid of His presence or they could repent and enter into fellowship with Him. If they

The Apocalypse: The Revelation of the Redeemer

continue He said very clearly what the outcome would be in verse 16, "*I will spue you out of My mouth.*" Thirdly, He counsels them concerning:

C: REWARD! Verse 21 This is spoken to those that know Him. The reward is based upon "*overcoming.*" This is not to be understood as something that man does in his own strength. The example for every one to follow is stated in the verse, "*Even as I overcame.*" How did Jesus overcome? It was not by being lukewarm, but by self-denial. He gave Himself on the cross. To those that overcome He promises that they will sit with Him in His throne.

Conclusion:

Is it possible that you find yourself spiritually in Laodicea? Do you remember a time when you walked with Christ in surrender, and your affection was on things above? Can you hear Him as He knocks on the door of your heart? I am told that Holman Hunt was visiting the art gallery where his famous painting of *Christ Knocking at the Door* was on display. He was visiting with a fellow artist. The friend asked, "Haven't you made a mistake, there is no latch?" Mr. Hunt then said to the man, "*It is not a mistake; the latch is on the inside.*" If the door is opened it must be opened from within. If we will open, "*He will come in and sup with us.*" This is His desire and it should be ours as well.

Come...Up
Revelation 4:1-3 and 10-11

Paul declared that when the Lord Jesus returns in the rapture that we will be *"Caught up."* In Revelation 4:1 we hear the Lord say, *"Come up hither."* Without being overly dogmatic I believe that this is a clear picture of Christ calling His church unto Himself in the rapture. I recognize that in theological circles this is controversial with some. Yet it is my heart felt conviction that John, who represents the church is being caught up in the presence of God before the earth experiences the tribulation that is to be visited upon the earth during the tribulation period that will soon follow the removal of the church.

Before this great and terrible Day of the Lord, He calls His church, *"Come up hither."* It is this blessed truth that we want to focus our attention upon for the next few moments. Note first,

I: THE REVELATION! Verse 1, *"After this..."* These words cause us to naturally ask the question *"After what?"* Chapter 3 has concluded the pre-written history of the church and the church is no longer in the earth. The reality is that the church is not again seen in the Revelation until she is seen coming with Christ in Revelation chapter 19. All that transpires in the chapters that follow, with the exception of chapters 4 and 5, is the tribulation that is to be visited upon the earth. Now there are things that are going to be revealed to John and through the Word to you and me that will transpire when the church is with her Lord.

There are three things revealed to John and through him to you and me. First we have:

A: THE ACCESS! Verse 1, *"Behold, a door was open in heaven."* The Lord Jesus is the Door! John 10:9 informs us, *"I am the Door."* A door is to provide access but there is an interesting

The Apocalypse: The Revelation of the Redeemer

thing about this door, it is "*Open.*" The access is available. It was and it still is because Jesus will receive those that come to Him and those that come to Him now, as the Door, will enter this door when He comes to gather His church as His bride.

This door was open for entrance, the door to His heart is still open but a sad reality is that one day that door will close. Modern man does not think so, but the people in Noah's day did not think it would rain because it never had. It did rain and when the people that had scoffed tried to get in the door was shut. The second truth is:

B: THE ANNOUNCEMENT! Verse 1, "*The first voice was as of trumpet which said, 'Come up hither.'*" If John had not already experienced what he had in chapter 1 he would probably be overcome with fear. It is clear that now he is aware of Who is speaking. This announcement is clear and concise. There are two things involved in this announcement that are worthy of note. First, it is a **trumpet announcement;** "*Was as of a trumpet.*" We all know that trumpets do not talk, that is as we understand talking. However, most of us have heard a professional playing a trumpet and we have said, "He can make that trumpet talk." This is not what John is referring to in this usage. The trumpet was used to announce, to alert, to awaken and even to sound an alarm. This reinforces First Thessalonians 4:16, "*With the voice of the archangel and the trump of God.*" Secondly, it is a **triumphant announcement**. "*Saying come up hither.*" This is the church hearing the call from heaven to rise for the meeting in the air. Thirdly,

C: THE AFTERMATH! Verse 1 reveals this in the expression, "*I will show thee things which must be hereafter.*" The aftermath is the "Great and terrible Day of the Lord" that is going to be poured out upon the earth. Most of us have great difficulty in accepting the fact that such a thing would be allowed by God. If I understand the scripture it is not only allowed by God it is appointed by God. The world has experienced a similar event in the days of the flood and there is another destined for the earth. This is what the Revelation is about. It is sharing with us God's dealing with His world in order to restore it to its former state before sin and corruption deluded it. Secondly we have:

II: THE REDEEMER! Verses 2-3 John shares that *"He was immediately in the Spirit."* This ought to be enough to reveal to us that if we are going to have a proper view of the Savior that we must be "Filled with the Spirit;" otherwise we will have a distorted view of Him and that will affect everything with which we are involved. The pattern adopted in chapter 1 is holding in that before the aftermath is shown to John he again views the incomparable Christ. There are two things to note in these verses about the Redeemer. First,

A: HIS POSITION! Verse 2, *"A throne was set in heaven and one sat on the throne."* We sing often, *"He is exalted, the King is exalted on high."* This position is the only one He, because of Who He is will occupy. This is reminiscent of the experience of Isaiah in chapter 6 where *"He saw the Lord high and lifted up."* We know that Jesus said of Himself, *"And I, if I be lifted up I will draw all men unto Me."* He was lifted on the cross to purchase our redemption; He is lifted now in heaven but where is He in this service and in our hearts? When we enter do we remotely think that we are privileged to engage in the worship of the awesome, living, holy, loving God of creation and the One that controls His universe? If His position is proper we can not but help to focus on Him in everything that transpires while we are together. Secondly,

B: HIS PRESENTATION! Verse 3 This verse is so rich with Who He is and what Christ did for mankind that it is almost beyond mans ability to even slightly fathom its depths. We will note them in a limited manner. First we have *His Purity* in the expression, *"Was to look upon like a jasper."* The jasper is clear which symbolically represents the absolute purity of Christ. There is not a single flaw in Him. Think of the purest thing you possibly can and it does not begin to compare with His purity. Second we have *His Power* in the expression, *"And a sardine stone."* The sardine is our ruby. The color represents the precious blood of Christ that was shed for our redemption. The power of Christ is demonstrated on the cross by His commitment to the Father's will in the giving of Himself to provide man with the opportunity to experience full salvation. Thirdly, *His Promise* is shared in the

The Apocalypse: The Revelation of the Redeemer

words, *"And a rainbow round about the throne."* After the Lord had judged the earth with the flood He placed His bow in the clouds as a constant reminder that He would not again destroy the earth with water. Note that when we see a rainbow we see only half of it, here it is round about the throne indicating that it is an unbroken circle; meaning that His promises are as good as His word. Fourthly, *His Purpose is shared* is shared in the expression, *"In the sight like unto an emerald."* The emerald is green and green is color of life or living. The purpose of Jesus coming into the world was to impart life, life that never ends because it is eternal in Him. Our third major thought is:

III: THE RESPONSE! Verses 10-11 We are introduced to the twenty-four elders in verse 4. From the description given one thing is clear they are those that have experienced redemption. Their *clothing* and *crowns* give ample testimony to their relationship with the One on the throne. What kind of response would be appropriate? Their response is shared in verses 10-11 and it is the response that I believe our God longs for from you and me. It is a two-fold response. First, we have:

A: THE WORSHIP OF THE SAVIOR! Verse 10 states it in the words *"The four and twenty elders fall down before Him that sat on the throne, and worship Him that sat on the throne."* There are some exciting truths revealed in these words. First, we have the *position of the worshippers*, *"fall down before Him that sat on the throne."* He is on the throne and if they fall before Him they are at His feet. This is the place of worship! It is possible that herein lies the reason there is so little worship; our pride keeps us standing erect having the attitude that I am not going to bow the knee. We gather to worship and if we are going to worship Him we must abandoned our pride and with humble hearts prostrate our selves before Him. Secondly, we have *their presentation in worship*, *"And cast their crowns before the throne."* They cast their crowns as they are willingly prostrating themselves before Him.

We have almost reached the place that we view church as a "bless me parlor." That is something of a "spiritual" pep rally. Services provided the opportunity for you and me to engage in the worship of the true and living God and to bow before Him. If we do the celebrating will be a natural outflow of being in His presence. Many are trying to replace worship with celebration and the end result is little more than a temporary satisfying of emotion. Secondly, we have:

B: WORTHINESS OF THE SAVIOR! Verse 11, *"Thou art worthy, O Lord, to receive glory and honor and power: for Thou hast created all things, and for Thy pleasure they are and were created."* They have given evidence of this in verse 10 by the casting of their crowns and in so doing recognizing that everything is to be given to Him for He alone is worthy. Glory belongs to God and He will not share His glory with any. The word *"Worthy"* is *Axios* in Greek and it was used of the Roman emperor when he marched in a triumphal procession. Here is the key: **we worship who or what we consider to be worthy**. What are you worshipping?

Conclusion:
Do you agree that the One that occupies the throne is worthy of worship? He has promised that He will save and secure you. Will you now trust Him as Lord of your life?

At a day known only to God the call is going forth, *"Come up hither"* and those that have received Jesus as Lord of their lives will be *"Caught up to meet the Lord in the air."* Does that include you? If you profess to know Jesus are you presently engaged in a lifestyle of worship? Or has pride robbed you the present tense joy of knowing and serving Him?

Beholding the Throne
Revelation 4:4-9

When the scene opens in Revelation chapter 4 we are immediately transported from earth to heaven. We, through the witness of John, are allowed to gaze upon things that are beyond our comprehension. If we would partially fathom the depths of what is before us we must recognize that a major key to grasping these verses is the word *"throne."* The things that transpire in this chapter are either at, from, before, around, beneath or center in the throne. The word is used 12 times in this chapter and 37 times in the book. There is one truth that must be understood and that is that God is now as He has always been on His throne.

God prepared His throne and it is forever established. It is permanent and the power to keep this universe in operation flows from His throne. If that is true and Biblically, at least as I understand the Bible, it is we should be interested in this throne and even asks ourselves what kind of throne is this in Revelation 4? The primary aspect of this throne is judgment. Does that sound harsh? It is believed by some and the number continues to expand that God is going to make some marvelous allowance for the unrepentant. Even if we did not have the record of the Revelation there is a single verse in Hebrews 9:27 that is sufficient to inform and warn of judgment that is forthcoming to all. In light of this we would do well to spend some time beholding the throne. There are three things that we want to observe as we behold the throne in these verses. First, we have:

I: THE ELDERS AROUND THE THRONE! Verse 4 May I share that I have in excess of 75 books on Revelation and prophecy. Most of these are by conservative scholars. Yet, it is almost impossible to find common consensus among them as to who or what these twenty-four elders represent around the throne. Let us examine this group and see if we can gain some insight into who they are and represent. There are three things we want to observe about them. First,

A: THE COMPANY! Verse 4a, *"And round about the throne were four and twenty seats: and upon the seats I saw four and twenty elders sitting."* The word *"seat"* is the same word that is used for throne. Just as a secondary thought it is thrilling to know that God's people are numbered. I do not have a clue as to how many there are, or where I fall in the number but I do know that there is a number known to God. Let us notice two things about this company of elders. First, *they are redeemed.* Revelation 5:9 is sufficient to inform us that these are where they are because they have been redeemed by the blood of Christ. There are many suggestions and speculative responses about this company. Some suggest that these are a special order of angels but the word used for elder, *presbuteroi* is never used for angels only humans. From the song and context it is clear that this can only refer to those that have experienced salvation. Secondly, *they are reigning.* They are *"sitting upon thrones."* What are they doing? They are not running about in frenzy, or filled with anxiety and worry about what is going to happen. They are sitting, implying that they are reigning with Christ. Some suggest that the number 24 implies that it is both Israel and the church. However, nowhere is Israel promised that they would reign with Christ. Further, these are already in heaven and the tribulation is yet to take place upon the earth. The tribulation is that designated period of time known in the Bible as *"Jacob's trouble;"* or God dealing again with the nation of Israel. The number 24 really speaks of being inclusive, that is all those that have been redeemed during the day of grace that comprise the church of the Lord Jesus. Secondly, we note about the elders:

B: THE CLOTHING! Verse 4b, *"Clothed in white raiment."* Do you recall what Jesus said to the rich poor church? *"I counsel thee to buy of Me...white raiment."* It is true that we do see angels in white but as John MacArthur states "white garments are usually the clothing of believers." The white clothing represents the imputed righteousness of Christ that the believer receives at salvation. These are individuals that have experienced deliverance from the penalty, power, and the presence of sin through the applied blood of Jesus Christ. This is the experience that awaits us. We are saved presently from the penalty of sin. We are still confronted by the power and presence of sin. The question for our hearts in this hour is have I received His imputed righteousness through the new birth? The company and clothing assures me that this group of elders comprises the church. Thirdly, we have:

C: THE CROWNS! Verse 4c, *"And they had on their heads crowns of gold."* As far as I am able to determine only the church receives crowns from the Lord. These crowns in a practical manner speak of two things. First, *their royalty*. We are informed in chapter 1:5-6 that the believers have been elevated to the position of *"kings and priest."* Even better this is a *"kingdom of priest."* Peter reminds (1 Peter 2:9) us that we are a *"royal priesthood."* This is not merely something that is going to be but something that has spiritually already transpired. The tragedy is that we are not living in our present spiritual position. Secondly, the crowns speak of *their rewards*. There are two Greek words that are used for crowns. We sing about one of them often in the song, *"Bring forth the royal diadem and crown Him Lord of all."* That is not the word used here. The word here is *Stephanos* and it is the victor's crown, it is given to those that successfully competed and won the victory in and through Jesus Christ. The reality is that rewards are not yet given and will not be given until Christ raptures the church. John is seeing what will happen after the judgment seat of Christ. The challenge for you and me is not to focus upon crowns or rewards but to faithfully run the race that is set before us.

Who are the elders around the throne? My studied opinion is that they represent the church and only the church of Jesus Christ. Our second major thought is:

II: THE EMANATIONS FROM THE THRONE! Verse 5-6 The emanations from the throne inform us that judgment is on the horizon. There is coming what should be a sad reality for us. That is the Day of Judgment is close for this world that has rejected every offer of mercy. The only reason God does not judge the world now is that He is seated upon a throne of grace. In this day the shocking truth is that grace has passed. What is emitted from the throne? There are three extremely important truths that we should observe. First, we have:

A: THE STORM! Verse 5, *"Out of the throne proceeded lightnings, thunderings and voices."* There is a truth that must be noted. Man can not stop or alter that which proceeds from the throne of God. The lightnings, thunderings and voices indicate that a devastating storm is soon to be visited upon the earth. As we view our world with all its wickedness we might ask, "How can it possibly get any worse?" The judgment that is about to be visited upon the earth is not what man has called natural disasters, but the wrath of God in tribulation! This is *"justice day"* for the earth. As God has dealt with the earth in grace, He will now deal with it in justice.

The lightning, thunder and voices are what many call signs. And they are but they are signs of the storm, and not the Savior. He has already raptured His church when this storm devastates the earth.

Secondly, we have emitted from the throne:

B: THE SPIRIT! Verse 5, *"And there were seven lamps of fire before the throne, which are the seven Spirits of God."* This indicates the completeness and fullness of the Spirit of God. (For a complete description please study Isaiah 11:2; Zechariah 4:1-10). I am not sure that when we get to heaven and are privileged to gaze upon the throne of God that we are going to see *"seven lamps of fire."* We must remember that John is seeking to transmit a heavenly scene to earthly minds. It is important to note that the Holy Spirit now takes on His judicial character, fire. This is a symbol of divine judgment at His revelation.

John MacArthur has an interesting observation. Torches are associated with war in Judges 7:16, 20 and Nahum 2:3-4. "John's vision reveals God as ready to make war on sinful, rebellious mankind. The Comforter has now become the Consumer of those who reject Him."

There is a third truth that we now consider. That is:

The Apocalypse: The Revelation of the Redeemer

C: THE SEA! Verse 6, *"And before the throne there was a sea of glass, like unto crystal."* While the sea does not exactly emit from the throne it is probably a part of its base. Moses saw a similar scene when he saw the God of Israel in Exodus 24:10. The sea is not literal because we know that there will not be a sea in heaven. What can this possibly have to say or do with us? In the Old Testament the tabernacle and in Solomon's temple there was a laver for priestly purification, which in New Testament terms that indicates confession of sin before seeking to enter or minister to God or on behalf of His people. The point is that in heaven the sea is solid which indicates that there is not a need for confession. This informs us that then we will then be totally free from sin. We will then enter into the state of perfect sanctification. While this is not possible in this life it is nonetheless the goal for which believers strive.

The third thought is:

III: THE ESCORTS ABOUT THE THRONE! Verses 6-9 This is probably among the most controversial areas in the book. It would be easy for us to allow our imaginations to run rampant. That however, is not our purpose. I do want to share this truth. It is easy to say something indicates or represents something in this passage and then turn over three pages and say that the same thing represents something entirely different. I do not believe that is handling the Word of God properly. There are two thoughts for us to consider about this escort. First, we will observe:

A: THEIR DESCRIPTION! Verses 6b-8a The King James calls these escorts *"beast."* The New American Standard calls them *"living creatures."* It is my opinion that they would be better understood by the term "living ones." The word used in Revelation 4:6 is *zoa* from which we get our word zoo. The word used in Revelation 13:1 is *theria* which means a *"vicious-wild-beast."* W.A. Criswell states that these are the same as the ones in Ezekiel's vision recorded in chapter one of his book. It is these living ones that we want to focus our attention upon for a moment. In observing their description we note their *function* in verse 6, *"full of eyes before and behind."* This indicates that they have awareness and that they are alert. These are in my opinion the same living ones that were placed outside the Garden of Eden to protect the way of the tree of life. Their number indicates that they have to do with the world since they are four in number and four is the number of the world. They are associated with protection and in this case they serve as protectors of the holiness of God. We also have their *features* in verse 7, *"And the first living one was like a lion, and the second living one like a calf, and the third living one had a face as a man, and the fourth living one was like a flying eagle."* The lion represents *strength*. The calf or young ox represents *strength*. The face of a man represents *sense* or reasoning ability. The eagle represents *speed*. Some commentators believe that in these we have illustrated the character of Christ as He is presented in the four gospels. The lion is *kingly* as represents Christ in *Matthew's* gospel. The young ox represents the *servant* and represents Christ in *Mark's* gospel. The face of the man reveals Christ as the *Son of Man* and represents Christ in *Luke's* gospel. The eagle is *heavenly* and represents Christ in *John's* gospel. There is a second thing we notice about this escort. That is:

B: THEIR DEVOTION! Verse 8, *"And the four living ones had each of them six wings about him; and they were full of eyes within: and they rest not day and night, saying, 'Holy, holy, holy, Lord God Almighty, which was, and is, and is to come.'"* A portion of their devotion is revealed first in their *"wings."* Isaiah 6:2 shares some insight into the *"wings"* of these living ones. There we discover that with two they covered their face, with two they flew, and with two they covered their feet. The wings have to do with the speed of their service to God. Which indicates their devotion to the One on the throne. A second portion of their devotion is revealed in their *worship*. But observe that even the highest of the created beings do not look upon full deity. They cover their eyes signifying something of the tremendous reverence and respect that they possess for the holiness of God. If these unregenerate beings have this deep reverence and continually (*rest not day and night*) engage in worship what should be the response of those that have experienced His salvation?

The Apocalypse: The Revelation of the Redeemer

Conclusion:

Are you presently a part of the living body of Christ that shall one day be in His presence and engage in worship and celebration? If not may I simply say to you that the terrible judgment that is going to be visited upon this earth is nothing to be compared with the eternal hell that awaits you in endless separation from the loving heart of God. Jesus loves you and He waits to receive you, do not wait any longer but yield to the call of His Spirit while you have the opportunity.

When the Search Concludes
Revelation 5:1-14

In the original manuscripts there are no chapter divisions. Therefore, in chapter five our focus is again upon the throne. In this message we are going to focus our thoughts upon something that is in the hand of the occupant of the throne. It is a scroll like book. This chapter is fundamental in our understanding the events that are forthcoming upon the earth.

There are a number of books mentioned in the Bible. Among them are the book of life, the book of deeds, and the book of testimony. But this (apart from the record of the individual's salvation) in the total plan of things is by far the most important. This book is the official document that contains the great events that climax the history of the earth. It is interesting that throughout history there have been predictions and even those persons that have sought to determine the destiny of the earth, yet the destiny of the earth is about to be unfolded in the Revelation.

This book that we will focus upon is referred to by Daniel in chapter 12:8-9, *"And I heard, but understood not, then said I, O my Lord, what shall be the end of these things? And He said, go thy way, Daniel for the words are closed up and sealed until the time of the end."* The book closed up and sealed has since been in the possession of Him that gave it. Ezekiel also refers to this book in chapter 2:9-10 where he saw lamentations, mourning and woe. This should be enough to more than arouse interest. It should be sufficient for us to devote a portion of our time in seeking to understand the weighty matters that are about to be presented.

There are three basic thoughts in these verses that we seek to explore. The first is:

The Apocalypse: The Revelation of the Redeemer

I: THE BOOK THAT IS SEALED! Verses 1-4 The very presence of this book probably causes some questions. The Greek word for *"book"* is the word for scroll. There was something different in that normally the scroll was only written upon the inside. This one is written on front and back. This says to us that it is *"filled up."* It would be like a person writing on the front and back of a sheet of paper, rolling it up and then placing a seal to insure that it would not be opened. This was done seven times; signifying that the sealed book was completely sealed. There are three truths that need consideration. The first is:

A: THE CONTENTS! If this book is sealed with seven seals how can we possibly know anything of its contents? We can learn much about the content of this sealed book by noting two things about it. First, we will consider the *meaning* of this book. In passing simply note the *position of scroll*; verse 1, *"In the right hand of Him that sat on the throne."* Remember that the One on the throne is sovereign God. He is the Creator and Controller of this world. It is important to understand that the book in lying in His hand. He is not holding the book in a tight fisted manner. We desperately need to understand that our God is not a tight fisted tyrant that delights in punishing and with holding good things from those that love Him. The book is lying in His hand waiting for someone to take it. Things that are in His hand are never pried out. He is waiting to either bestow blessings or to receive burdens. Then we have the *power of the seal.* Verse 1, *"Sealed with seven seals."* The seal signifies ownership. Every one needs to be reminded periodically *"The earth is the Lord's and the fullness thereof."* The meaning of this sealed book is alluded to in the account of Jeremiah. (Jeremiah 32) Before he was taken into captivity he purchased some property from his cousin. Then he is carried into captivity but when he returned he had the title deed of the property he had purchased before captivity. According to the Old Testament three things could be redeemed; those being a wife, a servant and land. When Jesus died He made provisions for the purchase of the first two and when He comes again the third will be completed. When we are saved we become part of the bride of Christ and are no longer salves of sin. Thus the first two but when He comes in the rapture then the earth will once again be under His rule. The earth was given to man but through his sin he lost the right to rule over it. It is now under the control of Satan but this is destined to change. This leads to the second thing we want to note about the content of the sealed book. That is the *message* of the book. Again we will consider two things that will share insight into the message of the book. First, we have the *subject* of the book. Its subject is full redemption. He that opens the seals is the Lamb still bearing the marks of His crucifixion. The full redemption is that of the creation of God. Secondly, we have the *song* of the book in verse 9. Redemption has its root in the past, but its final fulfillment lies in the future. Remember Paul's words, *"You were sealed with the Holy Spirit of promise, which is the earnest of our inheritance until the redemption of the purchased possession."* The possession has been purchased, but it has not been fully redeemed. Secondly, we have:

B: THE CHALLENGE! Verses 2-3 When John sees the sealed book he hears the inquiry of what is designated as a *"Strong angel."* This angel proclaimed so loudly that the entire universe heard the challenge in verse 2 in the words, *"Who is worthy to open the book and to loose the seals thereof?"* The word *"worthy"* actually means morally fit. It seems as if a search is ensued as indicated by the words in verse 3, *"And no man in heaven."* The words, *"no man"* literally means *"no one"* and it includes the host of angelic beings. We might think that surely one of them, possibly Michael or Gabriel would be able to take the book. But not so! Surely one of the great saints of old now in heaven could step forward and accept the challenge to open the book. Possibly Abraham, Moses or Elijah could step forward and take the book and open it. However, that is not the case. Then one that is now upon the earth could take the book and open it but the verse declares, *"No man in earth."* Those words leave us in a state of bewilderment don't they? They smack our ego, our pretense of goodness and our exalted opinion of ourselves. The reality is that when the verse declares that *"No man"* that it says exactly what it means. Not in heaven, not in earth and not under the earth. If the enemy could take this book then he could control the events that are destined for the earth. But it is beyond the reach of the underworld. Is it possible that this challenge is presented to reveal

The Apocalypse: The Revelation of the Redeemer

to John and through him to you and me that God and God alone controls the events that are forthcoming to the earth? Thirdly, we have:

C: THE CRYING! Verse 4, *"And I wept much, because no man was found worthy to open and to read the book, neither to look thereon."* There are two things that will help us understand something of this crying. First, we have the *loud lament*, *"He wept much."* The words *"wept much"* actually means a loud audible and open cry. This prompts the question of why is John crying, after all he is in heaven. It is not because he is weak but because he knows there is an inheritance that will be unclaimed because no man was found worthy to open and read the book. This would leave much that is undone including the retribution of the wicked, the restoration of Israel and the reign of Christ. John cries as a result of a broken heart. What cause our tears? Are we crying over the uncounted millions that do not know Jesus as Lord or because our team lost the ball game? In the crying we have secondly, the *lack of liberty* presented in the words, *"Neither to look thereon."* This is revealed in the fact that not only could no one be found to open the book, no one was found that qualified even look at the contents.

Do you join John in crying about the seven-sealed book? We should not be overly concerned about this book if we are not concerned about opening the book that He has put in our hands. This is the book that we need to allow the Spirit of God to put in our hearts.

Our second major thought is:

II: THE BLESSED SAVIOR! Verses 5-7 John's heart is broken. He is weeping because if the book is not taken and opened this world will stay under the control of the enemy. In verse 4 it is *"a strong angel"* that announces that a search is made for one to take the book that is sealed yet, this angel concludes, *"No one was found worthy to take the book and to loose the seals thereof."* However, in verse 5 it is *"One of the elders"* that responded to the cry of John and the announcement of the angel that steps forward and say, *"I know One."* It is an elder, one of the redeemed, one that knows declares, *"There is One."* The elder says to John,

"*Weep not.*" That is the message that our Lord has given his church and that is the message that His church is to continue relating, "*Weep not,*" because there is One that will do for you what no one has been able to do.

The elder then says, "*Behold.*" That is a word that is used to secure our attention, that declares that there is something important that is about to be shared. As we look at the Blessed Savior there are two truths that I want us to observe. First, we have:

A: THE DESCRIPTION! Verses 5-6 reveal that He is described in a three-fold manner. First, He is described as:

1. The Lion of the Tribe of Judah! Verse 5 This speaks to us of **His strength**. Judah is the lion tribe. When Jacob was blessing his children, Judah, his firstborn, came and stood before him. (Genesis 49:10) Jacob said, "*Judah you are like a lions whelp and the scepter shall depart from Judah until Shiloh is come.*" The word Shiloh means "*The one whose right it is.*" As John describes the Savior as "*The lion of the tribe of Judah*" he is referring to His strength which includes His sovereignty. The nation of Israel anticipated a Messiah that would be the Lion of the tribe of Judah. The verse further demonstrates His strength when John says; "*The Lion of the tribe of Judah hath prevailed.*" The word "*hath*" informs us that it is a completed act in the past and not to be repeated. The word "*prevailed*" in Greek is *Niki*, and it is not referring to either a missile or tennis shoes but it means "*Overcome, conqueror, victor.*" Thus John declares that the Lion has already purchased victory. He prevailed in life in the times of *trial*; He prevailed in times of *temptation*, He prevailed in the *terrors* of death, and He comes forth in *triumphant* strength to conquer. Secondly, in His description we have:

2. The Root of David! Verse 5 If there is perhaps even the remotes doubt that this is Jesus simply read Revelation 22:16, "*I Jesus...the root of David.*" This indicates that He is the **source**, I am the One from whom David came. Why does it not say that He is the root of Abraham, Moses or Elijah? Why David? Abraham is of the *promise*, Moses is of the *law*, and Elijah is of the *prophets* but David is preeminently associated with *kingship*.

The Apocalypse: The Revelation of the Redeemer

Jesus will be king over this entire world. Thirdly, He is described as:

3. The Lamb! Verse 6 This reveals His **sacrifice**. John knew Jesus in the flesh; he was there when Jesus was the Lamb of God on the cross. He now recognizes that He is the same Lamb. Israel was looking for a Lion but they failed to understand that before He was the Lion He must be the Lamb. Observe that the *"Lamb has been slain."* The Greek word for *"slain"* is *sphazo* and it indicates one slain violently, ripped and torn. It is the word that is used to describe the blood, the sacrifice and the suffering of the one offered at the altar. Remember Isaiah said, *"He was wounded for our transgression, bruised for our iniquities, the chastisement of our peace was upon Him and He was led as a lamb to the slaughter."* This is the sacrifice; Jesus Christ violently ripped, torn and slain from the foundation of the world. This is the price paid for our redemption.

He saw this Lamb standing. This little word *"stood"* is powerful because the Lamb is bearing the wounds of Calvary but he is standing. This is resurrection! John saw Jesus on the cross but now he sees Him alive bodily in heaven. This lamb is not lying, kicking or in panic. Hebrews (1:3) tells us that when Jesus ascended that He sat down. In heaven we see Jesus both seated, that is in relationship to the finished work of redemption but we see Him also standing and that informs us that there is something on the horizon that is about to transpire.

There is a precious truth in the word *"Lamb."* The common word that is used in the Greek for lamb is *ammos* and it is used 27 times as a reference to Jesus. However, *ammos* is not the word used in Revelation 5:6. It is the word *arinios* and this word is used only twice in the New Testament. First, in John 21:15 where Jesus said to Peter *"Feed My little lambs."* And secondly in Revelation 5:6 where it means a *"Little pet lamb."* In the Passover the Jewish families were instructed to get an *arinios*, a lamb of the first year, for its perfection and its beauty. That lamb was to be brought into the house and keep for four days. It was to be identified with that family and become a pet of the children. It was that little pet lamb that was slain at the Passover. Jesus came as God's gift of love and all He did was to identify with fallen man; to love man as he had never been loved; to give Himself for man. Man's response was to crucify Him. O, what a Savior! We now move from His description to:

B: THE DETAILS! Verses 6-7 Jesus is about to be presented not only as the *Redeeming One* but also as the *Reigning One*. As the Lamb that has redeemed He is worthy to possess. As the Lamb He is our *Savior* and as Lion He is *Sovereign*. There are three details presented. First, we have:

1. His Power! Verse 6, *"having seven horns."* This expression is taken from animals that use their horns as instruments of power. They used their horns to fight, as weapons to tear their prey or enemy. Thus these *"seven horns"* reveal the complete power that is in the Lamb/Lion. It also suggest to us that something rather than sacrifice or intercession. These *"seven horns"* suggest that this is aggressive power. This is the imperial power and authority that rest in the Lamb/Lion and He is about to exercise the power that is His. The second detail is:

2. His Perception! Verse 6; *"Seven eyes which are the seven Spirits of God sent forth into all the earth."* Please mark Isaiah 11:1-3 and study this passage. It says, *"In Him"* and it literally means *His heart will be the home* of the Spirit of wisdom, understanding, counsel, might, knowledge, fear of the Lord and quick understanding in the fear of the Lord. When Jesus rules He will rule with full knowledge. The third detail is:

3. His Possession! Verse 7; *"Took the book."* This is one of the most important verses in the Bible. When He takes the book the end begins. It is His possession. This book contains the destiny of the earth; it reveals the judgment of this world; how the anti-Christ will be defeated; how Satan will be bound and how Christ will sit upon the throne and reign.

Suppose someone asks Him, "What are the bases of Your claim to the title deed of the earth?" He could say, "It is Mine by creation for I created this world." He could say, "It is Mine because of Calvary, I redeemed this world." He could say, "It is Mine by way of conquest for I will take this world." This earth in totality is one day going to be reigned over by the Lamb/Lion.

There is an expression in verse 6 that we need to observe. That is, *"In the midst of the throne."* It is my opinion that John

The Apocalypse: The Revelation of the Redeemer

was so caught up in all the splendor, the rainbow and all that is transpiring that he did not see the Lamb that was standing in the midst. We can get so caught up in coming to church, listening to Bible teaching, listening to the music and the message that we miss Jesus. He is in the midst of your hurt and disappointment. If we will allow the Spirit of God to open our eyes and reveal to us Jesus we will discover that our hurt, problem, disappointment and need is lost in the glory of His person. Further, He that takes this book can and will take your burden and do what one else is capable of doing.

I do not know where you are but it is possible that He has brought you to where you are for you to realize that *"He is in the midst."*

Our third major thought is:

III: THE BENEDICTION OF THE SERVANTS! Verses 8-14 When the Lamb took the book there went a thrill through the heart of all living things. The four living ones, and the 24 elders, join in every creature in heaven and earth join in a glorious benediction to the Savior.

An interesting fact is that prior to this John was weeping and now he and all heaven and earth are filled with praise. Do you have any praise in your heart? The Psalmist declared in Psalm 150, *"Let everything that hath breath praise the Lord."* The benediction of the servants is presented in two ways by which we can also bless the Lord. First, we have the servants:

A: SINGING! Verses 8-10 One of the easiest and most effective ways we can bless the Lord is by singing. There are two things that we must observe about their singing. First,

1. They Sing to the Savior! Verse 8 May I inquire as to what if any difference it would make if our singing were to the Savior? How much singing would we do if we sang only when we were singing to Him? The reality is that we sing at almost every gathering. This, for the most part, is as it should be because music helps our hearts to be moved toward God. Yet, we need to realize that the Savior is the audience and that we are not singing to entertain. Those that sing are leading us in worship! When we sing heaven gets blessed! Their singing to the Savior involves two aspects. **First**, it involves *praise*. Verse 8 informs us that *"harps"* are used. Read Revelation 14:2 and 15:2 and you will discover that the harp is the celestial instrument of praise. Heaven is thrilled that the Worthy One has taken the book that is sealed. In heaven all pretense and make believe are vanished because all the focus is upon God for He is solely responsible for them being there. If we are going to join in praise to Him there it just makes sense that we practice now. **Secondly**, it involves *prayer*. Verse 8, *"Which are the prayers of the saints."* I do not mean to infer that in heaven we actually pray in the accepted form of presenting petitions. Neither does this infer that saints are mediators by which we reach Christ however, the verse tells us that the prayers that have been offered are in *"golden vials"* which consist of the prayers of all the saints of all time and they come into remembrance at this time. It is possible that the chief burden of many of those has not been fulfilled and that now all those prayers are about to be answered. It is possible that these are prayers that have said, *"Thy Kingdom come Thy will be done on earth as it is in heaven."* Those prayers have been heard; the timing has not been right and they could not be answered until now. The second thing for us to notice about the singing is:

    2. The Song they Sing! Verses 9-10 Do you have a song? The Psalmist declared *"He hath put a new song in my mouth even praise to our God."* This is a *"New song."* Do you like learning new songs? The sad fact is that in most church services there are about 15 songs that are rotated depending upon the occasion. There are two words upon which this song is built. Those words are (verses 9 and 12) *"Worthy"* and (verse 14) *"Worship."* The fact is we worship that which we consider to be worthy! This *"New song"* has three stanzas and they sing them all. The **first** stanza is *He loved us* in verse 9, *"Was slain."* This is Calvary. This is the place where a love that cannot be measured was manifested. While it is a love that can not be adequately expressed it is a love that can be experienced. This is unmerited, unconditional and unending love. The **second** stanza is *He loosed us* in verse 9, *"and hast redeemed us."* The word redeemed declares that He loosed or freed us. Those that have trusted Him have been loosed from sin and are free to serve Him. This is

The Apocalypse: The Revelation of the Redeemer

beautifully illustrated in John 11 where Jesus, referring to Lazarus said, *"Loose him and let him go."* The **third** stanza is *He lifted us* as verse 10 states, *"Made us kings and priest."* The word "made" indicates that this was not of our own doing. We have been lifted by adoption. Every redeemed soul becomes a part of God's kingdom. If you are saved you are indeed somebody! These words, *"made us kings...and we shall reign on the earth"* indicate that we are now *sons*. We become children of God and heirs and joint heirs with Christ. Luke 19 helps us understand something of our future reign with Him. In the parable of the nobleman Jesus said that some would reign over cities. We are sons and secondly, these words further indicate that we are *servants*. How? As *"priest we are to offer sacrifices to our Lord."* That is we are to praise Him because we are the receivers of His manifold goodness and grace. Therefore, we are to show forth praise to Him. Secondly, we have the servants benediction in their:

B: SHOUTING! Verses 11-14 John says, *"I beheld or I saw"* no less than 44 times. This informs us that he was an eyewitness of what is being shared. All join in the shouting to the One that liveth forever. Their shouting is twofold. First,

1. This is a Sevenfold Shout! Verse 12 The number seven informs us that this is a complete shout to the Savior. I am merely going to list them as they are presented to us in this one verse. **First**, it is a shout of His *power*. All power is His and He demonstrated a portion of that power in creation, over demons and death. In heaven all yield to His authority. He has the power to save, sustain and sanctify those that will yield to His power now. **Second** His *riches*. He was rich yet for our sakes He became poor that we might through Him become rich. Haggai 2:8 declares, *"All the silver and gold are Mine."* Have we learned that we possess nothing and that we are caretakers of His riches? In heaven all resources are not only His but they are at His disposal. We would be wise if we were to implement that in the earth. He is rich enough to redeem. **Thirdly**, we have His *wisdom*. Man boast of wisdom and knowledge as he makes advancements in the sciences. Yet, the reality is that man is simply discovering what He has created. Are we yielding our minds to Him now? **Fourthly**, we have His *strength*. When He comes the second time

(Psalm 24) it will be as the King of glory, the Lord strong and mighty. He has the strength for you and me to overthrow evil and overcome temptations. **Fifth**, we have His *honor*. He is honored in heaven and dishonored in earth. He is praised there and blasphemed here. If we are going to give honor to whom honor is due we must turn to Christ. **Sixth**, we have His *glory*. Man seeks to takes His glory for himself. There men will think more highly of Him than they do of themselves. Are we giving Him the glory due His name? **Seventh**, we have His *blessing*. The word means to be happy. Is He happy with our lives? It would make a tremendous difference in how we lived if we sought to live lives that make Him happy. If we will ponder what He has done for us we will realize how blessed we are and that we should desire to bless Him as well. What are we willing to do to make Him happy? Secondly,

    2. This is a Surrendered Shout! Verses 13-14; *"Fall down and worshipped Him that liveth for ever and ever."* The entire universe joins in shouting the worthiness of the Lamb that has taken the book. The elders then lead in the *worship* of the Lord that was and is, and is to come. A proud heart does not have the desire to worship the Lord Jesus. There are those that might say, "Man I was hoping that this thing of worship would be over when I get to heaven" No! Then we will worship properly and it will be the absolute desire of our hearts to worship the Worthy One. The host of heaven says, *"Amen."* Can we say *"Amen"* to the word of God to us?

Conclusion:
In heaven there is worship and praise to and for the Worthy One. Surely it would be a display of wisdom on our part if we join in worship and praise to Him now. Do you have a song? He is willing to give you a *"New Song"* if you will place your trust in Him. Where has your shout gone? How long has it been since you have engaged in the worship of the Worthy One? Are you yielded to His Lordship and if not why not?

The Horsemen Are Coming
Revelation 6:1-8

We are entering what many designate as the main action of the book. We have encountered some pretty amazing things in the first five chapters. We have observed the glorified Christ, the church, the church caught up into heaven, and the worship of the worthy One in heaven. Now we approach a different theme: The judgment period of the earth is on the horizon. This is the action by which, in the judicial proceedings of God, our Lord takes the back from the hands of Satan the inheritance forfeited by man through sin. This is the destruction of the powers of darkness, and the bringing of light, life and liberty. He that holds the title deed of the earth by creation and redemption is about to take possession of His purchased property and begin to open the seals of destiny.

Chapters 4 and 5 are scenes in heaven. The believers have been taken out, raptured and rewarded. God's people must be removed before the fire of His judgment can fall. An illustration of this truth is presented in the Old Testament in the record of Lot. The angel of the Lord said to him, "*I can do nothing until thou be come thence.*" Lot was a compromising Christian, vexing his soul with the filthy conversation (manner of life) of Sodom. Yet, he was one of God's. Peter presents him as a "*Preacher of righteousness.*" He was in New Testament terms saved. After Lot is removed from the city doomed to destruction, the flames, the brimstone and the judgment of God fell. So will it be again upon the earth.

The judgment period takes place from chapter 6:1 to chapter 19:4. These judgments are executed in three series; (1) The seals, (2) the trumpets and (3) the vials. The seven seals cover the entire judgment period. The trumpets are in the last seal and the vials are in the last trumpet.

These judgments are future. They have not been fulfilled as yet. The earth has witnessed on a much smaller scale some of the judgments that are forthcoming but it cannot be said that the kingdoms of this world are become the Kingdoms of our Lord and His Christ. This is future!

Someone has pointed out the following comparison of Matthew 24 and Revelation 6. If one can believe Matthew chapter 24; then he can, without difficulty believe Revelation chapter 6. Note the comparison:

Matthew 24 Revelation 6
False Christ Verse 5 Seal one Verses 1-2
Wars Verses 6-7 Seal two Verses 3-4
Famine Verse 7 Seal three Verses 5-6
Pestilence Verse 7 Seal four Verses 7-8
Martyrdom and Kingdom Seal five Verses 9-10
Preaching Verse 9 and 14
Earthquakes Verse 7 Seal six Verse 12

Jesus said in verse 8, "*All these things are the beginning of sorrow.*"

These events do not take place at the same time. For example it is probably that there will be a three and one half-year difference between the first and second seal.

There are many debates as to whether or not the details are to be regarded as literal or symbolically. We cannot say that either all is literal or all is symbols. Language and context must determine the question of literalness or symbolism. Are the horses and horsemen literal or symbolic? It is my studied opinion that they are symbolic of the nature of the judgments and calamities that are to come upon the earth. Notice the words in verse one, "*As it were.*" This phrase indicates the use of symbolic language. The horses are used here in a figurative sense, prophetically of judgment upon the earth in the last days (Zech. 1:8-11 and Revelation 6:1-5).

Remember that Christ has been acclaimed as "*worthy*" in heaven while He is being rejected upon the earth. Now the earth must receive Him, but first the righteous judgment of God must be meted out to the inhabitants of the earth that have rejected Him. We now turn our attention to the seals of Revelation six. The first seal:

I: THE COUNTERFEIT! Verses 1-2 There is nothing original about Satan. There is little that God has created that Satan has not sought to counterfeit. There are a couple of illustrations of this presented in the record of scripture; one, simply recall Moses experience when he stood before Pharaoh. He threw down the rod and it became a snake, the magicians duplicated the miracle. This reveals something of the power of the enemy. The difference was that Moses snake devoured the snakes of the magicians. Another is found in Matthew chapter 25 where we read of the *"Ten virgins."* The five *"foolish virgins"* could not be dictated by their appearance. So it is with Satan's counterfeit in Revelation chapter 6. The reality is that God will *"send them a strong delusion that they will believe the lie"* (11 Thessalonians 2:11). Observe that John says, *"I saw"* and *"I heard"* indicating that he was, by the Spirit of God, an eyewitness of the events that were going to come to pass.

A: THE ANNOUNCEMENT! Verse 1 Preparation is being made to open the first seal. There are some interesting things for us to consider. (1) *To whom is this spoken*? There are those that suggest that these words are spoken to John. If he were talking to John there would not be the need of crying in a voice of thunder. The commands, *"Come, go and proceed"* are not to John but to the riders of the horses that are to come. (2) *Who is speaking*? It is one of the living ones. When the subject deals with heaven the elders speak (the elders do not appear again until chapter 19:4). When the subject deals with the earth one of the living ones does the speaking. (3) *The way it was spoken. "As it were the noise of thunder."* This is the tone of majesty and might. Thunder portends a coming storm. The first mention of thunder is in connection with God's judgment upon Egypt (Exodus 9:23). This voice as a clap of thunder announces the beginning of the tribulation period, the time of Jacob's trouble. The thunder of Divine judgment upon the earth rolls with increasing power for seven years until the lightening of Christ Second Coming to the earth strikes. The announcement is the beginning of Daniel's seventh week (Daniel 9:27). Secondly, we have:

B: THE ANTICHRIST! Verses 2 Lehman Strauss in his book *The End of This Present World* shares some interesting insight into the subject of the Antichrist. Let us not be deceived as to who the rider of this horse is. Some have suggested that this is Christ. Consider that it is Christ that pulls aside the curtain in order for us to see the impending judgment; when He does so He must then change into the garb of a soldier and come forth riding a white horse. The idea is somewhat confusing. There is another problem; namely, all four horsemen have a common denominator. To say that the rider of the white horse is Christ is to associate Him with all the events that are connected with the other three horses. Another point is that the rider of the while horse in chapter six appears at the beginning of Daniel's seventh week while the rider in chapter 19 appears at the end of the week. This rider is none other than the counterfeiter, Satan's man in the flesh, the Antichrist. There are four things to be considered about the Antichrist. A simple definition of the word "anti" is opposite. First we have:

1. The Person! Verse 2 clearly reveals this in the words "*He that sat.*" Is this a person or a principle? There is a principle of Antichrist but this is "*the*" not "*a*" Antichrist. If there is a principle it originated with a person. Paul, in 11 Thessalonians 2:3 uses the expression, "*Man of sin.*" The word "*man*" (*anthropos*) is not used for any except a human being. Moreover, the use of the article "*the' man of sin, "the' son of perdition, "the' wicked one*" indicates that is indeed individual person.

Lehman Strauss shares that there are indications that the Antichrist will be a Jew. Jesus said in John 5:43 "*I am come in My Father's name, and ye receive Me not; if another shall come in his own name, him ye will receive.*" Daniel 11:37, "*Neither shall he regard the God of his fathers.*" It is not likely that the Jews will acclaim as their Messiah a man that is not of their own race. Strauss offers this bit of speculation that might have merit to some. His thought is that the only time in scripture (Luke 22:3) where we are informed that *Satan entered into anyone is when he entered Judas.* He suggests that there is the possibility that the

The Apocalypse: The Revelation of the Redeemer

Antichrist could be Judas resurrected. The issues that I have with this is that it gives to the devil the power of resurrection and I am not convinced that he possess that power. Secondly, we have:

2. The Pretense! Verse 2 shares this is done in the words *"He that sat on the white horse."* A number of commentators identify this rider as Christ based upon the fact that this horse is white and Christ comes forth riding a white charger in chapter 19. The point is that he is pretending to be the Savior of the world. In addition, it was the style of the victor to ride into the city on a white charger of victory. This in itself is a pretense. The pretense of the Antichrist is witnessed further in the fact that he is wearing a crown and so does Christ in revelation 19. There is a marked difference in the crowns. The Antichrist is wearing a *"Stephanos"* crown that one could win here, as in a race. The crown that Christ wears is a *"Diadem"* and it is the crown of a reigning, sovereign monarch. Thirdly, we have:

3. The Plan! Verse 2 reveals this in the words *"He had a bow."* After the church is removed this man will come on the scene offering peace and security to the nations of the earth. He is coming with a bow but no arrow. His plan is a bloodless conquest. He is going to write a treaty with the Jewish people by which they will have their homeland, enable them to rebuild their temple and reestablish the Mosaic order of sacrifice.

He will use deception as a part of his plan. The covenant that he makes will be kept for approximately 3 and ½ years. Our world is fast approaching, if we are not there, the place that it would gladly receive such a man. Fourth, we have:

4. The Purpose! Verse 2 states this in the words *"Conquering and to conquer."* This can be translated as "victory after victory." He is the liberator of the earth, at least in the eyes of the earth. He is the conqueror of all the problems of the world. He manages to give each one what he wants. The entire military, economic and political resources of the world are at his disposal. He comes in the name of peace but his purpose is to possess.

This informs us that the anti-Christ is on the march. He is Satan's man, totally dominated by the devil and it is his intention to take possession of the world. How can this be possible? A portion of the answer is that the church (the salt of the earth) is no longer here to offer any resistance to the work of Satan and sin. These have been sent a "strong delusion" and they believe "the lie." All of this is transpiring as a result of man's rebellion against God. He has refused God's offer of grace, now he will receive God's judgment.

This leads us to consider the second horseman:

II: THE CONFLICT! Verses 3-4 Another living one says, "*come.*" John saw another horse; this one is red. This indicates fighting and bloodshed. The rider is the same. It is possible that these events overlap somewhat since the horses involve the same rider. There are two things to consider about this conflict. First,

A: HE RECEIVED POWER! Verse 4, "*And power was given unto him.*" This naturally causes one to inquire as to where the rider receives this power? The word says, "*It was given unto him.*" But who gave him this power? Does Satan have power over the earth now? Surely, he is the god of this world, the prince of the power of the air.

Remember that God originally gave dominion and power of the earth to man. Man forfeited his dominion when he sinned.

The antichrist power is given to him by God Himself! Does that statement bother you? He receives this power in order to bring glory to God. Does God use the ungodly to glorify His name? Yes, remember Pharaoh. His power will be used to dominate the earth. We recognize that he is now dominating the earth in several areas but in this day he will dominate but it will be to ultimately bring glory to God. Secondly,

B: HE REMOVES PEACE! Verse 4 reveals this in the expression "*To take peace form the earth.*" It is almost impossible for us to imagine anything as awesome as this. We have a measure of peace but at best it is unsettled. During this day there shall be no peace. At this time men will be killing one another because a sword has replaced the peaceful bow. The Greek word is *Machaira* and it refers to the short, stabbing sword that a Roman soldier carried into battle. This was a "*sword*" that could be hidden and with this they "*killed one another.*" This was also a weapon used by assassins. This indicates a hand to hand fighting. There will be international warfare with nation fighting nation. It also refers to civil war, religious war, race wars but it means more. It indicates that this will even be families against families. But observe that the rider of the horse has what is called a *"great sword."* This again reflects upon the intensity of the battle and that peace is taken from the earth.

We now give our attention to the third horseman:

III: THE CATASTROPHE! Verses 5-6 This is the natural result of the worldwide conflict of verses 3-4. The rider is the same; the color of the horse is now black. The use of the word, *"behold"* indicates that this was a shock; it was not expected. Black is a sign of famine (Lamentations 5:10). Each seal reveals a greater intensity of the events that will be transpiring during the tribulation. There are two truths for us to consider. First, we have:

A: THE INSTRUMENT HE CARRIES! Verse 5 He is not carrying a weapon of war, not a hidden knife for hand to hand warfare, rather he is carrying a *"pair of balances."* He is dealing with the staff of life, bread, i.e., wheat and barley. There will be rationing as never before. This is natural because the people that have been producing food will be either so involved in fighting or killed that food will not have been produced. Famine is a terrible death. The Bible declares in Lamentation 4:9, *"They that be slain with the sword are better than they that be slain with hunger."* Jesus said in Matthew 24:7, *"And there shall be famine."* Death is death but most individuals have a particular way that they do not want to die. I have always had a horror of drowning. It is reported to be among the easiest ways to die, but I really do not know how anyone would know that. In our world there are in excess of a billion people that are hungry. Millions are in danger of starvation. The American dog has a diet of higher protein than most of the people of the world. But all of this is child's play when compared with the worldwide famine that will be experienced during that day.

Secondly, we have:

B: THE INFLATION HE CAUSES! Verse 6 reveals this in the words *"A measure of wheat for a penny and three measures of barley for a penny."* There are two things to consider about the inflation he causes. First there is the *extreme prices*. The *"penny"* was what a working man wages would be for a day. With it he could buy enough food to feed himself. If this man worked all day for enough money to feed himself what would his family do? In John's day eight measures of wheat sold for a penny, now the price has increased eight times. If he could not afford the wheat then he could buy three measures of barley and feed his wife and one child. But barley was low in nutritional value and commonly fed to livestock. Both of these scenarios represent starvation wages, and signify severe famine conditions. Secondly, the *excluded people*, *"Touch not the oil and the wine."* There are different opinions about these words. Some believe this refers to the basic staple items of cooking that will become priceless. I think it refers to those few individuals that have these possessions and hold the masses in a kind of slavery. They are not as yet affected by the inflation.

The forth horseman is:

IV: THE CALAMITY! Verses 7-8 reveal how terrible the coming tribulation will be upon the earth. This is beyond human comprehension and many of us would rather not think about the dark days that are to be experienced by the world of individuals that have rebelled against Christ. However, the calamity of the forth horse is destined to come to this earth. We will focus our attention upon two truths. First,

A: THE DESCRIPTION! Verse 8 informs us that John looked *"And saw a pale horse."* This is an ashen yellow-green like color. It is the only horse that has a rider that is named, death. This is the aftermath of war and famine but it goes much further that what has happened. The word *"hell"* is *"Hades,"* and here means death and the picture is that of Death's victims being buried. Secondly, we have:

B: THE DESTRUCTION! Verse 8, *"And power was given unto them over the forth part of the earth, to kill with sword, and with hunger, and with death, and with the beasts of the earth."* At the current population of the earth that would mean about 1.5 billion people being killed. The expression "and with death" probably refers to pestilence and probably refers to disease as being the cause of many of the deaths. It is possible that the wild

The Apocalypse: The Revelation of the Redeemer

beast refers to rats that will be roaming everywhere and defiling what food there is to eat.

Conclusion:
John MacArthur says, "The first four seals clearly describe awe-inspiring, frightening judgments without parallel in history. There is nothing that has happened since John had this vision that could be the fulfillment of these judgments. There will be no escape for impenitent unbelievers from the terrors of the Tribulation, or from the infinitely worse terrors of hell. In the words of the writer of Hebrews, "How will we escape if we neglect so great a salvation?"

The Price of Commitment and the Failure to Do So
Revelation 6:9-17

D. H. Lawrence said, "God is only a great imaginative experience." The tragedy is that those words had been flesh for generations before he said them. However, this world is in for an awakening. The sad reality is that for the vast majority of the world it will be to late. Yet, in spite of the efforts of the enemy there will be multitudes of individuals that will come to know Jesus as Lord during the time of the tribulation. We are introduced to a portion of them in the fifth seal. It seems that Revelation 6:9-11; as well as others sections are in chronological order. The church is no longer in the earth, and yet, there will be multitudes that come to know Jesus as Lord. If the church is not here and the Holy Spirit is no longer present as He is in this day of grace how will individuals be saved? While we do not know the particulars we can say that any conversion will as it has always been, by faith. We know that the Bible is already translated in more than 1100 languages. There are many questions that we can not answer about the fifth seal. We do, however, know that the scene sifts from earth to heaven. Here we witness under the altar the souls of those that either died as a result of coming to know Christ in the first portion of the tribulation or it is as a result of the efforts of the witness that we will meet later in the book. It is my opinion that it is a combination of both.

There are two thoughts that I would like for us to consider as we look at the opening of the fifth and sixth seals. First,

I: THE MARTYRS! Verses 9-11 The action of the fifth seal is not seen. We only have the results. Not every one that dies is a martyr. These are designated as martyrs for the reasons they die.

The Apocalypse: The Revelation of the Redeemer

Here we have a glimpse of the brutal persecution that will be experienced during the time of The Great Tribulation by those that come to know Christ as Lord. There are two things presented to us about these martyrs that should challenge and compel us to be more devoted to Jesus Today. First, we have:

A: THE VISION OF THE SLAIN! Verse 9, *"And when He had opened the fifth seal, I saw under the altar the souls of them that were slain."* There are two questions that immediately demand our attention. First, *where are these slain?* They are in heaven. But there is more, they are *"under the altar."* This is a reference to the altar of sacrifice. It is important to note that are under the altar, that is they are not on the top of it where the blood was applied for sins and where judgment was experienced. They are under the altar, signifying that the judgment has transpired, that forgiveness has been experienced and that condemnation is past. Secondly, *who are these slain?* The church has been removed. We saw them in the elders in chapter 4 and 5 in heaven. They are not Old Testament saints because these have not as yet been resurrected. Who are they? It is my studied opinion that these are tribulation saints. There are two things I want us to carefully note as we contemplate this vision of the slain. First, they were slain:

1. For the Word! Verse 9, *"...that were slain for the Word of God."* This does not mean that they walked down the street carrying a large red Bible but as John MacArthur says, "They will correctly interpret what they see going on around them in the light of Scripture. They will proclaim from the Bible God's judgment and call on people to repent and believe the gospel." We have great difficulty in fathoming the time when people will be persecuted for something that we take so lightly. Secondly,

2. For their Witness! Verse 9, *"And for the testimony which they held."* The word *"held"* is a word that means bore. These were not silent but spoke and show with their life that Jesus Christ had become the most priority of their lives. For these reasons these were slain. In Fox's Book of Martyrs there is the account of Rawlins White. He was a fisherman in the town of Cardiff. Rawlins was not an educated man, yet it pleased God to keep him from error and idolatry to a simple knowledge of the truth. He had his son taught to read English, and after the little boy could read pretty well, his father every night after supper had the little boy read a portion of the Scripture, and now and then a part of some other good book.

After King Edward died, Queen Mary succeeded him. This opened the door for all kinds of superstition. White was taken by the officers of the town, as a man suspected of heresy, brought before the Bishop Llandaff, and committed to prison in Chepstow, and at last removed to the castle of Cardiff, where he continued for a year. Then he was brought before the bishop and counseled by threats and promises. But Rawlins would in no wise recant his opinions. The bishop then proceeded by the law and condemned him as a heretic.

Before they proceeded to this extremity, the bishop proposed that prayer should be said for his conversion. "This" said white, "Is like a godly bishop, and if your request be godly and right, and you pray as you ought, no doubt God will hear you; pray you, therefore, to your God, and I will pray to my God." The bishop tried mass and then the threat of death. Rawlins still refused to recant.

Rawlins was taken to the place where he was to be burned. His wife and children stood weeping. As he approached the place a priest stood that addressed himself to the people. But as he spoke of the sacraments, Rawlins cried out, "Ah, thou hypocrite, dost thou presume to prove thy false doctrine by Scripture? Look to the text that follows; did not Christ say, 'Do this in remembrance of me?'"

Then some that stood by cried out "Put fire! Set on fire!" which being done, the straw and reeds cast up a great and sudden flame. In which flame this good man bathed his hands so long, until such time as the sinews shrank, and the fat dropped away, saving that once he did, as it were, wipe his face with one of them. All the while he cried with a loud voice singing Psalms and hymns and quoting Scripture. Before he fell into the flames he said, "O Lord, receive my spirit!" He choose to fall in the fire rather than deny the One that had saved him. Something like that will be the brutal treatment of the people of God during this time. What do you and I believe sufficiently that we are willing to die for rather than change our minds? Perhaps a better question would be what is there that I am willing to live my life for tomorrow? Secondly, we have:

B: THE VOICE OF THE SAINTS! Verses 10-11 present a picture that we are not comfortable with in this day of grace. In this day however, grace has expired for the earth and it is time for retribution. It is amazing at the number of individuals that glory in the doctrine of salvation by grace through faith but who revert to law to keep themselves saved. As we consider the voice of the saints we want to notice three things. First, we have:

1. Their Request! Verse 10, *"And they cried with a loud voice, how long, O Lord, holy and true, dost Thou not judge and avenge our blood on them that dwell on the earth."* They cried with loud voices not to get God to hear them but to express the urgency of the need and strong emotions. We must realize that they are now making this request in a time of judgment. It is much like the imprecatory Psalms. This is not a time for pardon but punishment. It is also worthy of note that these martyrs used the Greek word *despotes* for Lord, which means *"Master," "Ruler."* We should also note that they base their appeal upon the attributes of God. Because He is *holy*, He must judge sin and because He is *true*, He must honor His Word. Their request is stated in the words, *"How long...till you judge and avenge our blood on them that dwell on the earth?"* The word *"earth"* refers throughout the Revelation to the ungodly How unlike the prayer of our Lord and Stephen but it is in keeping with a time that is destined to experience the judgment of God. They are requesting God to deal with them according to His Word. Secondly, we have:

2. Their Robes! Verse 11, *"And white robes were given unto them."* This is a long flowing garment. This is not to be understood as some kind of body prior to their resurrection. This robe informs us that they are in fact redeemed. It symbolizes the imputed righteousness that is given when one receives Jesus as Lord. Please note the word, *"Given."* They did not achieve this on their own merit but they received a gift just like those that know Jesus in this day of grace. John MacArthur says, *"They symbolize all the glory that redeemed saints will enjoy in heaven."* Our joy in this day of grace is in the reality that we received His imputed righteousness when we in faith repent of our sins and ask Jesus to come into our hearts and live His life in and through us. The real question is not whether or not these are literal robes but have I been robed in His righteousness? Thirdly, we have:

3. The Reply! Verse 11; *"Rest yet a little season."* This is not instructing them to cease their request but to enjoy the heavenly joy that is theirs. The reason they are to rest is that others will follow. Verse 11, *"Until their fellowservants also and their brethren, that should be killed as they were should be fulfilled."* There may be two groups of people intended by the terms *"fellowservants"* and *"brethren."* There are those that believe that the first were those that were alive and willing to die like the martyrs, though they may not. The second group were those who will be killed because of their faith in Christ and their testimony concerning the things that were taking place in light of the Scriptures.

We are not, in this day of grace, being asked to become martyrs. We are being challenged to live, not die, for Christ and the cause of righteousness.

II: THE MADNESS! Verses 12-17 This is one of the most devastating scenes in the entire Bible. When we reach the opening of the sixth seal we are at the mid-point of the tribulation period. The antichrist has been revealed; he has desecrated the temple and declared himself to be God. There is a contrast between chapter five and six. In chapter five there is a praise service. In chapter six there is a prayer service. However, this is not what we would call a normal prayer service. This is a time when men are crying for the rocks and the mountains to fall on them and hide them from the wrath of the Lamb. This is a time of madness. It is moral, ethical, religious and economic madness like this world has never witnessed. It is almost impossible for us to conceive of a time when men will seek to hide in dens and caves to escape the worldwide judgment that is being experienced by the inhabitants of the earth. As terrible as this scene is it is not the final judgment! There is one outstanding difference between the opening of the sixth seal and the first five. This seal begins judgment from

The Apocalypse: The Revelation of the Redeemer

heaven. The others originated in the plan of God but man was the instrument used in them being experienced. This one begins the judgment from heaven upon a world that has rejected His offers of salvation in and through His Son. There are three things for us to consider in these verses about this madness. First,

A: THE CHAOS! Verses 12-14 There is a question about the events of these verses that must be answered, i.e., are these events literal or are they symbolic? It is my conviction that these are literal events. Yet, in their literal fulfillment we have some powerful practical principles. The record reveals that there are three earthquakes mentioned in Revelation (Rev. 6:12, 11:13 and 16:18). The word for earthquake is *seismos* which literal means, "a shaking." We get our word seismograph from this word. This is the apparatus for detecting earthquakes. This world has experienced some tremendous shaking by earthquakes. In November of 1989 there was a powerful earthquake that hit San Francisco bay area that resulted in the World Series being delayed. The effects of earthquakes upon people are often devastating. For weeks many will not sleep in a house. Many move from those regions that are prone to experience earthquakes. Indeed this world has been shaken many times but there has never been anything to compare with the earthquake that is coming during the tribulation period. When an earthquake occurs there are upheavals, unrest, a dividing and a falling down. Where there was order there is now disorder. When there was union there is now division. This also happens in the social, economic and governmental order of things. For this reason I believe that this has some very powerful practical principles for us. For example this "shaking" reminds me that the foundation of what is in existence at the beginning of the tribulation period will be so shaken that the disorder, division and disarray will be present in the structure of social, economic and government to the extent that the people of the earth are going to be filled with panic.

The chaos continues in the words, *"And the sun became black as sack cloth of hair, and the moon became as blood."* This has happened on a smaller scale in history. It happened during the plagues in Egypt and at Calvary. Further, in May of 1780 the sun became dark at noon. People were in a state of panic. Chickens went to roost and the cows came in because they thought it was night. Individuals thought surely that the end of time had come. The blackness reminds me of the chaos of man's world when the love of God is no longer manifested. His love is now available to all men but in this day that love that has been rejected will no longer be available. Isn't that a terrible thought!

Verse 13, *"And the stars of heaven fell unto the earth, even as a fig tree casteth her untimely figs, when she is shaken of a mighty wind."* We call these shooting stars. In November of 1833 this happened for a period of three hours. Jesus said in Luke 21:25-26, *"There shall be signs in the sun and moon and stars, the powers of heaven shaken."*

In addition verse 14 states that, *"The heaven departed as a scroll when it is rolled together; and every mountain and island were moved out of their places."* We know from the Scriptures that there are at least three heavens. The first, mentioned in Genesis, is really the atmosphere. There is one beyond that and then the third heaven, which is the dwelling place of God. Paul was caught up to the third heaven. Which heaven is departing as a scroll? It is my opinion that it is the first and possibly even the second. When you pull down a window shade and release it quickly it will go to the top and flutter around. This is something of what is meant. How can this happen? Democritics (460-370 B. C.?) discovered what we now know to be the atom. Later it was stated that our universe was made of atoms. The word "atom" actually means that which can not be divided. However, man discovered during the waning days of World War II that the atom could be divided and a bomb was developed and dropped on Hiroshima. Since then the world has developed nuclear weapons and it is possible that what is described in verse 14 is the result of a nuclear explosion. The madness is witnessed secondly in the;

B: COLLECTION! Verse 15 This is an unusual collection in that it is a collection of men. There are seven groups of people mentioned in verse 15. John MacArthur says, "The king of the earth refers to the heads of state throughout the world. The great men are the high-ranking officials in government. The commanders are the military leaders, while the rich are those who control commerce and business and the strong may well be the influential.

The Apocalypse: The Revelation of the Redeemer

Together they comprise the elite elements of human society. These are the very people who ignored the warnings of God's impending judgment and persecuted those who proclaimed it."

Today it is popular to say, "All men are created equal." Is that true? We are created equal in that we are created in the image of God but we are not equal. If we were we would all make "A's" on our report cards and there would be no need for the Olympics because everyone would be equal in ability. Individuals are not equal mentality or in the use of their talents. Our abilities are surely varied. In the spiritual arena men are not equal. There are some that mature and others remain as babes in Christ. Further, in the area of the gifts of the Spirit men are not equal in that some have more gifts than do others. What do these seven groups of individuals have in common? What can the king share with the slave? With all the differences in these they have in common they have rejected Jesus Christ as Savior and are gripped by the terror of the judgment that is being experienced. The point is that God is no respector of persons. In this day the playing field is level. Some of the very men responsible for the martyrs under the fifth seal are now facing the wrath of the Lamb. I am reasonably sure that some of those individuals thought that either their money or position would assure them of a life devoid of trouble but they are awakened to the reality of the judgment of God. The third truth about this madness is:

C: THE CRY! Verse 16-17, *"And say to the rocks and the mountains fall on us, and hide us from the face of Him that sitteth on the throne, and from the wrath of the Lamb: for the great day of His wrath is come; and who shall be able to stand?"* Jesus spoke of the day when men would cry unto the mountains and rocks in Luke 23:30, *"Then shall they begin to say to the mountains, fall on us: and to the hills, cover us."* The reality is that it is too late to cry because there is no hiding place in that day. These men could have been hid in the Rock of Ages rather than crying out to the rocks to hide them. They are seeking to hide from God and His wrath. They are not the first to try to hide. Adam tired to hide in Eden when God came to fellowship with him after he had disobeyed the command of God not to eat of the tree of life. From that time forward man has sought to hide from the all Seeing Eye of the Holy One without success. But please note that they are trying to hide in the very places that are being shaken. This informs us of the mental state of the heads of state during this day of divine visitation by God.

There are two expressions in these two verses that should arrest our attention. The first is in verse 16, *"The wrath of the Lamb."* We do not think of a lamb as being the aggressor but in this day this is not the little pet lamb, this is The Lamb of God that shed His blood for the salvation of man that is also the Lion that rules as a sovereign. The second expression is used in verse 17, *"Who shall be able to stand?"* The answer to this question is not difficult. In that day no one will be able to stand against the wrath of the tribulation.

Conclusion:
We are a blessed people in that we can now live for Jesus and it cost us practically nothing. The call and challenge for you and me is two fold. First, we are to hear and heed His call to salvation in this day of grace and secondly, allow the Spirit of God to so burden our hearts for those for whom Jesus died that we are willing to become instruments that He can use to share the transforming power of grace that is available to them.

Who will Be Saved in the Tribulation
Revelation 7:1-17

We might think that chapter seven is merely a continuation of the devastation of chapter six; after all the opening of the sixth seal brings worldwide judgment from heaven upon the earth. However, there is more to the plan of God than you and I can fathom. Revelation chapter seven naturally divides itself into two divisions. The first is contained in the first seven verses and it has to do with the sealing of His servants, as well as how God will deal with them in the great day of His wrath. The second portion has to do with the Gentiles and them being brought into the kingdom of God. It is my opinion that these that are saved during the tribulation are those individuals that have not had the opportunity to receive Jesus as Lord during the day of grace. I personally do not believe that those that have rejected His love and said "no" to the gospel a hundred times are suddenly going to have a desire to know Him. These are going to be deceived and believe the lie of the antichrist. Yet, there will be multitudes that are brought into the kingdom of God.

We might think that the opening of the seventh seal would simply see more havoc and devastation running wild in the earth. The seventh seal is not opened until chapter 8:1. What we have is a mighty wave of evangelism. This will be one of the greatest experiences of evangelism in the history of the earth. This will come to pass as a result of the 144,000 Jewish evangelists that share the message throughout the earth that Jesus was the Messiah and we missed Him.

Chapter seven begins with these words, *"Four angels standing on the four corners of the earth."* The number four is the number of the world and it is used four times in these verses. This refers to the universality of God's administration. God is in charge of His world. He is now; He will be then and forever. Everything is moving according to His timetable. The world may think that it is running itself and doing what it desires but the reality is that God is on the throne and He is in control.

The winds of verse one are striving to be loosed on the earth, but Almighty God holds them in check. Where we would look for havoc none exist. There is a judgment that is ready and probably even restless to fall upon this vile and evil world, but for the moment it is delayed. Why? There are two thoughts presented in these verses that will help us answer that question. First, we have:

I: THE SUSPENSION OF JUDGMENT! Verses 1-3 Chapter 6 ends with the question, *"For the great day of His wrath is come and who shall be able to stand?"* Men have already cried for the rocks and mountains to fall on them and hide them from the face of the Lamb. The answer to the inquiry of chapter 6 is that no one in his own might, ability, cunning or wisdom will be able to stand. Yet, Revelation 7 reveals to us that there will be those that will stand. These stand for a specific purpose during this time. Judgment is stayed. There are three things to consider about this suspension of judgment. First,

A: THE INTERLUDE! Verse 1 reveals this in the words *"That the wind should not blow."* The earth is ripe for judgment. Yet, the winds of judgment are not blowing. There is an interlude. There is an interlude between the 6th and 7th seal, between 6th and 7th trumpet, and between the 6th and 7th vial. There is calmness from the Lord. This has been called the answer of God to a prayer similar to the one Habakkuk (3:2) prayed, *"In wrath remember mercy."* There is an interlude of the mercy of God to provide individuals with the opportunity to come to know Christ as the Messiah. This has been something of the pattern of God throughout history. Before the flood there was an interlude of opportunity of 120 years. Before the final plague in Egypt of the death of the first born there was an interlude provided by God for an opportunity to apply the blood and come to Him. Often before there is a crises God gives this time of mercy. In a strange sort of way we are living in an interlude in that this is the day of opportunity to share the gospel but just as the interlude of chapter

The Apocalypse: The Revelation of the Redeemer

7 will end so will this day of the grace of God expire. Secondly, we have:

B: THE INSTRUMENTS! Verse 2 reveals they are *His angels*. Angels are a fascinating study. If you investigate you will discover that they are more predominate in the Old Testament, further their ministry is present in the New Testament. You will discover that their ministry is more predominate after the church is no longer in the earth than they are in this day of grace. I do not mean that they are not present, active and at work in this day. They are but in this day of grace it is not the instruments of angels that God uses as much as it is those individuals that have experienced His salvation. In this day the angels are His ministers, servants and instruments of discharging His work in the world. Verse 2, *"And I saw another angel descending from the east having the seal of the living God and he cried with a loud voice to the four angels to whom it was given to hurt the earth and the sea."* One of the exciting places in the Old Testament where angels intervened is Genesis chapter 19. The Lord is going down to destroy Sodom and the angels go to the city and are instruments used by Him to deliver Lot from the destruction that is to come. In the New Testament there is the record of Acts 12 where Peter is in prison and the angel comes and leads him out prison. I believe God, in this day of grace, uses angels to protect His children. The third thing for us to consider is:

C: THE INSTURCTIONS! Verse 3; *"Hurt not the earth, either the sea, nor the trees, till we have sealed the servants of our God in their foreheads."* Observe the word, *"till."* This is a word meaning that the restraint is temporary. These judgments will come in God's own time. We must remember that there is a *"till"* that is ours. This one will last until the coming of the Lord Jesus or we meet Him in death. This is when our opportunity of seeing individuals saved will come to an end. God is giving this opportunity to those that inhabit the earth to place their trust in Christ as the Messiah. Our second thought is:

II: THE SEALING OF THE JEWS! Verses 4-8 The judgment is suspended until as verse 3 makes very clear, the servants of God are sealed in their foreheads. Do you suppose that means that there is going to be a visible mark on their heads? I really don't think so. Who are the 144,000? Have they every knocked at your door? They think they have! There are three things for us to note about the sealing of the Jews. First,

A: THE SEALED! Verses 4-8 Who are these that are sealed? The Seventh Day Adventist says that this is their communion. The Jehovah's Witness says that when Judge Rutherford died that heaven was sealed, closed up and they are not among them. They are working for a place here in the earth during the reign. It is not my practice to call names but I do believe that if poison is out there and we know it we ought to name it to others. You would not allow a three-year-old to play with rat poison would you? If you have the time, and if you are secure in your faith, the next time they come to your door be Christian and cordial. Accept the literature they will provide if they will share their name and address with you. Go to their house the next day and share the simple gospel with them.

There are those that say this is spiritual and refers to the church. A great crime of some is to take the blessing that belong to Israel and give them to the church. These are biological Jews.

Note the list that is presented in these verses. (I do not remember where I first came across this information.) You will discover that they are not in the order of their birth. Verse 5, *"Of the tribe of Judah"* but Judah is not the first-born. Who was? Ruben! The first-born was the one that received a double portion, the size of the family not withstanding. The first-born was the ruler and the priest of the family. Ruben sinned and Judah received that position. David is of the tribe of Judah and our Lord is called *"The Lion of the tribe of Judah."* Judah means *"confession or praise of God."* Ruben is listed next. He is the oldest; his name means, *"viewing the son."* Gad is listed next but he is the 7th son. Seven is completion and his name means *"a company."* Next is Aser and he is the eight son. This is the number of new beginnings. His name means, *"blessed."* Nephthalim is the 6th son. His name means a *"wrestler or striving with."* Manasses is not a son of Jacob but of Joseph. His name means *"forgetfulness."* Simeon is a son of Jacob by Leigh. You talk about havoc in a home this had to be it. There are children by four women and they

The Apocalypse: The Revelation of the Redeemer

all lived in the same house. His name means, *"hearing and obeying."* Levi is listed but he was not listed in the giving of the land. Levi sinned in taking revenge on those that defiled his sister. Levi becomes the priestly tribe. His name means, *"joining or cleaving to."* Issachar is next and his name means, *"reward or what is given by way of reward."* Zebulon is the tenth son and his name means *"a home or dwelling place."* Joseph is listed. Does this strike you as being odd? Joseph was not listed as one of the tribes going into Canaan. His two sons are. His name means, *"added or an addition."* Benjamin is the youngest and listed last and his name means *"a son of the right hand."* If you put this all together you have a description of the people of God in that day. I do not think they are in this order by accident. These people are confessor or praisers of God looking upon the Son, a band of blessed ones, wrestling with forgetfulness, hearing and obeying the Word, cleaving unto the reward of a shelter and home, an addition, son of the day of God's right hand, begotten in the extremity of pain. This is what Israel will be in that day. Secondly,

B: THE SUBSITUTION! Verse 8 shares this in the words *"Of the tribe of Zabulon were sealed 12,000; of the tribe of Joseph were sealed 12,000."* Which tribe is omitted? It is Dan. The tribe of Joseph is substituted for the tribe of Dan. Why? When there was idolatry in Israel it is listed as being *"from Dan to Bathsheba."* Dan is guilty of idolatry. The history of Dan is one of idolatry. He is the first one to open his borders to idolatry and the first to give himself to idols. Dan is placed aside. In this day of grace God can and does place aside those that continue to rebel and refuse to follow Him. There are some that believe that the antichrist will come from the tribe of Dan.

The third thing about the sealing of the Jews is:

C: THE SEAL! Verse 2 states, *"Having the seal of the living God."* The phrase, *"The living God"* is used to show a distinction between God and gods. What is this seal? In Abraham it was a seal in the flesh. We know that when we were saved that we were sealed by, with the Holy Spirit of promise. I do not know what this seal is but I know that it does three things. First, it shows *possession*. When one is sealed the devil can do what and all he will but he cannot have what is sealed because it belongs to God. Before God will surrender a purchased possession it will die an untimely death. You may know some to whom this has happened. Secondly, it signifies *protection*. It is the seal of the king, the living God. Thirdly, it signifies *perseverance*. They are sealed so they persevere through the tribulation and give their lives for the Messiah they have come to know.

Do you suppose we would like it if there were a seal that revealed if we were really the purchased possession of God?

The third thought about who will be saved in the tribulation is:

III: THE SALVATION OF THE GENTILES! Verses 9-17 We have learned from the first eight verses that there will be a great host of Jews saved during this time of tribulation. However, we are now presented with the reality that others will be saved as well. It is my studied opinion that this great host will be saved as a result of the ministry of the 144,000 Jewish evangelists. This should not be interpreted as a "second chance" for those that have blatantly rejected the opportunity to experience salvation during the day of grace. Paul's words remind us that after the church is removed God will send them a strong delusion and they will believe "the lie." These are words that should challenge us in this day of grace to take advantage of every opportunity to share the gospel of Jesus with the peoples of the world. The point is that in this day men are not going to possess a "want" to experience the salvation of Jesus. There are six things we want to observe about the salvation of the gentiles in these verses. First, we have:

A: THEIR POSITION! Verse 9, *"After this I beheld, and, lo, a great multitude, which no man could number, of all nations, and kindred's, and people, and tongues, stood before the throne, and before the Lamb."* There are two things that immediately present themselves to us for consideration. First, is the **number**; *"A great multitude which no man could number."* How large is God's glorious kingdom? The word tells us that these that come to know Him during this time of tribulation are innumerable. Further, they come from all tribes, nations and kindred's of the earth. This is enough to inform us that the Gospel is going to be presented in that time period. It is not necessary for the gospel to be presented to the ends of the earth before Jesus comes for His church. It is my opinion that the truth of the gospel being presented to the ends of the earth refers to this time period and not prior to His coming. This is or should be exciting. It is a joy to realize that the number is beyond mans ability to count. I mention the number to simply say that there is also a number that will constitute His church and when that number is completed Jesus will come for His bride. The blessing of this truth is that I am in that number. I do not have to wait for a time of calamity, crises or judgment to open my heart to him in repentance. I am in that number in the day of grace. Secondly, we have their **nearness**; *"Stood before the throne and before the Lamb."* The church is seated in glory and these are standing. This does not imply that these are any less saved or precious to God because they are standing. It simply says that their position is one of nearness to God. This can easily be compared to/with the believer in this day of grace. We are as near the heart of God as we desire to be. Moreover, our nearness to God is not dependent upon others. It is a decision of ones own will and his willingness to keep short accounts with God as the Holy Spirit empowers him or her to walk in obedience with God. Their position is one of standing before the throne. The believer's position is one of standing before the throne as an intercessor lifting to the heart of God those individuals that do not know Jesus and pleading that they may have their hearts open in this day of opportunity.

Secondly, we have:

B: THEIR PURITY! Verse 9, *"Clothed with white robes and palms in their hands."* These words reveal two things to us about their purity. First, they are **redeemed**; *"White robes."* These robes are symbolic of purity. These are a part of those that have come to faith in Christ during times of great tribulation. White robes are referred to three times in these verses. The Greek word for robe is *stola*; from which we get our English word stole. This is a scarf that one wears around the shoulders. There is an animal that is called an ermine and it is pronounced ur-min that is of the weasel family. In the summer its coat is brown but in the winter its fur is purest white and it's tail is black. If you had a lot of money you could buy an ermine stole. An ermine robe would be an extremely expensive item. The white robe referred to here is a *stola*, an outer garment that is worn to signify dignity and position. These are redeemed. Secondly, we have in their purity they're **rejoicing**; *"Palms in their hands."* This phrase is used one other time in John 12 where Jesus is making His entry and they take the palms and spread them in the way. Here palms are a sign of rejoicing. These are rejoicing because God has brought them out of great tribulation. Thirdly, we have:

C: THEIR PRAISE! Verse 10, *"And cried with a loud voice, saying, 'salvation to our God which sitteth upon the throne, and unto the Lamb.'"* They are praising God for three things. First, they praise Him for His **grace**; *"Salvation to our God."* Can you imagine what heaven would be like if works saved us? You would ask one person how he got to heaven and he would respond by saying, "You just would not believe all the suffering and hardships that I endured." Another might say, "We went into mission work and lost our children to disease and finally my wife and I died but we finally made it." Finally you ask one person and he says, "I really don't deserve to be here, if I got what I deserved I would be in hell." Salvation is of God and not of our works or abilities. We believe the doctrine but most of us are guilty of adding something of works to the work of grace to keep ourselves saved. Secondly, they praise God for His **government**; *"Which sitteth upon the throne."* It is thrilling to know that God is in charge, that He is the One that occupies the eternal throne. It is easy for us to think that God has forsaken His world and that the inmates are running the asylum but the reality is that God is upon His throne, totally in charge of His world. The One that sits upon the throne knows all that is taking place in our world as well. The amazing thing is that this One that is in charge is One that loves us and desires what is best for us. Thirdly they praise Him for His **gift**, *"And unto the Lamb."* In heaven the redeemed praise God for Jesus! It is or at least should be appropriate for those of us that know Him here to praise Him now. It would be fitting for us to pause often and say, "Now thanks be unto God for His unspeakable, indescribable and immeasurable free Gift, the Lord

The Apocalypse: The Revelation of the Redeemer

Jesus Christ." If we are going to praise Him there we ought to be getting in practice here.

Fourthly, we have:

D: THE PRICE! Verse 14, *"These are they which came out of great tribulation, and have washed their robes, and made them white in the blood of the Lamb."* Is that possible? If you wash something in blood what color will it be? It will not be white but when man that is dirty, vile and sinful is washed in the blood a miracle takes place and he comes out white. It is apparent that the blood of Jesus is magnified in heaven. There are those that make light of the blood of Jesus but there is no salvation apart from the blood of Jesus Christ. It is the blood that cancels our sin.

Fifthly, we have:

E: THE PRIVILEGE! Verses 11-15 reveal that we are a privileged people. Our privilege is that we are living in the day of grace where the gospel of Jesus Christ is proclaimed and individuals have the opportunity to hear and heed the message of repentance. Their first privilege is that of **worship**. Verse 11 states, *"And all the angels stood round about the throne, and about the elders and the four beasts, and fell before the throne on their faces, and worshipped God."* Worship is taking place in heaven at all times as verse 12 indicates, *"Saying, Amen: Blessing, and glory, and wisdom, and thanksgiving, and honor, and power, and might, be unto our God for ever and ever. Amen."* We are privileged to join in the worship of the living God. What a privilege to simply bow before Him and worship Him in His Spirit. There is an exchange between one of the elders and John. John must do as we often do and say, "I don't know, but you do." Secondly there is the privilege of **work** shared in verse 15, *"Therefore are they before the throne of God, and serve Him day and night in His temple."* There is no night in heaven. This is a reference to the Old Testament temple. In the Old Testament the Gentiles could not even come into the temple. They came to the outer court and now they come into the very presence of God and serve Him. Since we are going to serve Him in heaven, what we are doing here should be training for us to serve more completely there.

Sixth we have:

F: THE PROVISIONS! Verses 16-17 These are very meaningful verses. They present two provisions that will have a great meaning to those that will come through the great tribulation but they also have a relevant spiritually application to our hearts. First, we have the **bountifulness of the Savior** in verse 16, *"They shall hunger no more, neither thirst any more; neither shall the sun light on them, nor any heat."* He will feed and lead His children. This will be special for those that come out of the great tribulation because not having the mark of the beast they have not been able to buy or sell and have experienced sever times of trial. I want to make a spiritual application in that when we come to know the Lord Jesus we do not have to hunger or thirst anymore. We can set our feet under the Lord's Table and dine with the King and receive any and everything we need in Jesus presently. Secondly, we have the **banishment of sorrow** in verse 17. *"For the Lamb which is in the midst of the throne shall feed them, and shall lead them unto living fountains of waters: and God shall wipe away all tears from their eyes."* Do not think that those in heaven are now crying. I know there are some that suggest that the ones already with the Lord are looking down on us and trying to get us to move in a particular direction or not do some things. How much glory would that be? This possibly refers to a time following the Great White throne judgment. I do not know how God will do it but I am convinced that a person will not know that a spouse is not in heaven. This is the time that He will wipe all tears from the eyes. There are some things that do not mix. Glory and grief do not reside in the same heart. Sorrow and rejoicing do not abide at the same time in the same heart. We know that in the presence of the Lord Jesus there is glory and rejoicing. No, I don't know how God is going to do it but He will wipe away all tears from eyes.

Conclusion:
May I make a present application of these truths to our hearts? God has given us an interlude, He is now showing mercy and you can now receive His mercy and grace. Further, the instruments that He is using are His Word and the witness of those that have experienced His salvation.

Why Heaven was Silent
Revelation 8:1-13

Verse one of Revelation eight is one of the most unusual verses in the entire Bible. This is true because throughout eternity past there has always been worship, praise and celebration in heaven. Heaven has been a place of activity but now all things come to a sudden stop. Have you been present when a large choir and orchestra was singing and suddenly everything just suddenly stopped? In chapter eight the seventh seal is opened. In chapter five the occupant of the throne has a seven sealed book which contains the title deed of the entire earth. A search is made in heaven and earth for one to be found worthy to open the book. One is found! He is the Lion of the tribe of Judah. He takes the book and begins to open those seals. In chapter six, six of those seals are opened. Chapter seven is an interlude between the opening of the sixth seal and the seventh seal. When the seventh seal is opened we will be made aware of the fact that in the seventh seal there are seven trumpets. When the last trumpet sounds there are seven vials or bowls of wrath. This is the time of the great tribulation. There is also an interlude between the sounding of the sixth and seventh trumpet. This is from chapter 10:1 to chapter 11:15. There are two answers to our question of why was heaven silent. First, we have:

I: THE PREPARATION FOR THE SOUNDING OF THE TRUMPETS! Verses 1-5 The trumpets do not immediately sound. This is because there is some preparation that precedes the sounding of the trumpets. There are three things for us to consider. First,

A: THE SILENT PAUSE! Verse 1, *"When He had opened the seventh seal there was silence in heaven for about the space of*

half an hour." It is important that we observe that this is silence in heaven. Heaven the very place that has always been filled with worship and adoration, where there has always been activity and movement is now suddenly silent. The duration of this silent pause is "half an hour." That is not a long period of time if you are enjoying what you are doing is it? But in this suspense filled environment this could be a hundred life times in regard to waiting for what is forthcoming. Observe that heaven is not silent as a result of a command. Even God is silent. Why? Picture in your mind a trial. A person is being tried for a horrendous crime, the jury has been out for several days and they are anticipated to return with their verdict shortly. The courtroom is filled with individuals that are whispering about the case. The jury comes in and all activity ceases. The judge asks, "Have you reached a verdict?" "Yes, your honor" is the response. There is total silence because the verdict is about to be announced. This is something of the reason heaven is silent. The verdict of the wrath of God is about to be rendered upon the earth for its blatant rejection of Jesus Christ as Lord. Secondly, we have:

B: THE SOLEMN PREPARATION! Verse 2, "*And I saw the seven angels which stood before God; and to them were given seven trumpets.*" These are not ordinary angels. The definite article "*the*" informs us that these are the seven "*presence*" angels. They are angels that abide in the presence of God. They are not there to give God counsel or their opinions of how things should or should not be done. They are there to carry out the instructions of God. It would be wonderful if those that have experienced salvation in Jesus Christ could do likewise. They are special in that they stand before God and move at His bidding. Each of them has a trumpet. Trumpets are the most used instruments in scripture. They are used for various reasons; among them are to call people to worship, to work and to war. Each one has its own unique sound and the people knew what it was calling them to do. This is a time of solemn preparation due to the judgment that is soon to be experienced upon the earth. Thirdly, we have:

C: THE SAINTS PRAYERS! Verses 3-5, "*And another angel came and stood at the altar, having a golden censer; and*

The Apocalypse: The Revelation of the Redeemer

there was given unto him much incense, that he should offer it with the prayers of all saints upon the golden altar which was before the throne." There are those that think this angel is the Lord Jesus because he is involved in a priestly function. The only problem I have with this conclusion is that when the Lord Jesus is referred to in the Revelation He is called the Son of God or the Son of Man and it is clearly defined as to Who He is. This angel is ministering at the altar. There are two altars mentioned. The first is a reference to the brazen altar in the tabernacle where the sacrifice was offered. This is the place where the animal bore the judgment of the sin of the individual that presented it. This is where blood was shed and applied. Therefore, it is an altar of substitution. Observe that the sacrifice made access possible. It was after the sacrifice at this altar the angel gathered it up in the golden censer and went to another altar with all the prayers of the saints. What would you imagine is a part of the prayers that are being presented? It is speculation on my part but I can imagine that a portion is what Jesus taught in the model prayer when He instructed His followers to pray, "*Thy kingdom come.*" I believe this is what they were praying under the fifth seal under the altar. This angel, if it is Jesus, goes in and offers the prayers and verse 4 states, "*And the smoke of the incense, which came with the prayers of the saints, ascended up before God out of the angel's hand.*" The prayers are lifted to God. Verse 5, "*And the angel took the censer, and filled it with the fire of the altar, and cast it into the earth: and there were voices, and thundering, and lightnings, and an earthquake.*" What has been a place of grace and mercy has now become a place of judgment; He that has ministered in grace and mercy now ministers in judgment. There are some lessons that we ought to learn about prayer. First, prayer is *pleasing*; "The smoke ascended up to God." Secondly, prayer is *powerful*; it preceded the judgment that was to come. Thirdly, prayer should be *priority*; that is it should be what the saints of God are engaged in now.

Secondly, we have:

II: THE PUNISHMENT AT THE SOUNDING OF THE TRUMPETS! Verses 6-13 This period is during the last three and one half years of the great tribulation. Do you recall the record of Israel going into the land of Canaan? They received some rather strange instructions but when they complied and on the seventh day they blew the trumpets and the walls fell. The destruction of the city followed the sounding of the trumpet. There are three things that we want to give our attention to in these verses. First,

A: THE PORTION DESTROYED! Verses 7-8; 9 and 11 In the reading of these verses take note of the number of times we are informed that one third of several things is destroyed. Why is it only a third? Again it is speculation on my part but it could be that even in judgment God is willing to extend mercy. Secondly,

B: THE PUNISHMENT DEPICTED! Verses 7-12 I will briefly mention the trumpets that are sounded. The first trumpet sounds in verse 7. *"The first angel sounded, and there followed hail and fire mingled with blood, and they were cast upon the earth."* The word *"cast"* indicates that this was a deliberate action. Do you recall when God dealt with the Egyptians and sent plagues? The plagues were used as a means of saving God's people. These are coming not to save but to trouble God's people (Israel) because they have refused to come to God. It is my opinion that these are literal events that will take place in and upon the earth. However, at the sounding of the second trumpet we are again confronted with what could be figurative language. Note that in verse 8 we have the expression, *"as it were a great mountain burning with fire."* I want to use an extended quote from W. A. Criswell here.

"I have no quarrel, none at all, with those who look upon these things as being literally described. But, these things could also be symbols, pictures of the judgments of God. For example, in the second sounding of the trumpet the text says: *'And as it were a great mountain burning with fire cast into the sea.'* Then John will say of the third trumpet that sounds: *'there fell a great star from heaven, burning as it were a lamp.'* What the seer is saying here is that the thing was not a mountain, actually, but *'as it were'* a lamp a mountain burning with fire; that it was not a lamp, actually, but *'as it were'* a lamp, falling, burning. So, these

The Apocalypse: The Revelation of the Redeemer

things could represent, they could be symbols of the judgments of God in this earth.

Now, herewith are some suggestions concerning the possible meaning of these symbols: '*hail*' is sudden, sharp, interposition of judgment of God (Isaiah 28:2, 17). '*Fire*' is an unsparing evidence of the wrath of God in burning judgment, mostly in the form of war (Deuteronomy 32:22). '*Blood*' is death, moral death, spiritual death, and physical death. '*The earth*' is the civilized world, constituted, as we know it under a regular and established government. '*The sea*' is restless masses of humanity (Daniel 7:2-3). '*Tree*' represents the pride of human greatness, flaunting the presence of God (Daniel 4:10). '*Grass*' is men in general, people generally (Isaiah 40:6, 7). '*The green grass,*' of course, would be the finest, the flower, and the fruit of mankind. When a nation goes to war, whom does it destroy first? It is always 'the green grass,' the flower, the fruit, the finest of the land. When men go down to enlist in the army, the army picks out the finest of the group. It is only the finest of our manhood that fights in a war... '*A mountain,*' represents firmly established power or kingdom (Jeremiah 51:25). '*A star,*' as in Revelation 1, is a pastor, a teacher, a man of great authority standing before people. '*A lamp*' of course, is the congregation, the church. When the star falls it represents an apostate teacher who fills the earth with terrible, darkening doctrine. There is not anything on earth as tragic as the misleading of the people by teaching a wrong revelation, a wrong evaluation or wrong doctrine; the '*rivers*' and '*the fountains*' which are embittered by the doctrine, the salvation, the hope which are destroyed by false teaching. The teaching is poison. It darkens the skies above and embitters the sources of life beneath."

The sounding of the third trumpet is in verses 10-11, "*And the third angel sounded, and there fell a great star from heaven, burning as it were a lamp.*" Genesis 1:14-16 informs us that God placed the stars and Psalm 147:4 that He numbered them. In Job 9: 9- 10 we are told that they are called by name. This fallen star is called "*Wormwood*" that is bitterness. The things that are needed to sustain life, as we know it will be affected by the sounding of these trumpets. One third of the vegetation is lost;

that is food supply. Then one third of the commerce will be affected when the ships are destroyed. One third of the natural or fresh water is going to be destroyed when this star falls to the earth.

The fourth trumpet is in verse 12, *"And the fourth angel sounded, and the third part of the sun was smitten, and the third part of the moon, and the third part of the stars; so as the third part of them was darkened, and the day shone not for a third part of it, and the night likewise."* I believe that scientist will be baffled by the events that transpire. God created the sun, moon and stars on the fourth day and placed them for the benefit of mankind. Now, at the sounding of the fourth trumpet they will be rendered ineffective as far as any ministry to man is concerned. I do not pretend to understand the extent or severity of the punishment that is coming upon the earth. It is my opinion that it will be beyond man's ability to describe.

Thirdly, we have:

C: THE PROSPECTIVE DISMAY! Verse 13, *"And I beheld, and heard an angel flying through the midst of heaven, saying with a loud voice, 'Woe, woe, woe, to the inhabiters of the earth by reason of the three angels, which are yet to sound!'"* The next trumpets are called *"Woe"* trumpets. This indicates that as severe as the first four have been that the remaining three will be more severe.

Conclusion:

The days that are coming to this earth are dark both literally and symbolically. The events that will be experienced during the time of tribulation in and upon the earth can be avoided by those that live in this day of grace if they will open their heart in faith and repentance and receive Jesus as Lord of their life.

In this day the Son shine of His love is freely manifested to you. In that day the literal sun will not give forth its light. The darkness that you experience can easily be overcome by receiving Him.

Something Like Hell on Earth
Revelation 9:1-12

Verse 13 of chapter eight declares, *"Woe, woe, woe to the inhabiters of the earth."* The words, *"inhabiters of the earth"* refers not merely to those persons alive but to those whose lifestyles are according to the flesh, the rejecters of God. The flying eagle says, *"Woe, woe, woe"* because the devastation ahead is so dreadfully demonic that all that has transpired in the blowing of the first four trumpets will pale into nothingness in comparison to it. These trumpets of woe exceed the mere physical earth in their judgments. The blowing of these trumpets unlooses the hordes of demons imprisoned from their fall to create hell on earth.

The repetitiveness of the word *"woe"* reveals how serious and solemn these judgments will be. If it were not a part of my responsibility to declare *"the whole council of God"* I would be tempted to omit these trumpets of woe because they present a judgment so awesome in terror that there is nothing with which to compare it. This is the greatest out pouring of the judgment of God that will ever be experienced in and upon the earth. He has judged the earth before, the flood and Sodom are examples of this, but never as He will during the Great Tribulation.

The sounding of this trumpet reveals a blessed truth. Namely, God is in control. He may use saint, sinner or Satan to accomplish His purpose, but His purpose will be achieved. It also reveals a burdensome truth. That is, the opportunities to repent will one day be past and man will seek death and not be able to find it.

The passage we are considering contains two major thoughts that we will observe. First, note with me:

I: THE UNLOCKED PIT! Verses 1-2 Verse 2, *"And he opened the bottomless pit."* If it was opened it was first closed. The word *"bottomless"* brings to mind something large, without a limit, at least known to man. *"Pit"* conveys the idea of a darkened dungeon of sorts. In these verses notice first,

A: THE DECEITFUL PERSONALITY! Verse 1, *"I saw a star fall."* This is neither a planet nor a celebrity. This, in my view, is a person. *"To him"* in verse one and *"he"* in verse two are masculine. If this is indeed a personality who is he? Our verse will help us identify him. Observe his **position** in verse one; *"fall from heaven."* The word *"fall"* is in the perfect tense. It is literally *"fallen."* This had already occurred. John did not see the star actually fall. The majority of expositors believe this is a reference to the original fall of Satan recorded in Isaiah 14:12-14. In addition, remember the words of Jesus in Luke 10:18, *"I beheld Satan as lightening fall from heaven."* The position reveals the deceit. His desire is to appear as an angel so he will not be recognized. This *"fallen"* position describes any and everything he has a hand in today. It is fallen; it has nothing to do with heavenly things.

The identity of this deceitful personality is also observed in his **possession**; *"To him was given the key."* Please do not assume that this is the person of the Lord Jesus because of His (The Lord Jesus) having *"keys"* in chapter 1:18. This is not the Savior; this is Satan. Keys are a symbol of power and authority. However, the words, *"was given"* reveal that what he possess is delegated to him. He will be acting on behalf of another with greater authority. He is acting under the authority of God and his actions will ultimately bring glory to God. Secondly,

B: THE DEMONIC PIT! Verse 2 The Greek word for *"pit"* is *abussos*, from which we draw our word *"abyss."* It is something that can be closed and locked. The word is used nine times in the New Testament. Seven of them are in the Revelation; one is in Luke 8:31 where the demons ask not to go to the deep. The word is *abussos*; the other is Romans 10:7, *"Or, who shall descend into the deep?"*

When this word is used it always refers to the abode of chained fallen angels. It is this demonic pit that is unlocked.

The Apocalypse: The Revelation of the Redeemer

Verse 2 states it clearly, *"And he opened the bottomless pit."* When this is done the smoke blocks out the sun and the air is darkened. This is the beginning of hells visit to the earth. These imprisoned demons burst forth with an eagerness to do their hellish work. Try to imagine what it would be like if all the jails and prisons were opened and those persons were free to do whatever they pleased for twenty-four hours. This demonic pit holds those that have been in chains since their fall with **Satan**. What terror will transpire when they are permitted to indwell the bodies of unbelieving man, creatures and animals; what a judgment when hell is let loose on earth.

The second major division is:

II: THE UNLEASHED POWER! Verses 3-11 Verse 3 states that *"unto them was given power."* This is the release of demons on the earth. The words, *"like"* and *"as"* appear more in this section of scripture than any other place in the Bible. At his best John can only try to tell what it is like in human terms. As horrible, wicked and awesome as this may sound it can not begin to compare with what is actually going to transpire. There are two disturbing truths that we must confront. First,

A: SATANS PERSECUTORS! Verses 3-11, *"There came out of the smoke locusts upon the earth."* These are not, in my judgment, literal locusts. We know this because they do not eat grass etc. Further verse 11 informs us that they had a king over them. Proverbs 30:27 states that locust do not have a leader. These are supernatural demons that possess animal like creatures. This is true because demons do not have bodies, form or shape. They must indwell a person or thing to have form and shape. They are spirit beings. We are going to note three things about them. First,

1. Their Power! Verse 3, *"Unto them was given power."* Then we are told that this power was *"as the scorpions of the earth."* The scorpion sting, I have been told, is the most intense that can be inflicted on man. As horrendous as their power is there are some limits established by God. For example they are limited in their *domain* as verse 4 shares. They were commanded not to hurt the grass. This is opposite to what natural locusts would do. They are locusts' demons and their interest is in those who are not sealed. Who are the sealed and the unsealed? The sealed are the 144 thousand (7:1) as well as others (Rev. 22:4). This reveals the sovereign control of God. In the midst of hell on earth the saints of God are protected. The unsealed are, in my judgment, those that have rejected Jesus as their personal Savior.

They are also limited in their *damage* as verse 5 shares. They could not kill. They could only torment. The word *"torment"* came to mean in the Greek, *"to examine by torture."* They make existing on earth a living hell.

They were also limited in their *duration* as verse 5 reveals. That duration will be 5 months. God decides what they can do, to whom they do it and how long it lasts. Think of the unbearable anguish of mind, soul and body for 150 days, of not being able to experience any release or rest. Knowing this why would anyone reject Jesus and run the risk of missing the rapture. This should compel sinners to be saved and saints to serve. In addition to their power we have

2. Their Picture! Verses 5-11 It is important to again observe the words *"like"* and *"as"* in these verses. This is not a picture one would hang on their living room wall but it a picture of the persecutors of Satan. In this picture we want to notice first their **features** in verses 7-10. Their features reveal the character of Satan. They are *"like unto horses,"* but they are not horses. This informs us of their *irresistible* power and swift movement. Second, they have *"crowns like gold."* This is the *stephanoi* crown, given to the victor. Hence they are *impregnable* and cannot be stopped by the forces of man. Third, *"faces as the faces of men."* This speaks of their *intelligence*; they can use a rational line of thought. Verse 8, *"as the hair of women."* The glory of the woman is in her hair. Everything was covered except the hair. The hair was so arranged to become a seductive attraction. Satan is always this way. His goal is to allure and rip to pieces. Then *"as the teeth of lions."* Seeking prey to devour. Verse 9, *"as it were breastplates of iron."* They are *invincible* they cannot be stopped by man. They have no mercy. Verse 9, *"as the sounds of chariots."* This reveals a massive movement. They are prepared to challenge every phase of the world.

The Apocalypse: The Revelation of the Redeemer

Now, consider their **function** in verses 5 and 10. They have power to hurt men. Everything connected with the enemy of God is to hurt Jesus Christ Who hurt him on the cross. He hates everything about God and because he cannot hurt Jesus Himself his next target is the believer or to keep the unbelievers from receiving Jesus as Lord. That is why we should stay away from the things of this world. Their function is to ensnare, to hurt, harm, grieve and lead to death. Thirdly,

3. Their Prince! Verse 11 His name is given both Hebrew and Greek. In any language it is the same, destroyer. The devil is the prince of this world and his purpose is to bring about as much destruction as possible.

Secondly, we will now consider:

B: THE SINNERS PLIGHT! Verses 5-6 It is not as if these people were not warned, they were. There are at least 600 warnings in the Bible about hell and the judgment. If you were traveling down a road and saw 600 signs that declared this road leads to death and destruction and continued, you would be responsible for whatever happened.

The plight of the sinner is witnessed in two ways. First,

1. His Punishment! Verse 5 These are receiving exactly what they have requested. This aspect of punishment is while one is still in his physical body. What can man expect in a lake of fire? Secondly,

2. His Predicament! Verse 6 The physical torment is so painful that man will try to commit suicide to escape. This has always been apart of Satan's plan that is to drive individuals to suicide. The age with the highest rate of suicide is over 70. The longer you live with the sin the sicker you get of it. The second highest age is 50-70. Here men will do anything possible to die, but God will not allow it. It is God that controls the span of life. The unbeliever does not normally like to talk about the reality of death. That is why he refuses to talk about meeting God. In this day men are seeking death. Imagine falling on a sword and it bends or bullets bouncing off like rubber. These will not be permitted to die until God says it is time.

Conclusion:
Earnest Hemmingway said in an article in 1960 that you can sin and get away with it. Later, he blew his brains out. In this day the brighter way will be the way of death.

How can God allow all of this to happen? When man turns his back on God, God must and will judge sin.

The person that builds his life on sin builds it on a crumbling cliff next door to hell. God cries, *"Turn ye, turn ye."* What is your response?

Just when You Think it Can't Get Any Worse
Revelation 9:12-21

The first woe, the sounding of the fifth trumpet which is the woe of hell being let loose on earth has past. One might expect a "let up" of sorts after 5 months of torment by these demons from the bottomless pit. One could even hope that man would desire God and flee to His extended arms of love. But this is not what will occur. Man will wax worse and worse. The second trumpet of woe is sounded and judgment increasing in the earth. The tribulation days grow darker. Yet, the depraved heart, deceived by *"the lie"* of the antichrist is without repentance.

The second woe is more dreadful than the first. In the second one-third of the population of the earth will be killed by demonic power. The heartbreak is that man will not seek God during this devastating period of tribulation in the earth. The Bible informs us that it is the goodness of God that leads to repentance. We should know that seldom does anyone turn to the Lord in genuine faith as a result of something devastating transpiring in his or her life.

This passage of Scripture reveals clearly that the earth and those that reject the Lord Jesus will experience days of devastation that exceed the vocabulary of man. There are two powerful truths in this passage that we want to consider. First, observe:

I: THE SCENE FROM HEAVEN! Verses 12-15 All that transpires during these dark days is under the control of God and is a part of His judicial process. It is not the result of some insane, mad deity. It is not occurring because God is a spoiled tyrant. This scene from heaven reveals the absolute sovereignty of God over the affairs of the earth. We will note two aspects of the scene from heaven.

First we will consider:

A: THE ALTAR! Verse 13 There were two altars in the tabernacle. One is the brazen altar, the altar of burnt sacrifice, located outside the sanctuary in the court. The other was small, overlaid with gold, and stood before the veil of the Holy place. This was the altar of worship, of prayer, of mediation, and of intercession. The brazen altar was the altar of judgment upon sin. It was the altar of sacrifice, of pouring out of blood, of the slaying of the victim. In the golden censer, fire was taken from the altar of sacrifice and carried to the golden altar, were incense was burned to God. Blood was taken from the altar of sacrifice on the Day of Atonement and sprinkled on the four horns of the altar of prayer. This was done to teach that coming into the presence of God is based upon sacrifice, the shedding of blood, without which there is no remission of sins and access to His heart in worship. It is from the four horns that the cry comes to loose the bound angels. Heretofore, the blood of the sacrifice and the prayers of intercession have always been for mercy, for God's forgiveness, for His salvation. But now the cry of blood is for judgment and damnation. The very altar cries out against mans blasphemy, unbelief and rejection. It is a terrible thing to fall into the hands of the living God. (W.A. Criswell)

When there is a cry invoking judgment, the locality of it expresses where the sin has been which is to be avenged. The voice that cried against Cain for the murder of his brother cried from the ground that received Abel's blood. When a call for retribution comes from the altar, it is because of some crime against that altar. What is the crime? God's appointed way of forgiveness, through blood, has been set aside, that His system of atonement and salvation has been rejected and despised. Here the wickedness of the earth has elevated to the point of despising the cross, and redemption by the blood of Jesus, that the altar itself, which otherwise cries for mercy, is compelled to cry for vengeance.

Secondly observe:

B: THE ANGELS! Verses 14-15 The definite article *"the"* helps us to understand that these are designated for this particular

The Apocalypse: The Revelation of the Redeemer

task. Also note that they are *four*. This speaks of the universality of their operation. These are a part of the "angels" that fell when they followed Satan in his rebellion against God. There are several things about these angels that require our special attention. First, we have:

1. The Loosing! Verses 14 and 15. *"Loose the four angels…and the four angels were loosed."* If they are loosed they have been, up to this point, restrained. It is implied that if they had not been under this restrain that they would have been engaged in their activity all the while. In this day of grace there are demons that would, if allowed, kill all individuals that know Jesus. In this dark day the restraint will be removed and they will be loosed. 11 Peter 2:4, *"…reserved unto the judgment of the great day."* This could mean the day of their judgment or, a portion of it could mean the judgment of some one else by them!

Secondly we have:

2. The Location! Verse 14, *"Which are bound in the great river Euphrates."* Why is this specific location mentioned? It was, at least in my opinion; here that the powers of evil made their first attempts against the human race that resulted in the fall of man. Here the first murder was committed. Here is where mans first organized rebellion against God took place. It is the region where all the world's beginnings were made, where man first saw the light, fell and was banished. This is where Satan won his first victory. The river Euphrates is the only one we know of that remains. These angels, in mercy, are now bound in this location but they will be loosed during the days of the Great Tribulation.

Thirdly we witness:

3. Their Length! Verse 15, *"Which were prepared for an hour, and a day, and a month, and a year."* They are held in bondage until they are loosed for a particular time for a particular judgment. The length of time is speculation. Some suggest the length will be 13 months, 1 day and 1 hour. The actual length is not the most important issue. We should be aware that God is moving according to His Sovereign schedule and that the length of these angels is under His control.

Fourth we have:

4. The Languish! Verse 15 These four angels are loosed from their restraint against inflicting death and torment upon men, and now, in judgment, are permitted to act out their evil will upon earth's guilty inhabitants. One-third of the population of the earth will be slain by them. One-third of the vegetation and water has already been reduced. If the total population of the earth was 6 billion people that would mean that 2 billion people will be slain. Verse 18 states this number to add intensity as well as helping us with the details of how this will actually happen.

The second major thought is:

II: SATANS HAVOC! Verses 16-21 A casual reading of these verses will reveal that we are not dealing solely with flesh and blood. Just as the locusts were demon spirits so are these horses and their riders.

We know that Satan counterfeits all that is Godly and good. We have recorded in 11 Kings chapter 6 an account of a spiritual army. Briefly the account reveals that Elisha and his servant are trapped and the servant is growing rather anxious. Elisha prays and asks the Lord to open his eyes and allow him to see that those that are with them are more than those against them. The Lord removes the scales from his eyes and he then sees that the mountains are full of horses and chariots of fire. Logical reasoning will lead one to conclude that Satan has his spiritual army and that one day they will march at his command. First we observe:

A: THE DEVASTATING HOST! Verses 16-19 This is a part of Satan's army. It is possible that this is an army of men possessed and driven by demons. There are two interesting things presented to us about this devastating host. First,

1. Their Number! Verse 16 It is as if John gives up on counting. The number is approximately 200 million. This is the combined power of the devil and man acting in their own evil interest and yet, at the same time, they are ignorantly carrying out the judicial will of God.

The *wonder* of this devastating host is seen when we realize that an army one mile wide and 87 miles long would be needed to comprise this host of 200 million. What an awesome power! This should help us to fully realize that even in this day of grace that

The Apocalypse: The Revelation of the Redeemer

we, in and of ourselves, are no match for the tremendous power of the enemy. Secondly,

2. Their nature! Verses 17-19 We can observe their nature by considering their **description** in verse 17. John calls them horses while he says they are not proper horses. Their heads are like lions heads. Their tails are like serpents. They have riders, and yet the riders are part of themselves, to whom no separate actions are ascribed. They are covered with coats of mail. They do not eat, nor does it appear that they are capable of being wounded or killed. *"Out of their mouth issues fire, smoke and brimstone or sulfur,"* the very elements of hell.

This could be modern warfare but I do not have any problem in this being a literal demonic expression that is used by Satan to inflect torture upon the inhibitions of the earth.

We can observe more of their nature by considering their **destruction** in verses 18-19. The *weapons* are presented in verses 18 and 19. They are *"fire, smoke and brimstone."* This is not symbolic. These are the elements of hell hurled upon the guilty while they still live in the flesh. Their destruction is witnessed in the *way* they destroy men. They stifle and kill by what they belch from their mouths, and they hurt and injure with their snake-headed tail (verse 19). The fire would scorch and burn men to death and the smoke or sulfur would stifle and smother them. These are called *"three plagues"* and the description is life is destroyed by each separately and joined together.

The idea of the serpentine tail suggests a capacity for lashing with painful and disabling strokes; the snake's head suggest the capacity to bite and sting.

There will be one out of three persons killed by this hellish army. When the death angel past through Egypt it probably resulted in one out of ten dying and it produced a cry from the guilty but nothing like that happens in this day. Secondly, we witness:

B: THE DEPRAVED HEARTS! Verses 20-21 Note that two-thirds of the earth's population is still alive. It is possible that even in wrath God remembers mercy. What effect does all this have on those still alive? One would think that they would repent but just the opposite is true. Their hearts are made harder by their experience. This was true of Pharaoh and it reveals that the old nature is totally depraved.

How is this possible? 11 Thessalonians 2:10-11 shares how this will be fulfilled in Revelation chapter 9. *"And with all deceivableness of unrighteousness in them that perish: because they received not the love of the truth, that they might be saved. And for this cause God shall send them strong delusion, that they should believe a (the) lie."* The lie is the antichrist. There are two things presented to us in these verses that can help us understand something of the depraved hearts of man during this time. First,

1. The Arrogance of the Depraved heart is seen in verses 20 and 21. Here we are informed that these, *"yet repented not."* They refused to bow to the One that was capable of doing something about it. But they reveal their depravity in that they *worship* that which was built by them. Verse 20 declares, *"which neither can see, nor hear, nor walk."* All over the world men are worshipping rocks, animals and the devil. The truth is revealed that there is no good in man apart from God.

Verse 21 reveals how *wicked* man will be in this day. One can readily see that wickedness is elevating more and more with each new day. Secondly,

2. The Activity of the Depraved Heart is seen in verses 20 and 21. Note the words; *"worship devils."* This is not idle talk. It is a matter of fact that devil worship has reached alarming proportions throughout the land. This is associated with idolatry.

Verse 21 list *"murders."* Ours has become a crime-oriented society. This reveals how little we esteem human life. How long has it been since you wrote a letter opposing abortion? This is an area that should concern us. When a people murder the unborn innocent then they will become selective of those that should live. After the unborn it will doubtless be the older individuals that are removed.

"Sorceries" is listed next. This comes from the Greek word from which we get our English word "pharmacy." The word specifically includes tampering with ones own or another's health by means of drugs, potions, and intoxications, which is often associated with magical arts and incantations.

The Apocalypse: The Revelation of the Redeemer

"*Fornication*" is listed next in verse 21. This word is used so as to inform us that marriage will then hardly be recognized. It is sex without love and with as many partners as one chooses.

"*Thefts*" concludes the list. This is the disregard of other's rights and the practice of fraud, theft and deceit. The attitude of getting what you desire in any way will only be intensified during this day.

Conclusion:
One can easily see that things are going to get worse during these terrible days of the Great Tribulation. There is one great difference in that day and our day, individuals can now bow freely to the Lord Jesus and receive His mercy. In this day men will not have that desire because of their believing Satan's lie. Imagine society a million times more wicked. That does not being to reveal what lies ahead during these days.

The Angels' Announcement and Assignment
Revelation 10:1-11

From the conclusion of chapter 9 one might expect to hear the sounding of the seventh trumpet. That does not occur until chapter 11:15. This is the second of three interludes in the book. The first was between the 6th and 7th seal. That is chapter 7, the sealing of the 144,000. The third is between the 6th and 7th bowls or vials in Revelation chapter 16.

Why are these pauses present? It is possible that it is a pause for mercy. In wrath God remembers mercy. This will serve as a means of encouraging the believers in the tribulation. Imagine their thoughts. They have not been saved for more than three years. Think of what they have witnessed. The universe has been shaken. The sun and moon darkened. The stars have fallen. They have witnessed judgment and an army of 200 million demons has killed one-third of the earth's population. It would be easy for them to be discouraged and conclude that God has lost control; that He is no longer on the throne and the devil has won. It would be easy to think I'm next; all has been in vain.

Revelation 10 is Gods pause to comfort them by assuring them of His grace and control. He is saying, "I know it looks bad but I'm still the 'I Am' I am still on the throne."

Chapter 10 is a preview of the triumph of the Son of God. In chapter 10 there are three major thoughts that we need to carefully consider. First, note with me:

I: THE MIGHTY ANGEL! Verses 1-4 There are those things that distinguish this angel from the host of angels in heaven. It is designated as a *"mighty angel."* There are three things presented to us about this mighty angel that should bless our hearts. First, let us notice:

The Apocalypse: The Revelation of the Redeemer

A: HIS AFFINITY TO THE SAVIOR! Verses 1-2 This angel is not named and while there are many similarities between this angel and the description of The Lord Jesus in chapter 1:12-17. It is probably not the person of Jesus Christ. John MacArthur is especially helpful in clearing up this point. He points out that the Greek word for another is *allos*, which means another of the same kind. If it referred to Christ it would be *heteros*, that is another of a different kind. Secondly, whenever Jesus Christ appears in Revelation John gives Him an unmistakable title. Third, there are other strong angels that appear in Revelation (5:2; 18:21) that cannot be identified as Christ. Fourth, The Lord Jesus could not make the oath that this angel makes in verse 5 and 6.While I do not agree that this is the person of The Lord Jesus I do believe that this strong angel is what W.A. Criswell calls "a full ambassadorial representative of the Lord." It must be remembered that this is the tribulation and God is dealing with Israel.

In these verses there are those things that reveal his affinity to the Savior. First, we have: **His Coming!** Verse 1, *"Come down from heaven."* This informs us where He is from. It informs us that heaven is aware of all the activity that transpires upon this earth. This is in the present tense. That is as John saw this it was the present activity. Our Lord came from heaven to earth the first time. However, the time for His ultimate triumph has not yet arrived. If this were the Lord it would indicate a coming other than the one when He comes to reign. Secondly, we have: **His Clothing!** Verse 1, *"Clothed with a cloud."* Deity is often associated with clouds. God appeared in the tabernacle in a cloud at the mercy seat. That was His Sheniah glory. It was the evidence that He was present. He led Israel by a cloud. The cloud directed them. He directs us by His Spirit from within. In Matthew 24:29-30 we read, *"And they shall see the Son of man coming in the clouds of heaven."* Matthew 26:64 declares, *"And coming in the clouds of heaven."* Revelation 1:7 states, *"Behold, He cometh with clouds."* Note that verse 1 is singular not plural. He is *"Clothed with a cloud."* This is surely a reference to the Sheniah glory of God that will accompany this mighty representative of the Son of God. Thirdly, we note: **His Covenant!** Verse 1, *"And a rainbow* *was upon His head."* In Greek the definite article is used to designate this as *"the"* not *"a"* rainbow. This is a particular rainbow. What rainbow is this? Chapter 4:3 has the answer, *"Rainbow about the throne."* The rainbow is associated with the covenant of God. Genesis 9, *"I will not destroy the earth again with water."* The rainbow upon the head in Revelation 10 is seen as the fulfilled promise of God. He promised as early as Genesis 3:15 that He would send One to the earth to deal with man's sin and that promise was fulfilled in Jesus Christ. God keeps His promises or covenant. Peter declared in 11 Peter 3:9, *"God is not slack concerning His promises."* Everything will come to pass as God has said it would. He is as good as His word. He cannot lie. The rainbow here reminds us of mercy that is now available but will one day expire. Fourthly, we have: **His Countenance**! Verse 1, *"And His face (countenance) was as the sun."* This is probably because of where he has been and the fact that he is reflecting the glory of the Person on the throne of eternity. A reasonable question for each of us would be "What is reflected by my countenance?" Fifth, **His Columns**! Verse 1, *"His feet as pillars of fire."* They are ready to walk throughout the earth in judgment and justice. In chapter 1:15 we read about the Lord Jesus, *"His feet like unto fine brass, as if they burned in a furnace."* That was a reminder of the judgment He bore at Calvary. Here the feet are *"As pillars of fire."* This is not in the furnace of substitution for the sin of the world. This is a reminder that at this time the judgment is by fire and justice flows from them as this mighty angel walks!

We now move from the affinity that this mighty angel to the Savior to:

B: HIS ACTION THAT IS SOLEMN! Verses 2-3 This is given to encourage and strengthen the saints that are experiencing the tribulation. This is a reminder that God is in absolute control of His world. As we observe his solemn action we will consider three things about it in these verses. First, **His Possession**! Verse 2, *"And He had in His hand a little book opened."* This naturally causes us to inquire as to the nature of this little book as well as how it happens to be in the possession of this mighty angel. It is in his hand doubtless because God desires to reveal to those that

The Apocalypse: The Revelation of the Redeemer

are dwelling upon the earth that they are squatters. This is the identical book we are introduced to in chapter 5. This is the title deed to the entire earth. He has it in His hand. Also note that there is one significant difference in the book now. It is now opened. The Worthy One, Jesus Christ, has cut the seals. The word in Greek indicates that it is opened never to be closed again.

Any possession to be proper must be based upon legal ground. This mighty angel that holds the title deed to the earth is by his action declaring that Jesus purchased all that Adam forfeited at Calvary. The title deed being in the hand of this mighty angel is a clear indication that the One that purchased the earth will rule over His purchased possession at the time when judgment is completed. *"The earth is the Lords and the fullness thereof the world and they that dwell therein"* and in that day He will possess His possession. Secondly, we note: **His Position!** Verse 2, *"And He set His right foot upon the sea, and His left foot on the earth."* The full significance of this action is nowhere stated in Scripture. Deuteronomy 11:24 declares, *"Every place wherein the soles of your feet shall tread shall be yours."* There has been much confusion about *"sea"* and *"land."* I believe it declares that just as this representative of Jesus Christ positioned himself over all that the One he represents, being the heir to the throne of this earth, will one day perform the needed action to possess it. That is, it will be under His feet, and that His sovereign control will be expressed. He came to have dominion over all creation, if this is to be reality all things must be put under His feet. That does include you and me. Thirdly we have: **His Pronouncement!** Verse 3, *"And Cried* (the Mighty Angel) *with a loud voice, as when a lion roarth."* This is not a cry of fear. It is a loud cry but it is as a *"lion roareth."* The lion roars when it is ready to finish off its prey. It is the deathblow. This is the pronouncement of conquest completed.

This mighty angel is declaring that The Lord Jesus is ready to finish the conquest that was commenced at Calvary. He will and all that has been going on will be brought to its conclusion by Him.

We now consider:

C: HIS ANNOUNCEMENT THAT IS STRANGE! Verse 4, *"Seal up those things which the seven thunders uttered, and write them not."* The announcement is clear and concise. Therefore, what the seven thunders uttered is not known. Why was John instructed to *"write not?"* It is speculation but it could have been for one of two reasons. First, it is possible that it was so *devastating* and terrifying that mankind could not bear the knowledge of these things. Or secondly, it could be that it was so *delightful* that words were not adequate to convey what was being witnessed.

John had witnessed one-fourth of the population of the earth destroyed. He wrote it. When he saw the demonic horde of 200 million torturing one-third of the population he wrote it. But here what he heard was not to be written.

If you are not a Christian, if you cannot say, "I'm ready to meet Him as Savior and not as judge" then I plead with you to make the decision of all decisions in surrendering your heart as the throne of Jesus Christ. If you do not know Jesus you are missing the best of this life and will face eternity in hell.

The second major thought is:

II: THE MARVELOUS ANNOUNCEMENT! Verses 5-7 I do not desire to be overly repetitive but it is imperative that we fully understand that the things John witnessed in all of chapter 10 is a preview of what will transpire. He sees it as if it is in the process of happening. He hears the mighty angel's announcement of these events as if they were actually taking place at that very moment. They are not. The actual events will be experienced when Christ comes in power and glory. It is a future happening with present consequences.

This marvelous announcement involves two great themes. First he announced that:

A: THE DELAY IS PAST! Verses 5-6 The last words of verse 6 *"That there should be time no longer"* are more literally translated as *"There shall be delay no longer."*

Before we address the question of what delay is past it is noteworthy for us to consider the fact of the mighty angel's oath. The act of lifting up the hand to heaven is explained in verse six by the words, *"And sware."* It is true that Jesus declared that man is not to swear by heaven or earth. Why then is it acceptable for Him to use an oath in these verses? There are at least two differences. One His words apply to the age of the church in the earth. Further, it applies to you and me and not directly to Him. That does not imply that He has a standard for us that does not apply to Him, rather it stresses the importance of the event. Under the law God swore, and here Christ swears to attest the authority and finality of His own statement.

To make an oath one must swear by someone or something greater than himself, else it is nothing more than a mere statement. Christ confirms His promise with an oath. The great events yet to happen in the earth, as announced by God, must surely come to pass. Christ has staked His very existence on their fulfillment.

The words, "That there should be no more delay" declare that in the midst of the tribulation there is one more trumpet judgment. He is declaring that when the seventh trumpet sounds, all evil in the earth will be put down without further delay. Sin has been reigning, and righteousness has suffered throughout man's day on earth, but now things must change (Strauss).

It can be said in a different way that we are living in a day of delay. That is the delay of His coming for His church. This delay will one day pass. He will come for His own. Now, in the delay, we are to be doing all that we possibly can to share the "good news" with every man in the earth.

Secondly, He announced;

B: THE DISCLOSURE OF THE PURPOSE! Verse 7, *"But in the days…"* inform us that something unusual is going to transpire when the delay is past. What is it? *"The mystery of God should be finished."* What is the "mystery of God?" It is not the mystery of the church or kingdom. Mystery in the scripture means something known to God but it is not the general knowledge of man. There may be partial understanding by some, but not all by all. The mystery was given to the prophets and apostles. They shared with us as much as God allowed. So what is the "mystery of God" in verse seven?

W.A. Criswell says, "The mystery of God is the long delay of our Lord in taking the kingdom unto Himself and in establishing righteousness in the earth. The mystery is why God does not intervene."

The mystery is the secret of allowing the devil and man to have his way in the earth and His delay in reinstating mans lost inheritance. Friday ask Robinson Crusoe, "If God is as great, powerful and awesome as you say why doesn't He kill the devil?" There is a designated day when the forbearance of God shall end and the mystery will be revealed. Then and only then will man be able to grasp the purpose of God in allowing evil, sin and wickedness to run loose in the earth.

The third major thought is:

III: THE MAGNIFICENT ASSIGNMENT! Verses 8-11 The voice he heard is the voice of God. John sees himself in this vision. His assignment is two-fold. First, he is to:

A: EAT THE SCROLL! Verses 8-10 Before he could eat the scroll he must act obediently. The voice had instructed him, *"Take the scroll out of the mighty angel's hand."* This is simple yet profound. In verse nine he did what he had been instructed to do.

To *'eat"* means to devour as well as digest. He is to devour and digest the truth. He is to feed and feast on the word; that is absorbed it into his life. Jeremiah 15:16 states, *"I did eat."* Psalm 119:103 states, *"How sweet are Thy words unto my taste."* 1 Peter 2:2 declares that we are to *"desire the sincere milk of the word."*

Do we have a hunger for the Word of God?

He is told before he eats the scroll that it will be both sweet and bitter. How is this possible? Remember what is being dealt with. It is Christ returning to take possession of this earth. This will be both sweet and bitter. The sweetness is for the saint. Jesus will reign as king, conquer Satan and establish His kingdom. The bitterness is that this will be a time of wrath, judgment, vengeance and hell.

Indeed the second coming is a bittersweet truth. Because this is true we need to be doing our best to reach the lost with the Gospel of Jesus Christ.

Secondly, he is to:

B: EXAULT THE SAVIOR! Verse 11 *"Thou must"* and must is an imperative. He is coming in judgment do not hide the truth rather proclaim the truth of His coming.

This He will do in a larger ministry. *"Before many people and nations and tongues and kings."* Why is this so important for us today? Someday there will be no sweet only bitter for the sinner. One day the delay will be past. People must hear the truth now while grace is available then His coming will be sweet and not bitter.

Conclusion:

D.L. Moody had preached and said to his audience, "Go home and think about being saved," that night the Chicago fire happened and one-half of the congregation perished. Mr. Moody said, "I never again ask people to think about being saved but to act in faith and to be saved."

God's Last Call
Revelation 11:1-19

If it were not such a serious matter one could have a hilarious time reading what many have said about Revelation 11. Dr. W.A. Criswell shares some of the following, for example one said, "The temple is used here figuratively for the faithful portion of the church of Christ." Another stated "The command is given to John to measure the temple to call attention to the size of the church." Another believes the altar is the church. One thought the outer court signified a part of the church. Another declared that in the Revelation the Holy City is always a type of the church. Still another said, "The two witnesses represent the elect church of God, embracing both the Jew and Christian, and the witness she bears concerning God in the Old and New Testament." These are only a portion of the many but they are sufficient to reveal to us the necessity of allowing the Holy Spirit the privilege of making known what He inspired.

One of the great truths of this chapter is that God in His mercy pleads with sinful man till the end. But the end does come.

There are four thoughts presented in this passage. First we will observe:

I: THE TEMPLE IS MEASURED! Verses 1-2 The use of the *"Temple"* is sufficient to inform us that we are exclusively on Jewish ground. There is nothing in these verses that can be representative of the church.

John is no longer merely observing these events. In a manner unknown to man he is involved in this work himself. There is an application of this truth for each of us. Spiritual observation results in specific involvement.

There are two thoughts to be considered. First,

The Apocalypse: The Revelation of the Redeemer

A: THE AREA EMBRACED IN MEASURING! Verse 1 It is the "Temple of God." We will deal more clearly with this in a moment. Before we do, consider the *instrument for measuring* shared in verse 1 in the words, *"And there was given me a reed like a rod."* It is not the rod of John it was *"given him"* for this purpose. The *"rod"* was a common reed that grew in the region. They were lightweight and were cut into 10 feet lengths for measuring, much like we would use a yardstick. It was a surveyor's tool.

When *"rod"* is used in Revelation it carries with it the idea of correction or judgment. Verse 1 also shares with us the *instructions for measuring*. John is instructed to *"measure."* This has two basic meanings. First, it was used for measuring out chastisement or judgment. It was like a general laying out a war plan. Second, it was used for claiming or showing ownership. Both ideas are involved in the tribulation. The reason is that man has made such a mockery of worship; that the house is abused therefore, it will be judged by Him. John is instructed to measure a *specific place*. He is to measure, *"The temple of God."* What temple is this *"temple of God"*? There have been three and will be two more. The first was Solomon's, the second was Zerubabbals; the third was Herods; the fourth will be the tribulation temple; and the fifth will be the millennium temple. The temple referred to in chapter 11 is the tribulation temple. It will be built after the rapture with the assistance of the antichrist. Matthew 24:15 states, *"When ye shall see the abomination of desolation, spoken by Daniel, stand in the holy place..."* He is also instructed to measure a *specific people* as verse 1 states, *"And them that worship therein."* This however is not righteous worship it is ritual worship. These are going through a form but failing to measure up. They fall short. Remember he is measuring with a rod given to him by God. It is not according to the standards of man but Gods. These have made a mockery of worship and will be judged by God.

Secondly we will consider;

B: THE AREA EXCLUDED IN MEASURING! Verse 2, *"Do not measure the court."* The temple involved three areas; the brazen altar, the Holy place and the Holiest of Holies. The courtyard was not included and here we are told why it will be excluded in that day. "For it is given unto the Gentiles; and the holy city shall they tread under foot forty-two months." That is three and one-half years. I believe this to be the last three and one-half years of the tribulation. The Gentiles time will not end until Jesus comes to reign in power (Luke 21:24). Zechariah 14 indicates that the Gentiles will trample Israel just prior to Christ coming in glory on the Mount of Olives. During this time two out of three Jews will be killed.

The second major thought is:

II: THE TWO MESSENGERS! Verses 3-10 There is and has been so much speculation about these messengers that I am merely going to share what the scriptures state. There are two truths that we will consider. First,

A: THEY ARE PERSONS! Verses 3-6 These have been called almost everything conceivable. They are persons. They have bodies; they are clothed; they prophecy. That word is used of a person speaking. There are some interesting things to consider about these persons. **One** is their *number*. They are *two*. Under Jewish law two witnesses were required to collaborate a testimony. At the tomb there were two heavenly witnesses; at the ascension there were two men that were witnesses. They are designated as *"witnesses;"* this word in Greek it is *martus*. It came to refer to those that sealed their witness with their blood and it came to mean in English *"One who bears witness by his death."* **Two**, is their *name*. Verses 3-4 Here's where the imagination of man has run wild. There are those that say they represent the Old and New Testaments. They have been called John Huss and Jerome of Prague. Many conclude based upon similar signs that they are Moses and Elijah or Enoch and Elijah. Their thinking is Enoch and Elijah did not die and all men die (Hebrews 9:27). They must therefore, come back to die. They were the first astronauts! They already have bodies (they were seen with Jesus on the Mt. of Transfiguration) and there will be those that will not die a physical death when Jesus comes. Then some declare that Malachi said that Elijah would come before the great day of the Lord. True! However, Jesus said that if the people had received

The Apocalypse: The Revelation of the Redeemer

the kingdom, John would have been Elijah. It does not have to the literal Elijah. The best conclusion is that they are unnamed persons called for a specific purpose.

Third, is their *nature* as shared in verses 3-6. Their clothing helps us understand that they are expressing judgment and doom. They are anointed of God and give forth light in a dark world (verse 4). They have power to keep it from raining (verse 6). This usually was the punishment for sin. They can turn water to blood. These are signs. Signs are for unbelievers. They are used here to gain the attention and ear of the world. We want to declare that their actions are not in keeping with grace and that is correct. They are living in a day of judgment. There is a constant cry from the unbelieving world to get rid of them. Why? They are constantly announcing the coming judgment of God upon the wicked of this world.

The second thought about these two messengers is:

B: THEY ARE PERSECUTED! Verses 7-10 Make no mistake about it this wicked world has never nor will it ever welcome the world of anointed witnesses. There are two things we observe about their persecution. **First**, we have *the death of the messengers* in verse 7. The beast (anti-Christ) is finally successful in killing them. There is a blessed truth that we must not miss that is stated in verse 7, *"And when they had finished their testimony."* They were invincible until they had completed their work. The truth is that there is not enough power in hell to stop the work of the worker until God says it is finished. Likewise, there is not enough power in earth or hell to prolong it ones life when God says it is over. There is another truth that perhaps is not as blessed, but nonetheless true; that is, we like these messengers will one day finish our stay on this earth. If Jesus tarries we will go through the valley of death. And there may be a troubling thought connected with this, namely our death may not be in a manner of our choosing. We too may die at the hands of the enemy. It may come after an extended period of persecution. The challenge for us is to be ready to meet Jesus at any time.

Secondly, we have *the depravity of man* in verses 8-10. Verses 8-9 informs us that the depraved heart is filled with hate.

Their hatred is manifested in that they will not allow their bodies to be buried. The vilest of the vile were allowed a burial. The natural tendency is to get the body out of sight as soon as possible. This will not be the case under the antichrist. Their bodies will lie in the street and allowed to decompose. They are lying in the street of the city that throughout it time has been called the "Holy City." Here it is properly designated spiritually as Sodom and Egypt because of the vileness and violence that it harbors. The truth is she is not what she once was. It has been a decline in depravity. Verse 9 informs us that the bodies will be observed worldwide. This was unheard of 50 years ago. Those of a more liberal persuasion taunted others for believing such a thing could be possible. Now with television, satellite, computers and who knows what this can easily be seen in all parts of the world at the same time. Verse 10 shares with us that the depraved heart will be filled with happiness. This is the only mention of celebration in the tribulation. They are happy because God's servants have been killed. (What causes you and me to be happy?) This is celebration without Christ. Much like Christmas is to multitudes in our time. This was their "happy dead witness day." They were so happy they celebrated by giving gifts.

The third major thought is:

III: THE TERRIFIED MEN! Verses 11-13 Verse 11 closes with, "...*and great fear fell upon them*..." Verse 13, "...*and the remnant were affrighted*..." The word "*affrighted*" literally means terrified. In view of what has just transpired it is no wonder that men are terrified. Do you remember the last time fear gripped your heart? I can assure you that if you have been terrified that experience was not soon or easily forgotten. There are two thoughts presented to us about the terrified men that we will consider. First we will observe,

A: THE WISDOM OF GOD! Verses 11-12 it is the act of God in these verses that clearly reveals His wondrous wisdom. These verses reveal that what terrifies a man is directly related to his spiritual life. God's wisdom is presented in two great acts. **First** His wisdom is witnessed in *His apparent delay*, verse 11. These two messengers have been in the street of Jerusalem for 3

The Apocalypse: The Revelation of the Redeemer

and ½ days. It is significant tht He delayed more than 3 days. Why? The Jews believed that the spirit of the person hovered over the body for 3 days. He was just "sort-of-dead!" until after 3 days. You recall that Jesus delayed in going to Bethany till Lazarus had been in the grave 4 days. Here the entire world will be absolutely convinced that these messengers are dead. It is possible that you have thought that God has needlessly delayed in giving His answer or assistance only to realize, often as you looked back how wonderful it was when you recognized that He was right on schedule.

Someone might respond, "Well, if He was going to intervene why would He delay?" That is a part of His wisdom. The world must know that what is happening is His work and that He does it His way. The apparent delay is from our perspective not His.

Secondly, His wisdom is seen in *His awesome deliverance*, verses 11-12. The deliverance of the two messengers is so grand and glorious that the best word to describe it is awesome.

In these verses we are privileged to witness *their resurrection* as stated in verse 11, *"The Spirit of life from God entered into them."* The unbelieving world that denied the resurrection of the Lord Jesus will behold the event. This entire event will be on television worldwide. We are familiar with how reporters hunt for things to say. I can imagine that here they are already describing the clothing not only of the messengers but of the masses that are walking by their bodies. I can hear one as he says, "Well, they have been dead 3 days and 11 hours and 59 minutes. Then suddenly those bodies begin to show signs of life. They stand on their feet! What will be the response of the world? There may be a few that will believe that the rapture has occurred but not many. Terror not trust will fill most hearts.

What is observed here will be the experience of all those that have died in Jesus. The old spiritual says it this way, *"There ain't no grave goin' hold my body down!"* This is a Biblical fact!! When the Spirit of life from God enters there is resurrection.

We witness *their rapture* in verse 12. There is a *voice*, *"And they heard."* Who? The messengers; the world has turned a deaf ear to God and the gospel. They will not hear His voice; *"A great voice from heaven."* The scriptures inform us that throughout the space of time there have been voices from heaven. Some examples are: In the giving of the law; at the birth of Jesus; at His baptism; on the Mount of Transfiguration; just before the crucifixion and Saul on the Damascus road. Paul shares with us about "The voice of the archangel, the trump of God" that is to sound when Christ comes for His children. That voice may appear to be silent but be assured that He speaks even in this generation. His voice is not heard with the physical ear but the spiritual ear can hear from heaven by His Spirit. Take courage God is not silent or indifferent to where you are and of your needs.

There is further the *victory*. The voice said "*Come up hither. And they ascend up to heaven in a cloud.*" The victory is more than their being resurrected; it is their rapture to heaven in a "*cloud.*" This is the Shekinah glory of God. Resurrection without rapture would be more of the same misery and woe. The rapture; being called to heaven by God to be with Him is the ultimate victory.

We also have the *vision* in verse 12, "*And their enemies behold them.*" These people thought they were rid of these troublemakers. They were but not in the way they thought. This added to the terror of their heart because they knew that this was of God and they could do nothing about it.

One should be able to easily see why this deliverance is indeed awesome.

Secondly we have:

B: THE WRATH OF GOD! Verse 13 The earthquake of this verse is literal. It is not, at least in my view, some mystical or secret thing. What does the wrath of God mean? Who experiences God's wrath?

What does it mean? For some it means *horror*; verse 11, "*And great fear.*" For some it means *hell*! Note please that hell is for the *insignificant* people; "*those of the tenth of the city*" that was destroyed. Hell is also for the *important* people; "*the seven thousand men.*" The word is for the renowned; those of distinction. These are worldwide leaders. They are here to join the celebration. What they experience is entirely different from what they expected. This will be the case with multitudes in hell. It will

The Apocalypse: The Revelation of the Redeemer

not be one great party but a place of experiencing the wrath of God.

These terrified men *"give glory to the God of heaven."* However, do not think that they turn to God in repentance. The thought is "O.K. God we know You are there but that's all You will get from us." Man becomes more and more rebellious not repentant. What have the experiences of your life produced in you thus far; rebellion or repentance? For you it is not too late, you can still freely bow before Him and receive mercy.

The fourth major thought is:

IV: THE TRIUMPHANT MONARCH! Verses 15-19 The details of these verses are recorded in chapters 12-19. This is the third woe, the sounding of the seventh trumpet. Because these events will be presented in great detail I will merely introduce those things that we will be considering. There are three thoughts that we need to take note of right now. First,

A: THE SAVIOR WILL REIGN! Verse 15 *"...And He shall reign for ever and ever."* Here we are informed that these "were great voices in heaven." This is spoken of in the past tense but it has not as yet occurred. That is Gods way of telling us that this event is so sure that He speaks of it as if it were already a thing of the past. Also observe that in this case there are "voices." That is more than one. The universe joins in this burst of praise. God has waited since Adam for this event. I believe that all of heaven is excited that this long awaited event is taking place.

Take special note of the *place of His reign*, *"the kingdom of this world are become the kingdom of our Lord."* The place is this world. The kingdom of this world is presently ruled over by the "god of this world" that is, the devil. When the Savior reigns all wicked rulers shall be put down; their governments shall crumble and fall. This is Satan's day but one day the prayer of countless Christians "Thy kingdom come" will be answered and the Savior will reign.

Further, take special note of the *period of His reign*, *"...and He shall reign for ever and ever."* How long is that? He will reign for As long as God is! The point is that if any individual would display wisdom he will yield his own world to the exclusive reign of the Lord Jesus Christ now. He will be blessed by saying; "I want this man Christ Jesus to reign over me and all that is in my possession."

Secondly,

B: THE SAINTS WILL REJOICE! Verses 16-17 The living church in glory, sitting on lesser thrones, in response to the declaration made *"fell upon their faces, and worshipped God."* There are three simple, yet profound truths shared about this. **First**, we have *their position* in verse 16, *"fell upon their faces."* They are not now upon their thrones but on their faces at His feet. If the saints in glory will occupy this position then we will be the more blessed if we now find that position of surrender and submission at His feet. A reasonable inquiry in light of their position is "What is our present position?" Are we haughty or humbled by His awareness of us? How has it been since you enjoyed the "fellowship at His feet?" **Secondly**, we move from their position to *their practice* inverse 16, *"And worshipped Him."* It should be noted that one cannot worship the Sovereign, reigning Lord while sitting upon a throne. Worship will lead us to an acknowledgment of who He is and what He has done for us. In heaven the practice is worship. It is an unending period of worship, love and adoration. I really do not know what some people are going to do since they cannot, according to them, tolerate the joy of worship and praise! Why would I say such a thing? Multitudes profess to be Christian and yet they do not attend the services at the church, spiritual things bore them; they do not have a desire to worship the God of glory. If they are in heaven will they not be out of place? Is real worship the present practice of your heart?

Thirdly, we have *their praise* in verse 17. They are joining in praise to God for who He is, what He has done, and what He will do. In glory the theme is one of praiseful thanksgiving. I am convinced that this should be the theme of the Christian in this hour. How long has it been since you were in a private service of praise and thanksgiving?

Praise fills heaven and, it should fill our hearts. In heaven there is no selfishness, no pride, no vaunting of authority. There is no covetousness in the presence of God. There is but one thing

The Apocalypse: The Revelation of the Redeemer

and that is praise. The Christian should be able to rejoice that Christ will reign. Note that real praise flows from those that practice worship at His feet.

Our third thought in the matter of the saints rejoicing is:

C: THE SINNERS WILL REBEL! Verse 18 What is the response of the world to this event? *"The nations were angry."* That is the anger of the inhabitants of the earth because heaven will rule unbounded on the earth. This rebellion will grow and grow. Observe the reference to the *dead*. That is there is a time for sinners to be judged by God for their rejection of Christ. There is also a reference to the *dedicated*, *"...Give reward to servants and saints."* God is aware of all things. He has a payday for His faithful people. Further, there is a reference to the *destroyers*. This could be people but it may also be the demonic host that has carried out the destruction of the devil. The fact is saint, sinner, society and Satan are all going to be judged by God.

Conclusion:

This is Sovereign prewritten history. What one does with Jesus determines his destiny. It will be judgment and hell or repentance and glory. Each of us decides for ourselves what our future will be, no one else.

The Woman, War and Woe
Revelation 12:1-17

To understand the plan of the ages one must comprehended this chapter. It involves Christ, Satan, the nation of Israel and the archangel, Michael. There are three wars in these verses. There is war in the earth, verses 1-5; this is Israel's conflict with Satan in the past. There is war in heaven, verses 7-12 and another war on earth, verses 13-17; Israel's future conflict with Satan.

Revelation 12 is an opening of the curtain of eternity past. It provides us with some of the details that have been omitted in the trumpet judgments. In this sense it is much like Job. While he did not know the what's and why's, he did know the experience was real; but he did not know what was happening behind the scene with God and Satan.

The tribulation is in full force on earth. Yet, what we see is not restricted to the tribulation rather we are carried all the way back to where the conflict of the ages commenced. That same conflict continues now and will not conclude until the reign of Christ as King of kings over this earth. This conflict is not between you and me, nor you and the unbeliever. It is not even between the Christian and the devil. The conflict of the ages is between Christ Jesus and Satan and everything else is a part of that conflict but the conflict is between Christ and the devil.

In these verses we will consider three thoughts. First, we have:

I: THE WOMAN! Verses 1-6 There are four women mentioned in the Revelation. There is Jezebel (Revelation 2:20) who is corrupt and compromising. The great harlot (Revelation 17:1) that is the apostate church that will be in place after the rapture of the church; the Bride, the Lamb's wife (Revelation 19:7) the glorified raptured church. The other is the woman of Revelation 12. We will seek to identify her as we observe three things about her. First, we see:

A: SHE IS A SYMBOLIC PERSON! Verses 1-2; 5 She is a person however, she is a most unusual person. The word *"wonder"* is normally *"teras"* but that is not the word used here. The word here is *"semeion"* translated *"sign."* She is a person but she is also a sign or symbol. Who is she? There are those that believe she is Mary. This is unthinkable. It is ridicules to show Mary about to deliver her child, after the birth, death, resurrection and ascension of Christ. There are those that believe the woman is the church. That can not be. The child is the Lord Jesus and we know that the church did not give birth to Christ, but rather Christ founded the church.

There is a more preposterous teaching that believes that the woman is Mary Baker Eddy. The "man child" that she brought forth was Christian Science and the "dragon" is the "mortal mind." Dr. Ironside said of this "I need not take up the time of sane people with such."

It is my studied opinion that the woman of Revelation 12 is Israel. Remember she is a *"sign"* person. There are three things we should consider about this symbolic person that will assist us in identifying her as Israel.

First, we have *her clothing* in verse 1, *"A woman clothed with the sun and the moon under her feet."* That is the most unusual attire anyone could ever wear. There is a passage in Genesis 37:9-11 that will shed some light on the matter of identifying this woman as Israel by her clothing. It is Joseph's dream. There is the sun, moon and eleven stars bowed to him. Verse 19 indicates that Jacob understood those symbols to represent his entire family, Israel, *"Of whom concerning the flesh Christ came."* (Romans 9:5)

Secondly, we have *her crown* in verse 1, *"And upon her head a crown of twelve stars."* The crown signifies royal dignity; but why are the stars in the crown? They are twelve. In Joseph's dream there were only eleven. Why? He was not one of the stars bowing to himself. He is included here. The number twelve used here and in other passages in Revelation, denotes administrative rule in the hands of men. Israel is of this earth with earthly promises and every promise made to Abraham will be fulfilled, even to possessing the entire land promised.

Thirdly, we have *her child* in verses 2 and 5; verse 2 is in the present tense, which tells us this is a continuing action. Only of Israel can it be said that she brought forth this *"child"* that is none other than Christ Jesus Himself. This is the *"seed of woman;"* (Genesis 3:15) it was from the chosen people, the Israel of God, that Jesus Christ sprang in His human lineage.

Verse 5 reveals three interesting facts about this child, **first,** we have *His advent, "and she brought forth a man child."* That is the incarnation of Christ. This was God invading the earth. **Second,** *His ascension, "and her child was caught up unto God, and to His throne."* We are dealing with the conflict of the ages. There is no mention of His earthly life. Why? It is not important! What! It is not important for this purpose. It reveals that Christ was born and Satan could not stop it. That He was glorified and he could not stop that. Do you know one of the chief reasons the devil hates Jesus Christ? Because one day every knee will bow and every tongue will confess that He is Lord to the glory of God the Father. The fact is that if Satan had been successful in any one area of His earthly life the exaltation would have never happened. The ascension signifies approval. What is revealed is that Christ lived His life and conquered Satan. **Thirdly,** we have *His action, "Who was to rule the nations with a rod of iron."* That is His second coming. There are two time lapses in verse 5. The first, a period of thirty-three years, from His advent to His ascension; the second, a period of unknown time from His ascension to the end of the Great Tribulation when He shall indeed reign in power and glory.

A second thing to note about the woman is:

B: SHE SUFFERS PERSECUTION! Verses 3-4 We have the word *"Semeion"* used again. This is *"another wonder.'* There are three things we must understand about the suffering of persecution. **First,** we see a *portrait of persecution* in verse 3. We are not left to speculation as to who is persecuting the woman, Israel. Verse 9 informs us that the *"dragon"* is none other than the devil. Verse 3 shares a rather unusual portrait of the enemy of

The Apocalypse: The Revelation of the Redeemer

righteousness. The portrait **describes** him as *"a great red dragon."* Note the word *"great"* is used five times in this chapter. *"Great"* is above normal. *"Red"* informs us that he is a bloodthirsty murderer. *"Dragon"* refers to fierce fighting nature. The *"seven heads and ten horns"* probably have to do with his **domain**. This is, I believe, a reference to a *special place*. This is probably the revived Roman Empire that the antichrist will rule over. In addition, observe he has a *special perception* as indicated by his *"seven heads."* Seven is the number of completeness. The *"head"* refers to wisdom. Therefore, the antichrist will have complete worldly wisdom. He will be a master strategist, a great deceiver. His domain will also include a *special power* as indicated by the *"crown"* that represents authority. He will have authority over the world for this period of time. He thinks he is "doing his own thing" but in reality he is doing the will of God. He is an instrument that God is using to accomplish His ultimate purpose.

Secondly, we witness the *purpose of the persecution* in verse 4, *"For to devour her child as soon as it was born."* The devil has had this purpose since the divine pronouncement in Genesis 3:15. The history of the human race is a record of war between the seeds, the *"seed of the serpent"* and the "Seed of the woman." He hates any testimony to the truth about the Son of God, and he will resort to any method to silence such a witness, whether by *murder*, as when Cain killed Abel; or through a *mixture*, as when an unholy alliance was made between the sons of God and the daughters of men in Genesis 6; or through a *mad mans* decree to destroy the woman's child (Matthew 2:13); or by trying to get a *mob* to throw Him over a cliff (Luke 4:28-29); or by *maneuver* Christ to cast Himself down (Matthew 4:6). The purpose has not diminished. It is to devour. He knows that he can not devour Christ; he therefore, seeks to devour the people of Christ. From time past he has plotted against all that God promised. It was his purpose to destroy them in Egypt. That same purpose is seen in Esther. In that day it will be his purpose to devour Israel. Today it is his purpose to defeat the Church of the Lord Christ.

Thirdly, we observe the *persuasion of the persecutor* in verse 4, *"And his tail drew the third part of the stars of heaven,* *and did cast them to the earth."* This carries us back to the beginning of the conflict in eternity past. This refers to his rebellion against God. We should give him credit for wanting to be like God. He wanted the worship that was given to God for himself. He persuaded one-third of the angels to follow him. These had witnessed the unspeakable glory of God and yet they were persuaded to follow him. I have no idea what he may have promised but I know it was a lie. How many angels actually fell? Revelation 5:11 tells us of *"ten thousand times ten thousand and thousands of thousands."* That is millions and millions. These are the unfallen after the fall. One third of the original angels fell with Satan. These are demons. It is worthy of noting just where they were cast when they fell; *"And did cast them to the earth."* They are now doing everything in the power of hell to hinder the work of Christ and the worship of God.

The enemy is as persuasive as ever. He persuades us to sin, to get out of the will of God; to forsake prayer and Bible study, to think we are happier out of God's will. He persuades us to believe that sins pleasures really last. He persuades the lost to be religious without coming to Christ. He persuades man that he can make it on his own. He persuades man to believe that the Bible is not really God's Word to and for him.

Thirdly we note about the woman,

C: SHE IS SOVEREIGNLY PROTECTED! Verse 6 Most Bible scholars believe this will be in the area of Petra. The fleeing into the wilderness signifies a place devoid of natural resources. In this place God will sovereignly protect them. This will last for 1260 days or 3 ½ years. Here we see *the preparation*, *"She hath a place prepared of God."* This statement is true of every one of His children; both in this life and in the life to come. We also have *the provisions*, *"That they should feed her there."* They are provided for it (when) they are there. The "there" is His appointed place for them. He has a "there" for you! Are you in His divinely appointed "there" for you? We also have *the period*, *"a thousand two hundred and threescore days."* That is a definite, designated period of time. There will be 1261.This period of persecution will end.

The Apocalypse: The Revelation of the Redeemer

In the midst of all these things the woman, Israel was sovereignly protected. The child of God, in the day of grace, enjoys that same protection as he abides securely in the Person of Jesus Christ.

The second major division is:

II: THE WAR! Verses 7-12, *"And there was war ..."* This was not a one time scrimmage rather these words indicate a continual struggle. These words are descriptive of the history of man, but they do not refer to man! The location of this war probably disturbs many of us; it was *"In heaven."* We normally associate peace with heaven and rightly so but there is a campaign in heaven to defeat the child of God. The war is fought where sin originated! There are two truths shared about this war. First,

A: THE OPPONENTS! Verse 7 The opponents are Michael and his angels and the devil and his angels. The devil has always had access to heaven. His domain is the earth but he has access to accuse. Verse 10 declares that he is, *"The accuser of the brethren."* He is still doing that; i.e., accusing the Christian before God. He is there because he thinks he belongs there. His pride blinded him and he still does not believe that he was wrong in his rebellion. He will not withdraw voluntarily. Verse 7 of chapter 10 assures us that one day we will understand the mystery of allowing him to exist and cause so much pain, suffering and sorrow.

If war is required to remove him from heaven do we think it will be easy to dislodge him from those places that he has been allowed to make strongholds in our lives? Paul informs us that our battle is against the power of darkness.

Daniel 12:1 is probably fulfilled in revelation 12. Michael is the guardian of Israel. The child of God does not face nor fight the enemy in his own strength. The Bible declares, *"Greater is He that is in you than he that is in the world."* Yet, there is a constant war that must be fought in the power of the Lord.

Secondly, we note:

B: THE OUTCOME! Verses 8-12 share with us the blessing that victory belongs to God and His children. There are three thrilling outcomes of this war. **First,** *Satan is routed* in verses 8-9. This transpires during the last 3 ½ years of the tribulation. It is still future for us. The actual casting out of Satan occurs in the middle of the tribulation. Then persecution becomes more intense (verse 13). In verse 9 four titles of the enemy are used. Each of these reveals something of his diabolical nature. "*Dragon*" reveals his fierce fighting nature. He would rather fight than switch. "*Serpent*" reveals how crafty he is. Remember the garden and how crafty he was in dealing with Eve. His is as crafty now as ever. "*Devil*" reveals that he is a liar, slander and accuser. He still tells man that there are benefits in sin; that the wages of sin are delightful not death. "*Satan*" reveals that he is the adversary, the deceiver; the old trickster.

In Luke 18:10 Jesus saw this. In the Greek it is in the past which reveals the certainty of his fall. Remember with God there is no time. When He speaks it is as good as done. I believe it delights His heart when He sees one of His children taking Him at His word; that is bringing what has been spoken into present reality.

Secondly, in verses 10-11 the *saints were relieved*. The term "*salvation*" is not meant for the saving of a soul but it refers to deliverance. Observe the *motivation for their relief*. It is shared in the last words of verse 10, "*...for the accuser of the brethren is cast down, which accused them before our God day and night.*" The fact is that the majority of the time the accuser does not have to lie or make up anything to accuse us of...the truth is enough! When one is unfaithful he merely says to God, "See, I told You he was not true to You." When one strays he says, "I told You he was not walking right." We must have an advocate to stand between the Father and the accusations of the devil. In Jesus Christ the risen Lord we have One!

One great tragedy is that all too often we assist the accuser. We do this when we speak negatively about a brother, or when we try to make him look bad. Do you know an unlovely person that for some reason causes you to be filled with anxiety? Do you know a person that constantly criticizes you? If that person were moved would you be relieved? The motivation for the saints to be relieved is that the accuser is cast down.

The Apocalypse: The Revelation of the Redeemer

In addition to their motivation we also have *the means of their relief* in verse 11. There are three deeply significant things that were and are the means of overcoming the enemy. First, there is an *acknowledgment*, *"and they overcame him by the blood of the Lamb."* This, for us, refers to our cleansing. The *"they"* are the redeemed. The *"him"* is the devil and the *"blood of the Lamb"* is Jesus and His work for man at Calvary. It was His blood that defeated the devil. When one is washed in His blood he identifies with the Person of Christ. This provides one with a new position. He is now in Christ. Secondly, there is the *activity*, *"And by the word of their testimony."* This refers to our confession. Witnessing the truth defeats the devil and sin stops our speech for the Savior. This is a reference to knowing and using the truth against the darkness. Third, there is an *abandonment*, *"And loved not their lives unto the death."* This refers to our courage. This abandonment is an attitude of total surrender to the Savior even if it means self sacrifice. Where has surrender gone? Where is the attitude of *"For me to live is Christ"* to be found in our day? These three speak of the saints cleansing, confession and courage. These are available and must be appropriated to overcome the devil.

The third outcome is *the saints were rejoicing* as shared in verse 12, *"Therefore, rejoice, ye heavens, and ye that dwell in them."* Why? The accuser is cast down and the blood; the word and surrender have overcome him. There is rejoicing because the door of access is closed and barred forever. Yes there will be war in heaven between spiritual forces that are warring on the earth right now. The issue is which side are you on in this war? To be neutral is to side with the enemy.

The woman, the war and now:

III: THE WOE! Verses 12-17 Soon after this woe is pronounced, the woe trumpets begin. Satan is a mad caged beast in the earth where he has been cast. He shakes his fist at the sky and looks for ways to vent his frustrations upon mankind. The woe is the dark side of the heavenly victory. Verse 12 states, *"Woe to the inhabitants of the earth and of the sea."* This woe is war intensified. The enemy turns his full attention to the destruction of the people of God. There are some powerful truths that we want to consider as we observe this woe of verses 12-17. First,

A: SATAN'S MANIFESTED HATRED! Verse 12-13; 15 Note the word, *"wrath"* is used in verse 12 and the word *"wroth"* is used in verse 17. These are emotions of hate filled anger. These are not descriptive of a state of mind of blinded emotion. There are three special truths for us to note about his hatred. **First** we have *the time of his manifested hatred* in verses 12-13. He has always been a personality of hate. There are times when his hatred is more pronounced. This is one of those times. There are two things that bear upon the time of his manifested hatred. One he has been *dislodged*; cast unto the earth. This action has caused him to burn with a passion to destroy the people of the earth. Where is Satan now abiding? Some might suggest that he is in hell! No! Satan has never been to hell. He is going to hell and he knows of that place that has been prepared for him and his angels but he is not there yet. He is now the *"prince of the power of the air"* but he knows what is ahead for him. Two, he is aware of his *duration* as verse 12 states, *"...because he knoweth he hath but a short time."* The length of his days is 1260 or 3 and ½ years. His days are numbered. What would you do if you knew the number of days left to you? There are those that would waste them in every kind of pleasurable pursuit known to man. There are others that would seek to invest them, to make them count for God and man. If you knew the duration of your days would you have a time of evaluating your priorities, of repentance and renewing your commitment to God? The fact is our days are numbered and one day the last day on earth will be spent and we will meet the living God.

The time is when he cannot longer freely accuse the people of God to God.

Secondly, we have *the target of his manifested hatred.* Verse 13 shares with us the target is Israel; this is as it has always been. The world has witnessed many dress rehearsals for the coming hatred of Israel. The secret police, the knock on the door at night; the dreadful ordeal of days and nights without food, drink or sanitation, herded like cattle into concentration camps; the gas

The Apocalypse: The Revelation of the Redeemer

ovens and the firing squads of the past set the stage for the full production of terror that will be experienced by the woman, Israel. Israel has been the target since God chose Abraham. They are the target for the same reason; we too must learn that when any person answers the call of God and casts his lot on the side of righteousness he can expect to be hated by the enemies of God. The target in the day of grace is any person willing to stand for the person of Jesus Christ, His church and His cause.

The **third** truth for us to consider from verse 15; it is *a type of his manifested hatred, "and the serpent cast out of his mouth water as a flood after the woman."* The words, *"as a flood"* help us to understand that this is symbolic of a type of Satan's persecution. The word *"flood"* carries the idea of something of the overwhelming power of the destruction. This destruction originates from the mouth of the serpent, the devil. While one can not be dogmatic it is my personal opinion that this will be evil propaganda spread by Satan against the Jewish people.

The person that first said, "Sticks and stones may break my bones but words can never hurt me" was sorely mistaken. Words were and are the vehicle of communication. Words can bless or break.

What he says and or does will be overwhelming in power against Israel. This has already transpired to some degree. This is what Hitler did when he turned the German people against the Jews. He used words; and words still intimidate, cause injury and insult. Words of insinuation have resulted in misunderstandings that have ultimately ended in death. The reality is that one's words can be the means of lifting the Lord or lifting lies.

The second thing we notice about the woe is:

B: SATAN IS MARVELOUSLY HINDERED! Verse 14, 16-17 He is the god of the present world but here is One greater in power than he. There is One that knows his plans and has power to turn his cursing into blessings. These verses reveal that Satan is under the power and control of God. He is not an island unto himself but he is subject to the ultimate purpose of God. There are three things in these verses that reveal how he was marvelously hindered. **First** in verse 14 we have the *supernatural provision of deliverance*. The devil is doing his best to inflect the people of

God with deadly poison. He is persecuting them on every hand and in the midst of his best attack they are supernaturally delivered. Verse 14 may be a reference to a great airlift or it may refer to the swiftness of their deliverance. Regardless the deliverance was/will be supernatural in that God provided it. The woman/Israel is carried to the wilderness. This is a place of safety and security in the time of calamity. Note; it is *"her place, where she is nourished for 3 and ½ years."* Any provision in the wilderness will be supernatural. This will not tax the One that nourished Israel for 40 years in the wilderness. They are safe and sustained supernaturally. This is the present experience of the child of God. He is safe and secure in the will of God. He is sustained by God's grace in places that to the natural eye appear to be a wilderness.

Secondly, Satan is marvelously hindered by: the swallowing of the pollution of the dragon; verse 16, *"And the earth helped the woman and the earth opened her mouth and swallowed up the flood."* When Pharaoh pursued Israel and the Egyptians were overwhelmed by the sea, the song of Moses and his people was, *"Who is like unto Thee, O Lord! Thou stretchedst forth Thy right hand, the earth swallowed them."* (Exodus 15:11-12)

The *"opening of her mouth"* may refer to an earthquake to receive the attackers in their pursuit of Israel. It is not known how God will defeat the plan of the devil but God will deal with the dragon in a way that will glorify His own Person. This action further attests to the sovereign power of God. He that created the earth also controls the earth. In this same wilderness, when God's anger was visited upon Korah for his rebellion against Moses, *"The ground clave asunder and the earth opened her mouth, and swallowed them up...and the earth closed upon them, and they perished."* (Numbers 16: 31-33)

We do know that they failed to reach the woman in her place of refuge. The very ground opened to stop them in their hellish madness. It can be stated dogmatically that God is not limited in how He chooses to swallow up the pollution of the dragon. It is also encouraging to know that He is well able to minister to us in our need in the present hour.

The Apocalypse: The Revelation of the Redeemer

Thirdly, in verse 17, we note that *Satan's purpose is determined*. Satan is no quitter. When he is halted in one direction he turns to another. He is determined to win the war against the woman. When his attempts against the larger body are turned back by God he purposes to center his attention on those that *"keep the commandments of God, and have the testimony of Jesus Christ."* These may be a part of the 144,000 or their converts. The simple fact is he hates them because they love the Lord. He is no different today. He is just as determined in his purpose today as he will be in that dark day of rebellion.

Conclusion:

There are things that are certainly going to come to pass, however, in the midst of all the things that are uncertain, one can and should be certain about his/her own eternal destiny. This can be done only as one places his/her trust in the person of Jesus Christ. This does not remove those times of testing and trials but it does provide His presence in the midst of those times and the knowledge of His ultimate triumphant.

The Beast
Revelation 13:1-10

This chapter reveals the unholy trinity; the dragon, the first beast and the second beast. These are not animals but men. They are termed beast because of their cruelty. The hate filled hostility of Satan is presented in these verses. There is a mounting terror as the devil displays his total hatred of God. These events are transpiring in the last 3 and ½ years of the tribulation. Chapters 6-19 cover the entire 7 years period know as the tribulation. The seventh seal has been cut or opened. These were upon the scroll that was/is the title deed of the earth. The last seal contained seven trumpets. The seventh trumpet has sounded. In the seventh trumpet are seven bowls or vials of wrath of God to be visited upon the earth in rapid fire succession. This period of time is unparallel; the wrath of God upon rebellion plus all the wrath/hatred of Satan on the righteous.

Chapters 12-14 provide some of the details of this period as it relates to two powerful personalities; the antichrist and the false prophet.

There have been antichrists for a long time as revealed in 1 John 2:18 "...*even now are there many antichrist*." This one in Revelation 13 is the culmination of all that is against Christ. This one is characterized as being Satan's master piece; all that is presented as being against Christ, hate, lies and rebellion, is bound up in him. We should not be surprised that the antichrist will appear; Daniel, Jesus and Paul spoke of him. He is portrayed in Scripture along many lines. Some are lawless, mockery, murderer, fierce liar, ruler and willful king.

Remember the angel said, "*Woe to the inhabitants of the earth*!" Why? Satan is routed from heaven and now (in that day) will be on earth. He, Satan, indwells the first beast. As he

The Apocalypse: The Revelation of the Redeemer

indwells the first beasts, the antichrist will manifest all the characteristics of Satan himself. This is so much so that the two become somewhat synonymous. Satan is a spirit being and can not operate effectively in the world without a body through which to operate. He works his worse through the passions and personalities of people that are his willing subjects. When he desires to accomplish a great task he finds that person that will yield themselves to him and allow him to possess them. He did this with Judas and he will do it with the antichrist. He can not indwell believers but he will his own through his demons. One of the primary makes of the tribulation will be drugs and demonic possession. Satan becomes so identified with antichrist that they become like one, interchangeable. Let me illustrate with an opposite. Saul is on his way to Damascus when Jesus said to him, *"Why are you persecuting Me?"* He did not ask, "Why are you persecuting the Christians?" Why? Jesus so identifies with His own that what one does to a Christian he does to Christ. The opposite is true as well. We are focusing our attention upon the first beast, the antichrist of the tribulation period. Consider first,

I: THE APPEARANCE OF THE BEAST! Verses 1-3 We may find ourselves in unfamiliar territory. It may be a little deeper than some of us are accustomed to traveling. Therefore, we must be willing to give, as much as possible, our undivided attention and to think. There are four things to observe; first,

    A: HIS PLACE! Verse 1, *"And I stood upon the sand of the sea."* It more properly translated, *"And he stood."* The *"and"* connects verse 17 of chapter 12 with verse 1 of chapter 13. *"And the devil was wroth with the woman....and he stood upon the sand of the sea."* It is not John that stands but the dragon that we know to be the devil. He is the one that introduced all sin, sorrow and suffering into the world. (L. Strauss)

    This expression probably refers to the place of the Mediterranean area. It reveals that he devil has gained power over the people. *"Sand"* pictures the many people that make up the nations, *"The number of whom is as the sand of the sea."* (Revelation 20:8) The standing raised him above, as a leader; it separated him. The phrase indicates that the sand/people remained in this place while he occupied a different place; one of prominence and power. Secondly we have:

B: HIS PERSON! Verses 1-3 It is imperative that we understand what is and is not said. I will refer to other passages to verify and hopefully clarify what is presented in these verses. We will at this point move slow and deliberately. The purpose is not to confuse but to make clear. Therefore, we will observe two truths about his person. **First,** *he is a man* as verses 1-2 indicates. Verse 18 states it clearly when it declares that the number of the beast is the number of man. The person is a man that is real. Verse 1, "*...he rises up out of the sea.*" The sea represents humanity. Chapter 17:15, "*The waters...are people, multitudes, nations and tongues;*" Isaiah 57:20, "*But the wicked are like the troubled sea.*" We are not dealing with some incidental influence. This is the diabolical dictator of the coming world; this is a real man.

The person is a man that is representative (verse 1-2). If he is a real person how can he be a representative person? He has seven heads, ten horns and ten crowns; verse 2, "*The beast was like unto a leopard, bear and lion.*"

This indicates that he has multiplied dominion and regal power. This is a person with sweeping power that is reigning as a conqueror. These heads, horns and crowns present him in his relationship to the revived Roman Empire. Read Revelation 17:3 and 9-11 and witness a description of the empire of Rome. (Verse 12) The ten horns are ten kings of the tribulation period. This was neither in John's day nor necessarily in ours. This is as it will be seen in that day. The revived Roman Empire will be headed by the antichrist of the tribulation period. (Revelation 17:9-10) He will have authority over ten nations. The seven kings are in sequence; the ten are at the same time. The seven heads are seven world empires or the seven basic dominating governments at that time. When Daniel wrote he saw four. In John's day he said five are fallen. Those are Babylon, Persia, Greece, Assyria and Egypt; the one that is present is Rome. The one that follows is the revived Roman Empire. In chapter 17:11 we are informed that the eighth that will rule over that empire of the seventh.

The Apocalypse: The Revelation of the Redeemer

The person is real and representative. As we note his person we note **secondly** that *he is a monster*; verse 2. What does this mean to us? The *lion* represents Babylon; the *superior empire*. God is using descriptive language. This world empire had the characteristics of the lion or the king of the beast. Babylon was the purest, most regal and authoritative of the world empires. The *bear* represents the Persian Empire; the *sure empire*. It was like the bear, tenacious in its stand, like a bear rising up on its hind feet refusing to back down from its enemies rather charging ahead. The law of the Persians was one that could not be broken. The *leopard* represents the Grecian Empire; the *swift empire*. The chief characteristic of the leopard is it swiftness in conquering. This empire conquered the world in the shortest recorded period of time under Alexandria the Great. This one of verse 2 combines all of these into one. The greatest qualities of the greatest empires are wrapped up in this one. Note verse 1 ends by saying, *"and upon his heads the name of blasphemy."* This is his entire purpose. This refers to verbal persuasion.

Thirdly, we note in the appearance of the beast,

C: HIS POWER! Verse 2, *"And the dragon gave him his power."* That is, it was delegated from the devil. He was more powerful that he could be in his own might. A person becomes one with whatever controls him. The beast becomes one with the devil; one indwelt by Satan is one with him. This is illustrated in Ezekiel 28:11-13 and Isaiah 14:9-12. In the first the reference is to the King of Tyrus, and the second to the King of Babylon.

As this is true with the beast and the dragon it is true with the Christian and Christ; His power is delegated to us so that we are more than conquers through Him. Fourth, we have:

D: HIS POPULARITY! Verses 3-4 reveal two things about his popularity. **First**, *the world will follow a man*. Regardless of where you go you will always find others that will follow regardless of what the person stand for or against. In our time we have been amazed that individuals with above average intelligence would follow a man like Jim Jones. The fact is that anyone could, in a week's time, espouse any doctrine and gain a following. The world is being prepared even now to follow him.

Secondly, *the world will follow a miracle* (verse 3) and miracles generally attract people. Many see this to be the death and resurrection of the person of antichrist that causes the world to follow him. Many have said that this is Judas or even Hitler resurrected. One said to Napoleon, "Sir, I would like to start a new religion, can you tell me how to gain a following?" Napoleon said, "Go, get a crowd around you on a busy street and have someone drive a spear through you heart and in 2 or 3 days just rise from the dead." He did not follow the advice but that would do it! Verse 3 is not referring to a resurrected individual. Note, (1) the wicked are not resurrected until the great white throne judgment; this would be out of order. (2) It is not the beast that is dead; it is one of his heads, that is one of the heads of government and this is not to critical if he has six left. (3) I do not think it is taught in the Scripture that Satan possesses the power to raise the dead; that power belongs only to God. This is probably one of these world empires revived; that is the Roman Empire that will be revived at the end time. It will be of miraculous notice because we are working with a miraculous person, the antichrist. It happens so fast and miraculous that it causes the world to be amazed.

Secondly we have:

II: THE ACCLAIM OF THE BEAST! Verses 4 and 8 If there was a doubt as to the darkness of the depraved heart these verse remove it. Mankind, in this day, will be so deluded that he will willingly support anything or anyone that opposes God.

The acclaim of the beast is clearly presented in that he receives the worship of man. This is almost beyond belief but it will be a reality in this dark day. Note first,

A: IT WAS BLASPHEMOUS WORSHIP! Verse 4 One of the marks of the tribulation will be Satan worship, *"and they worshipped the dragon."* The *"they"* are those deceived by the devil; they believe his lie. The *"dragon"* is none other than the devil. No doubt some will say, "But there is already Satan worship!" There is, however, this will be worldwide. What we have now is nothing compared with what will be in this day. Observe that they worship Satan in the person of the beast, *"and* *they worshiped the beast."* In I Corinthians 10 Paul shares the truth that to worship anything other than Christ is to worship demons. It may be called a number of names but it is demonic.

One of Satan's most successful methods of damning mankind is false religion. In my personal opinion at least 90% of his work through his demonic host is through false religion. In this day it will be stated openly that Satan is whom they worship. Notice what the blasphemous worship does; it causes them to believe that the beast is beyond defeat. They ask, *"Who is able to make war with him?"* The implied answer is "no one, not even God!" The child of God knows that the real victory has already been announced in chapter 11 verse 15.

Secondly, we observe that:

B: IT WAS BLIND WORSHIP! Verse 8, *"And all that dwell upon the earth worship him."* Those that refuse will be executed. This verse literally reads, *"Whose names are not written from the foundation of the world in the book of life."* Even the tribulation saint's names were recorded before the foundation of the world. It blesses me to know that God has never been surprised nor has He ever had to revert to plan B!

Paul talks about how the devil blinds in II Corinthians 4:3-4; yet, it must be understood that for one to know the truth and realize that people are facing eternity in hell and never seek to share their faith says more about the professing Christian than about the lost person's ignorance. Moreover, something is wrong when we would rather sit in comfort than to shed tears of compassion while there is time. God does and will hold us accountable for truth.

In this day of tribulation it will be blind worship. But they, like the worldly-minded in this hour, will believe that theirs is the way and worship of the enlightened. In light of this truth how desperately we need to allow the *"glorious light of the gospel"* to shine in and through us in our present day of darkness.

The third major thought is:

III: THE ACTIVITY OF THE BEAST! Verses 5-7 The beast is not content to receive the worship of the world. He is active in seeking to do three things. First,

A: HE DEFIES THE SAVIOR! Verses 5-6, *"And there was given him* (the beast) *a mouth;"* this is a key word. He is the mouth of all time. He speaks against Christ and the family of God.

Daniel refers to the mouth of the antichrist in 7:9, *"A mouth speaking great things;"* Verse 11, *"...the voice of the great words which the horn* (antichrist) *spoke;"* verse 25, *"...and he* (antichrist) *shall speak great words against the most high..."* His mouth is boasting, arrogant and anti-God. His mouth in the tribulation period will use every media form available to defy the Savior. Man will be a puppet to speak as he speaks.

The same word is used in 11 Timothy 3:2 where we are told that in the last days men will be guilty of the same things.

In this day when believers tear each other down that is his mouth and his work for that is the antichrist method.

The second activity of the beast is:

B: HE DESTROYS THE SAINTS! Verse 7, *"And it was given him to make war with the saints."* Daniel 7:25 informs us that after he speaks words against the Most High, *"And shall wear out the saints of the Most High;"* that he will assault the saints.

It would be natural for us to inquire as to why God allows this to happen to His people. The word declares, *"It was given him,"* just as it was given Herod to imprison and behead John the Baptist; as it was given him to persecute Job, and just as it was given Pilate to pass the sentence of death upon Jesus. This is, at least for the present, a part of the great mystery that will one day be understood.

The duration of his destruction is forty-two months; this is a literal period of time. I mention it to say that there is a limit and his destruction does end. Yet, it must be understood that during these forty-two months he is victorious but it is temporary. Chapter 5:2, *"...and them that had gotten the victory over the beast..."* God never leaves His saints and the God of glory will ultimately win any war of the enemy.

The third activity of the beast is:

C: TO DOMINATE SOCIETY! Verse 7, *"And power was given him over all kindreds, and tongues and nations."* North and south, east and west, all peoples will be forced to submit to him.

The Apocalypse: The Revelation of the Redeemer

His authority will be acknowledged worldwide. This will come to pass as he unifies the nations. He will accomplish this by indulging in every evil passion that the depraved heart can imagine and with an unrelenting persecution. In this day compliance will not be optional. If a people do not freely join him they will be forced to comply by his arm of authority.

The forth major thought is:

IV: THE ADMONISHMENT TO BELIEVE! Verses 9-10 In this dark day there is an abomination to believe. There are three things to observe about this abomination. First note,

A: THE WAY! Verse 9, *"If any man has an ear, let him hear."* These words are addressed to the world. In chapters 2 and 3 the phrase is used but there it is addressed to the church and adds, "What the Spirit says unto the churches." Here there are no true churches.

The way to the heart is by way of the head. What is a man to hear in that day? Will he hear of the blood of Jesus? I think what they hear is revealed in verse 10.

Consider secondly:

B: THE WARNING! Verse 10, *"He that leadeth into captivity shall go into captivity: he that killeth with sword must be killed with the sword."* This was a proverb with a message of vengeance. The essence of the warning is "you reap what you sow." It declares that inherent in every system of tyranny and death is its own death. God warns if a man kills the saints or takes them into captivity the judgment of God will fall upon that man or nation. He has declared, *"Vengeance is Mine."*

Do you recall the record of Peter and his sword? He cut off the servant's ear. He was aiming at his head! Jesus said, *"Put up your sword, those that take the sword must perish with it."* Then Jesus said in essence, "I am not dependant upon fleshly means, if I desired to I could call twelve legions of angels." That is about 72,000. In the Old Testament we are informed that one angel single handedly took care of any army of 185,000. Yes, Peter put up your sword. The weapons of our warfare are not carnal.

The warning was that God will not allow this action to go unpunished. The warning for saint and sinner alike is to turn to

Jesus as the only source of strength and salvation. The third truth is:

    C: THE WONDER! Verse 10; *"Here is the patience and faith of the saints."* The wonder is the future belongs to God. Satan can rebel and have his beast but God will win and reign. It may be difficult at times to realize this truth. They were suffering but their faith was in God in spite of their present circumstances.

Conclusion:
The beast is at work today. He is seeking to convince man that there is a better way. He is using deception to damn the souls of men. Are you hearing and looking forward to reaping what you are sowing?

The Second Beast...The False Prophet
Revelation 13:11-18

The tribulation is the outpouring of God's wrath upon the earth. Satan, up to a point, will be the instrument of that wrath. His wrath is poured out for three primary purposes. The first is for purging. Israel has been polluted. The second is for punishment. The ungodly that have rejected all that is offered in Christ will experience God's wrath. The third is for preparation. It is a means of preparing for the second coming of Christ to earth to set up His kingdom to reign a thousand years.

In the tribulation Satan will release all the demonic hordes of hell against the earth. All that man depends upon will collapse. From an earthly perspective this period of time will feature two main characters. These are the antichrist and the second beast, the false prophet. These two become two world rulers.

The second beast is an extremely religious personality while the first is more political in nature. The second focuses all the attention upon the first. This is the nature of a prophet; he points to someone other than himself. Satan works through religious systems or structures. Why? It is the nature of man to worship. It might be a stick or stone; it can be a mountain or a man but man will worship. The issue, therefore, is not will man worship but what will he worship. That is why, in the tribulation period, there will be a worldwide system of religion. It will be a direct contradiction of the true church. Satan will counterfeit all that God is and does. Remember, he only counterfeits that which has value. Crooks do not counterfeit on brown paper. In this dark day there will be an unholy trinity. Satan will counterfeit God. The antichrist will counterfeit Christ and the false prophet will be the counterfeit of the Holy Spirit.

The antichrist is willing to overlook his personal feelings and to work with the false prophet to accomplish his purpose. There is a great lesson for us to learn in our present day from this. The purpose we are to be about is God's. We, as His people, are to work together to reach men with the gospel of Jesus Christ. If the enemy of righteousness can do this surely the people of God ought to be able to do the same.

There are three thoughts tht we want to consider in these verses about the second beast, the false prophet. First, observe:

I: THE PERSON OF THE BEAST! Verse 11 Who or what is the beast? Some call him a system; others say he is a state. He is called by some a philosophy and others designate the beast as the false church. He is called the *"false prophet"* a number of times. He is cast with the devil and first beast into the lake of fire. It would be difficult to cast a system or state into a lake of fire.

There are two tings for us to consider about the person of the beast, first note,

A: HIS DESCRIPTION! Verse 11, *"And I beheld another beast coming up out of the earth."* It is clear that *"beast"* does not refer to an animal. It describes for us something of his nature. There are two things that describe him. **First**, we have his *likeness,* *"and I beheld another beast."* The Greek word for *"another"* is *"alos."* It means another of the same kind. *"Hertrus"* is the word for another of a different kind. This beast is like the first beast. It is *"alos."* If I ask you to bring me a pair of glasses and I said "I want 'Hertrus' glasses" you could bring me sunglass or any ones glasses. If I said "I want 'alos' glasses" you would bring me glasses just like the ones I wear.

Jesus used this word when He said, *"I will send you another (alos) comforter."*

Secondly, we have *his location,* *"Coming up out of the earth."* The first one in Verse 1 came out of the sea. This is probably the sea of Gentile humanity; this one is from the earth. He is probably a Jew or at least part Jew from the land of Palestine. His location will help him accomplish his task.

Secondly we observe about the person of the beast,

The Apocalypse: The Revelation of the Redeemer

B: HIS DECEPTION! *"And he had two horns like a lamb and spoke as a dragon."* The enemy of God is especially subtle. His description is witnessed **first** in *his looks, "and he had two horns like a lamb."* He gives the appearance of being an innocent loveable being. Why would the beast want to look like a lamb? In the economy of the Old Testament man could approach God through the sacrifice of a lamb. Jesus was the fulfillment of all those sacrificial lambs. John the Baptist said, *"Behold the Lamb of God that takes away the sin of the world."* If God had His Lamb the devil will have a phony. This one is a wolf in lambs clothing.

His description is seen **secondly** in *his language, "And he spoke as a dragon."* He is a remarkable counterfeit. Jesus said that one of the ways to know man was by what he said. The mouth speaks forth what is in the heart. He looks like a lamb but his language reveals that he is an imposter. Religion can be the voice of hell even if it is espoused by a number of strong advocates, for example, it is the voice of hell if they deny the deity of Christ, His cross, heaven and hell; if this should be the case there is one that may look like a lamb but his language reveals he is from hell.

We move from the person of the beast to:

II: THE POWER OF THE BEAST! Verses 12-15 The power of the second beast is from the devil. He, Satan, gave the first beast power; the second beast exercises the power of the first. Simply stated his power is the power of Satan. There are two important truths for us to consider about the power of the beast. First,

A: HE HAS POWER TO PERSUADE MEN! Verse 12, *"And causes the earth and them that dwell therein to worship the first beast."* This individual must possess tremendous persuasive power because he is capable of turning the entire world into a religion that worships the antichrist. He will be a silver tongue orator. He will have the combined ability of Hitler, Armstrong, Smith, Russell and Jim Jones.

Consider this truth; we have individuals that hold forth the truth of the word of God and they cannot persuade those of the church membership or community to worship the true and living God. This individual will be able to do this. Prior to the *"beast worship*" a false religious system must be in place. We have the details of this in chapter 17; this is Babylon the great, the harlot; the false corrupt church will be established after the true church is with Jesus, he merely assumes control of the system that has replaced the true one. There will doubtless be those that will object and declare that man is too intelligent for such a thing to transpire. Man may be intelligent but by in large this is a world of followers. This second beast has such persuasive power that he can sell toothpicks to a beaver.

Secondly we notice:

B: HE HAS POWER TO PERFORM MIRACLES! Verses 13-15 It will be helpful to read Paul's words in 11 Thessalonians 2:8-11 at this point. From verses 13-15 we gather two important facts about his power. **First**, the miracles are *supernatural*! Verse 13, "...*great wonders...fire from heaven.*" All miracles are not from God neither are all supernatural happens from heaven. This is a supernatural miracle but it is a copy of the original. God sent fire in Genesis 19 to destroy Sodom. In Leviticus 10 Nadab and Abihu were consumed with fire from the Lord. In 1 Kings 18 Elijah said, "*Let the one that answers by fire by declared God.*" The devil knows prophecy; therefore, the beast will call fire from heaven. This is done to cause the world to *worship the beast*. The stage is being prepared. People are more and more taken with the supernatural, and more and more it is drawing the attention of the world. This enables individuals to walk by sight and not faith. **Secondly**, the miracles are *satanic*, verse 14-15. Do you recall the account of Moses before Pharaoh? The sorceries were able to duplicate the miracles but that did not indicate that they were from God. These miracles have as their purpose deception and not deliverance (verse 14). They are designed to cause the world to worship the first beast.

There is another proof that these are satanic miracles in addition to the worship of the beast, there is the *workmanship of the beast*. He made an image and was able to make it speak and execute judgment (verses 14-15). The image is a part of the "*abomination of desolation*" spoken of by Daniel and Jesus.

It is not my purpose to endeavor to explain what or how this is done. It is satanic. I do know that Satan is able to possess people and things. When he does there are times when he speaks and times when the person speaks. This is illustrated in Mark 5 and Acts 16.

If you have been underestimating the power of the devil these verses are/should be sufficient to challenge and to a great degree correct that thinking.

The third truth is:

III: THE PURPOSE OF THE BEAST! Verses 12-17 His purpose can be stated in four statements. First, his purpose is:

A: TO DECIEVE THE WICKED! Verse 14, *"And deceives them that dwell on earth."* He does this by means of signs and wonders. Jesus said in Matthew 24:24, *"For there shall arise false Christ, and false prophets, and shall show great signs and wonders, insomuch that, if it were possible, they shall deceive the very elect."*

The second purpose is:

B: TO DIRECT WORSHIP! Verse 12, *"And causes the earth and them that dwell therein to worship the first beast."* The spirit of antichrist directs, in our day, worship away from the person of Christ.

The third purpose is:

C: TO DESTROY THE WITHSTANDERS! Verse 15, *"And cause that as many as would not worship the image of the beast should be killed."* Those that refuse will wither be destroyed or flee to their provided shelter in what I think is Petra.

The fourth purpose is:

D: TO DOMINATE THE WORLD! Verses 16-17 This is his ultimate purpose. Observe, **first** *its scope* in verse 16, *"Causes all..."* Those with positions, prestige and prosperous will come under his dominance. **Secondly**, *its significance* in verse 17, *"No man could buy or sell."* That is control of the economic system. Five things are needed in order for him to m to control the economic system of the world. (1) Invent machines to house all economic data-done; (2) remove currency and use controlled credit...very much in process; (3) know everyone's economic status as well as their credit rating...done; (4) have all economic work done at the institutional level...done; and (5) have the government control more and more finance and do it in a central headquarters...done. The stage is being set for all these things are in readiness for the one indwelt by the person and power of Satan. **Thirdly**, verse 17 shares *its severity*. Without the mark of the beast a child cannot buy an ice cream cone and the realtor cannot close that million-dollar deal. Without the mark individuals will starve. The cost for following Christ will be high; the cost for not following Him will be higher (14:11).

Conclusion:
"*Here is wisdom.*" He has been dealing with the false now he speaks to the wise. Do not miss this! What? The number of the beast; it is 666. This is the mark of identification necessary to live in the day of tribulation.

Six is the number of man. That is one short of the seven of completeness. In the system under Moses there are six days for labor, six years to till; it always stops one short of God. The point, I think, is that all that has been presented deals with the highest level of man and it is still short of the perfection necessary to satisfy the demands of Holy God.

The antichrist is a six; the false prophet is a six; the entire system is a six; all that man can be is in and of himself is a six.

There has been a river of ink used to identify this person. I will not add to it. For now it reveals how incomplete man is apart from Christ. In that day it will be his identification.

There is presently in our world a false church; it is growing rapidly. How? (1) It always says what people desire to hear, not what the word declares. (2) It always does what the world does and (3) it offers an institutional salvation, not personal. This is now and in the tribulation it will be intensified.

A Preview of Victory
Revelation 14:1-11

To assist us in keeping our perspective I will seek to briefly review a few facts. The subject of the book is the Revelation of Jesus Christ. He came in humiliation that we might experience His grace. He is coming again in His full glory, not as Savior to redeem but as Sovereign to rule! This is the subject matter of this book. Its primary emphasis is not the rapture but the revelation. The book is outlined in chapter 1:19. Those events from chapter 4 are future. We have seen the glorified Christ in chapter 1; the churches in chapters 2-3; the church in heaven in chapters 4-5 and in chapters 6-11 we have Christ breaking the seals, He is unrolling the scroll taking back the earth. The sixth seal is opened in chapter 6:12. There is a pause, chapter 7 and the seventh seal is opened in chapter 8. The seventh seal contains seven trumpets. The seventh trumpet sounds in chapter 11:15. The seventh trumpet contains seven bowls of wrath. This begins in chapter 15. There is another pause of chapters 12-14 between the sixth and seventh trumpet.

We are now, in the book, at this location. The events recorded in this chapter actually transpire in chapter 19. This is a preview of the victory that will be accomplished by Christ. It is a chapter of hope and can be viewed as a table of contents. This chapter contains seven disconnected visions of victory. The first of these is a picture of:

I: THE WORSHIP OF THE SAVIOR! Verses 1-5 Please take the necessary time to carefully examine the contrast between chapter 13 and 14. In chapter 13 we have a false Christ and false lamb. In chapter 14 we have the true Christ and true Lamb.

These verses are a picture of worship. Worship is the natural result of Christ presence. It has been said that worship is the first responsibility of the Christian. There are two truths for us to consider in these verses about the worship of the Savior. First,

A: THE PERSON WORSHIPPED! Verse 1, *"And I looked, and, lo, a lamb..."* The world was focusing all of its attention upon the false lamb of chapter 13. But John sees the true Lamb, *"And I looked."* What is the focus of your attention in the midst of crises? This is the same one the Baptist had pointed out as, *"The Lamb of God that takes away the sin of the world."* There are two things for us to consider about the person worshipped. **First**, we have *His position* in verse 1. The Lamb is standing. This is an act that precedes activity. The Lamb was seen in chapter 5 as having been slain. He is in the midst and receiving the title deed to the earth. Where has He been? He opened the seals and occupied His position with the Father as the Intercessor. His position now is standing; one of authority and control. He has been behind the scenes but in total charge of all that was transpiring. He is never unaware of what is going on in the universe or our lives, hearts or heads. The issue for you and me is what position He presently occupies in our lives on day-to-day bases. **Secondly**, we have *His place* in verse 1, *"Stood on the Mount Sion."* There are those that believe this is the heavenly Jerusalem. There is a possibility that this could be in heaven; however, I believe that the context reveals that this is the earthly city of Jerusalem. In 11 Samuel 5:7 Zion is called the city of David. This is a reference to the triumphant return of Jesus Christ to reign in power and glory over the earth from His throne in Jerusalem. The details are in chapters 19-20. The person worshipped is the worthy Lamb that will reign over the earth. He desires to occupy that position and place in our lives today.

Secondly observe,

B: THE PEOPLE WORSHIPPING! Verses 1-5 There are 144,000 people worshipping the Savior. Who are they? They are the same ones of chapter seven. They were sealed Jewish missionaries and seven years later they are with Him on Mount Zion. They have been through the years of tribulation and every one of them is with Him. There are not 143,999; not a single one

The Apocalypse: The Revelation of the Redeemer

is missing. God has preserved them. Satan will do everything to stop them but he will not succeed. These are sealed with the name of the Father; this signifies ownership. They are secure! (Note John 6:39) They are safe! The safest place to be is in the will of God. That is the place of His protection, power and promise. These are literal Jewish missionaries during the tribulation period. The enemy knows this and has built a cult to confuse as many people as possible. There are six things worthy of our attention in these verses. **First** we have *their singing* in verses 2-3. There is sorrow, suffering and strife throughout the world but when the Lamb of God is brought in focus there is a song of victory. The voice is like a thundering Nigeria gathering volume until it individualizes into the voice of many harpers harping with their harps.

It is a song of redemption sung neither by the church nor by angels. The song is that the beast has been overcome. It is exclusively theirs. They sing with the harp. In the Old Testament there are 40 references to harps and it is always a reference to joy. If there is no victory there cannot be a song of joy.

These 144,000 proclaim the gospel and multitudes are saved. Today there are from 40 to 50,000 protestant missionaries around the world. Many of these are social gospel and cults such as Mormons and Jehovah Witnesses. We have less than 25,000 missionaries to reach a world of almost 3 billion people that are yet to hear of Jesus. During the tribulation period these 144,000 missionaries will make a difference. They will make this impact not only because of their song but **secondly** *their separation* as verse 4 reveals. These words do not relate to physical marriage. He is using this figure to illustrate purity. Who would it be? Men that never knew a woman or a woman that never knew a man? One of the great impacts of the beast and false prophet in the world will be immorality. In contrast these will be pure. They will be free from spiritual fornication. Separation speaks of their conduct. This is still a prime requirement for usefulness. The major problem with most Christians of this day is desiring to have a foot in both camps. We, for the most part, are not willing to pay the price of total commitment to Jesus.

Thirdly, we have *their surrender* presented in verse 4, "*These are they which follow the Lamb.*" The lamb usually follows. Note the next words, "*Wherever He goes.*" Like Caleb they wholly follow the Lord. They allow no rivals, refusals or restraints to mar their dedication to Him. Does the Lamb need someone to cry out against the flood tide of the darkness of sin? How many modern Christians can sing with meaning, "Where He leads me I will follow?" It may be sung but the practice of surrender is missing.

Forth they *were samples*, verse 4; "*...being the firstfruits.*" They were the sample of the crop about to go into the kingdom of Christ on earth. The firstfruits were a sign that a full harvest was to follow. Jesus was the firstfruits of the resurrection; the first resurrected never to die again. The guarantee of a full harvest is the fact that He lives.

Fifth in verse 5 we have *their sincerity*, "*And in their mouth was found no guile*" or, "*not a lie found in their mouths.*" How different they are from Satan's messengers! These are bold and honest in their message. Their lives were genuine, without deceit during this critical time in the earth. It is this group that is entrusted with the task of reaching the world before it is eternally too late. This is our situation as well. How sincere are we in presenting Jesus as the only hope of mankind? It is strange that many church members do not want "prospective members" to be "offended" by the truth of the Bible. We can forget about the place God wants us to be until we are the people He wants us to be!

Sixth we witness *their spotlessness* in verse 5, "*Without fault.*" This is practical holiness; the practice of holiness requires the practice of holy habits. These were single in their devotion and walk with Jesus Christ. This is still the measure of effectiveness. This was not necessarily what man though of them; verse 5 concludes with the words, "*...before the throne of God.*" This reveals that He sees man as he really is, from the heart outward.

These worshippers can sing because of the victory of the Lamb for them. This has translated in a life of separation, surrender, sincerity and being spotless.

The Apocalypse: The Revelation of the Redeemer

Each of us is a worshipper; something or someone. What is it? How would you measure your current surrender? Are you looking forward to meeting the Lamb, the living Lord Jesus? Do not wait for the circumstances or crises to confront you to surrender to His Lordship.

Secondly we have the picture of:

II: THE WITNESSING OF SALVATION! Verses 6-7 This is the last call to the Gentiles in the tribulation period. There is something frightening about the reality of God's last call; it does come! These have had many witnesses during these days and may have thought that they would have unnumbered opportunities to come to Christ. (How many shared the Lord Jesus with you before you surrendered your heart to Him?) The solemn fact is that there eventually comes the last call. What is true for them in that day is true for man in this day. There will one day be the last call for man to trust Christ; wisdom challenges, do not wait for a more convenient season!

We will focus our attention upon two basic facts. First we will consider:

A: THE PREACHER! Verse 6 This preacher is not Paul or James; he is not John the Beloved. There are three things about this preacher that are worthy of note. **First** he is an *unusual messenger*, *"And I saw another angel."* The word "angel" literally means, "messenger." It is quite certain that in this day of grace that angels do not preach the gospel. However, in the tribulation the wickedness of man and the power of Satan will be cause for God to use His angels as He did before Christ came the first time. The point for us is that this is not the normal manner of communicating the gospel. The angel said to Cornelius in Acts 10, *"Send for Peter."* God could use His unusual messengers today; however, I am grateful that He has made it possible for us to be a part of this ministry. Should we not seek to be useful unusual messengers for God? We should realize that if men are silent God can speak through unusual messenger. He has, through Baalam and He can use whatever means He chooses! **Secondly**, he has a *unique manner* as verse 6 reveals in the words, *"...fly in the midst of heaven."* The antichrist will not be able to halt this servant of God. His pulpit is the sky. He is beyond the reach of God's enemies. His unique manner is that of flaying. I mention this to simply emphasis that we should be rebuked for our tardiness and dawdling way of doing the kings business. We are not expected to literally fly but we are expected to move as the Spirit of God directs us and when He speaks to be ready to respond in positive obedience to Him. This is what Philip did in Acts 8 and we should be more than ready to follow his example. This, for the most part, would be unique!

Thirdly he has a *universal message* as shared in verse 6, "*...to every nation, kindred, tongue and people.*" He will herald his message to the Jewish remnant that will in turn carry it throughout the earth. This is or should be the method used in our day. It is a universal message because God's field of harvest is the world. As the love of God knows no boundaries so His message must reach the harvest fields of the world. He has declared that in this generation this is to be done not by angels but redeemed men that love the souls for whom He died.

We move from the preacher to:

B: THE PROCLAMATION! Verses 6-7 The preacher's proclamation has to do with the "*everlasting gospel.*" The word, "*gospel*" means "*good news.*" Everything about God is good news but all good news is not the gospel as you and I know it! I am sure it was good news to the people in the Old Testament that their sins could be forgiven by the blood of a lamb but that is not the gospel; it was good news to Israel that they were going to enter the promised land but that is not the gospel. There are two things for us to observe about this proclamation: **First**, we have the *proclamation defined*! What is the "*everlasting gospel?*" There are at least three (3) kinds or types of the gospel. (a) The gospel of the grace of God, also called the gospel of Christ, gospel of God, as well as the gospel of peace. This is salvation in Christ through His death and resurrection. This is not the everlasting gospel for that gospel was not preached until Jesus came to earth. (b) The gospel of the kingdom. This is the gospel that John the Baptist and Jesus preached. John in Matthew 3:2 said, "*...repent ye: for the kingdom of heaven is at hand.*" Jesus in Matthew 4:23 came "*...preaching the gospel of the kingdom.*" That message will be preached again during the tribulation period. This is not the everlasting gospel because it started with David and will end at the conclusion of the reign of Christ on earth. (c) The everlasting gospel is presented in verse 7. The essence of it is God always has and will punish sin and reward worship. This gospel reveals the everlasting character of God. It is the ageless news that God is righteous. This gospel might include the other two aspects but it reflects the character of God in that He will always reward righteousness and punish sin.

Secondly we see:

C: THE PROCLAMATION'S DEMAND! Verse 7 The everlasting gospel puts priorities straight. *"Fear God, and give Him glory; for the hour of His judgment is come."* It is not now the Day of Judgment but the hour of judgment.

The demand is stated in the words, *"and worship Him."* During the great tribulation, when false worship prevails, God will again stake His claim to the worship of man. Worship is the overflow of a heart filled with wonder, love and praise for God. Intelligent worship is pouring out one's being as a drink offering to God, the laying of one's life upon the altar, the giving of self without reservation to God. (Phillips)

In light of the message we have of salvation in the precious blood of Christ and the knowledge that Jesus can come at any moment are we allowing the Holy Spirit to transform us into "preachers" that proclaim the love and liberty of the Lord to those lost souls? If we do not who will tell the lost the good news of Jesus and salvation that is offered freely in Him?

Thirdly we have a picture of:

III: THE WORLD'S SYSTEM! Verse 8 This is covered in detail in chapters 17 and 18. We will give attention to it then. For now I will mention two things about the world's system. First,

A: IT'S DEFEAT! *"Babylon is fallen, is fallen."* Here is the announcement of the defeat of the end time religious system. The first Babylon mentioned in the Bible was founded by a God defying rebel named Nimrod (Genesis 10:8-10). It grew into the first Gentile world power that oppressed the nations.

The repetition, *"is fallen, is fallen"* informs us that her defeat is so certain she appears here as already "fallen." It represents, in the Revelation all that is anti-God. It is the harlot religious system of chapter 17 and the polluted economic system of chapter 18. It will fall as all that is opposed to God will fall.

Secondly,

B: IT'S DOMINANCE! *"She made all nations drink of the wine of the wrath of her fornication."* Here is a religious system in its most corrupt form. Multitudes are won to it and intoxicated by it. Her unholy alliance is her fornication. (Strauss)

Whatever seduces the affections away from the Lord Jesus Christ must be the object of God's wrath.

How does she have this dominance? Corruption and convenience that appeals to the masses will surely be part of her plan. This world system will, in God's plan, fall. Any system developed by man that omits God regardless of when or where will ultimately be defeated by God Himself. It may, for a designated period of time, be dominate and enjoy great success but it will not last. God will defeat it.

The fourth picture is:

IV: THE WRATH OF THE SOVEREIGN! Verses 9-11 He is not presented in these verses as the Savior but as Sovereign. He is not pictured here as redeemer but as the ruler. We will consider two thoughts about the wrath of the sovereign. First,

A: THE WARNING OF GOD! Verse 9, *"...if any man worship the beast;"* verse 10, *"The same shall drink of the wine of the wrath of God."* This is a fair warning to the inhabitants of the earth. The judgment of God does not fall upon men without their being told that it is coming. It is still in the future when the angel announces it. (Strauss)

This is true for man in this day. There will not be anyone able to offer an excuse when he stands before God. Have you received a warning ticket? That informs you that if you continue this way you will be fined.

Secondly we have:

B: THE WRATH OF GOD! Verses 10-11 This is wrath without mercy. The day of mercy has passed when these events

The Apocalypse: The Revelation of the Redeemer

transpire. Doom and destruction is for the individual that worship the beast and identifies himself with him. He identifies with him by receiving his mark either in his forehead or in his hand. All will see the mark in the forehead. Many will wear it with pride. The mark in the hand may be hidden and revealed only as needed. By contrast those sealed by God are all in the forehead. It will be for all to see. God does not call us to be secret or private followers but to be an example before the world of His grace.

There are two aspects of His wrath that we must consider. **First,** notice in verse 10 *the description of His wrath*. This is one of the most awesome descriptions in the entire Bible for the destiny of the damned. The words, *"without mixture"* mean "full strength." It is not diluted. There is no mercy extended. The word *"indignation"* means "anger or scorn resulting from injustice or meanness." Man has been indignant toward God now he receives indignation from God. **Secondly** in verses 10-11 we have *the duration of his wrath*. These verses provide us with a glimpse of hell. The word "tormented" in verse 10 is in the future tense because it refers to eternity and not time. If "fire and brimstone" are not literal they speak of something far worse than we can begin to understand. Remember Sodom!?

The words of verse 11 reveal the duration of hell, *"and the smoke of their torment ascended up for ever and ever."* The words *"forever and ever"* can be "ages to ages." It is applied to the duration of the throne of God in Hebrews 1:8. The expression *"no rest day or night"* tell us of their consciousness. It is not rest for the wicked but wrath.

This is not popular but hell is the eternal dwelling of the unsaved. How can this be? How will the saved live eternally in heaven? We will receive a body that will not die. Even so the lost at their resurrection will receive a body that never dies.

Conclusion:
Try to think of those that do not know Jesus. If they die without Him this will be their destiny. Do these facts disturb you? One hundred and twenty people die every 60 seconds; 7,200 people die every hour; 172,800 die every day; one million two hundred

thousand nine hundred every week; almost 63 million people each year; how many of those do you think are lost?

The good word is that hell is avoidable. Jesus has provided salvation for us in His grace. In the tribulation period they can choose the beast and hell or Jesus and heaven; that is your choice today as well.

The Winepress of God's Wrath
Revelation 14:12-20

These verses clearly reveal that the day of God's wrath will be experienced by the godless masses of mankind that have refused to heed the message of the everlasting gospel heralded by the 144,000 during the days of the Great Tribulation.

The mind of man can not conceive the magnitude of the wrath of God. The picture is graphic. It is enough to arrest our attention and thrust us forth in this day of grace as flaming evangels with the good news of full salvation in the blood of the risen Lord. This day of wrath is a day of reckoning for the earth for its constant refusal to acknowledge God and it is measured according to the blasphemies of the rebellious nature of man.

In these verses we will consider first:

I: THE PATIENCES OF THE SAINTS! Verses 12-13 There is a tremendous contrast in these verses and the ones preceding them. In these we witness compliance, commitment, relationship, rest and rewards of righteousness. The previous verses have revealed something of the everlasting torments of hell where there is no hope of rest.

The patience of the saints should arrest our attention primarily because of the tribulation that they are experiencing. They are not, as we, reading about what is forthcoming. They are a part of the event.

Before we really address the patience of the saints let us ask two questions. (1) *Who are these people?* These are people that, for the most part, were reached by the 144,000 or those reached by them shared their experience with them. These represent an unnumbered host of saved people; *"as the sand of the sea."* (2) *What is their patience?* The word *"patience"* means endurance but it is more than merely being tolerant of something. It really implies a steadfast endurance or the refusal to accept what many would call an easy way out. This is the day of easy-ism! It has captured the heart and hands of multitudes that profess to know Jesus as Lord.

Now we will consider how these saints were able to display patience. There are two thundering truths presented in verse 12. First observe:

A: THE BASIS OF THEIR ENDURANCE! Verse 12 How are they able to endure hardness and suffering? There are two reasons. **First**, we have *their compliance to the testimony of scripture*, *"...here are they that keep the commandments of God."* These saints did not waiver. The key was their knowledge of the word of God. To know and comply with the word of God is everything in the Christian life. The statement of Moody is still correct; he said, "This book will keep you from sin or sin will keep you from this book!" The Word must be a daily part of our lives. We must learn it as well as live it. It provides reproof, direction, motivation and wisdom. It is the mirror that reveals our hearts to us. It will provide strength for us to stand against opposition regardless of what it is. If this is true and if their compliance with the testimony with the scripture was the key to their being able to stand; how much time did you spend in the scripture yesterday; last week; month; year? Compare that time with your television time or newspaper or even your hobby. It is not really a problem to understand why the church of Christ is so weak. Neither is it a problem to understand why churches are not growing or to understand why psychologist offices are full.

It is impossible to comply with what you do not know. They were *"keeping the commandments of God"* in the worst of times.

The basis of their endurance is witnessed **secondly** in their commitment to the teachings of the Savior; verse 12, *"...and the faith of Jesus."* This does not refer to faith in Jesus. The definite article before "faith" is very instructive. It tells us that this is referring to the entire system of doctrine. It is what was taught and acted upon in their lives on a daily basis.

Salvation has always been free, yet, in this day the consequence will be almost unbelievable. We can trust Christ and people praise the Lord. We are not hunted down like animals. These will be and they will persevere. They have been/will be tempted to compromise the teachings of the Savior. They have made a commitment of total submission to the will of God. They were not willing to compromise for the sake of a few more days of existence. They would not compromise with the beast even if it resulted in their death!

Ours is the day of convenience and compromise even among Christians and in churches. In the dark day of tribulation there will be those willing to endure for the sake of the souls of others. Their basis needs to be ours in the dark day of temptation to set aside the principles of commitment and compliance.

The second truth to note about the patience's of the saints is,

B: THE BLESSEDNESS OF THEIR ESTATE! Verse 13 shares this in the words, *"The voice from heaven said write blessed are the dead!"* I have used this verse of scripture in many memorial services and the application is surely there, however, it applies directly to those that pay with their lives rather than worship the antichrist. The fact is death is the price, for the most part; people will pay for trusting Christ during this period.

The voice says, *"Blessed are the dead."* The word *"blessed"* is our word for "happy." Therefore, *"Happy are the dead!"* However, there are three things that make their estate blessed. **First**, we have *their relationship* in verse 13 in the words, *"Which die in the Lord."* The happy dead are those that in this life had a relationship to and with the Lord. How did they have this relationship? The same as we; they realized they were not automatically "in the Lord." They had heard the *"everlasting gospel"* and repented in faith and received Christ as their Messiah. A reasonable question would be do you possess a relationship that is sufficient to base your eternal destiny upon? If you are not sure it is time to make sure, for be assured that not all deaths are blessed. If yours is a relationship that you are willing to die by it should be one that you can and will live by as well.

Secondly note *their rest* in the words *"...that they may rest from their labors."* Death for these will be rest because there will be no more persecution from the beast and the false prophet. Take a moment and compare the unbeliever in verse 11 *"...no rest"* and the believer in verse 13 in their "rest." The early Christians viewed death as rest. These die in the Lord. The Spirit speaks to our hearts and He is calling us to be those that live for the Lord rather than die for Him at this time. These are experiencing the words of the hymn "There is a place of quiet rest." Where; "near to the heart of God." We can rest in Jesus now and in eternity we will be blessed.

Thirdly we witness *their reward* in the words, *"…their works do follow them."* In this regard note Paul's words in 1 Corinthians 15:58 *"…for as much as ye kno0w that your labor is not in vain in the Lord."* It is a part of the nature of God to reward those that seek Him and put Him first (Hebrews 11:6). What is following you that one day you will be rewarded for by God Himself? These were willing to die for their faith in the Lord Jesus Christ, are we willing allow Him to live in and through us. Our song ought to be *"I'll live for Him who died for Me."*

II: THE PUNISHMENT OF THE SINNERS! Verses 14-20 We are not overly fond of either of these words. They have an offence built in them. We find them even more unpleasant when someone dares to use them together. It is acceptable to speak of the reward of the saints but do not warn of the retribution of sinners. These verses reveal in a clear manner that there is a day of reckoning for everyone that refuses to receive Jesus Christ as their personal redeem and Lord. There are two important aspects of the punishment of the sinner that demand our attention. First, note:

A: THE COMING OF JESUS TO HARVEST! Verses 14-16 The words of verse 16 are arresting *"…and the earth was reaped."* That expression does not refer to the ground commonly called dust but rather to the host of humanity and it reminds us of the words of Paul in Galatians 6:7, *"God is not mocked: for whatsoever a man soweth, that shall he also reap."* There is going to be a great harvest of the earth. There are three facts we should consider. **First**, verse 14 shares *the identification of the Harvester*. John has been hearing voices from heaven now he is seeing something that is gripping his heart. What he saw could have been an angel but there are those things shared in the verse

The Apocalypse: The Revelation of the Redeemer

that, to my satisfaction at least, identifies the harvester as the Lord Jesus Himself. Those things are the *cloud* and the *crown*. The cloud reminds us of Acts 1:9-11; the crown is the victor's crown. What is being witnessed is the ultimate victory that He will experience at His coming. This is the last time the title *"Son of Man"* is used. David used it first in Psalm 8 to refer to the coming glory of the Son of Man when He is crowned Sovereign of the earth. **Secondly** verse 14 shares the *instrument of the harvest* in the words, *"And in His hand a sharp sickle."* I would simply mention the *position of the instrument*. It is in His hand. That is the hand of Jesus Christ. He declared in John 5:27 *"All judgment has been committed unto Me."* Mankind will be held in His hand or be judged by His hand. I would also mention the *power of the instrument*; it is sharp. I tried once to cut down a pine tree with a dull ax. I have the scar on my left foot to prove that it does not work so well. It will not fail to thoroughly do its work. The power is that it is so sharp that nothing of man can successfully stand before it. The sickle in His hand does not mean that He does not use angels for the actual reaping. He does, but this is later. This reveals that He is in total control of the operation. This instrument is used to separate the wheat and the tares preceding His visible return to reign in power and glory. **Thirdly** in verses 15-16 we have the *indications of the harvest*. What can or should we learn from this harvest by Jesus Christ? At least two things are strongly indicated. First, the *lawlessness of society is indicated*. The harvest of the earth is ripe; the word "ripe" in Greek (verse 15) is a word that means "dry, withered or lifeless." That is the inhabitants of the earth are fully ready for judgment because they are so corrupted with immorality, lawlessness and apostasy that God must judge them. The spirit of antichrist, which is rebellion and blasphemy, has so excelled that the time of harvest has come.

Why does *"another angel"* speak in verse 15? He comes from the temple in heaven. He is the messenger of the harvest. This informs us that God and God alone control all these events.

The second indication is the *longsuffering of the Savior*. The word *"ripe"* in verse 18 is *"overripe."* It should have been harvested long ago. The only reason it was not was the grace of God. God was giving the 144,000 time to proclaim the everlasting gospel. But please observe that the longsuffering of God does expire; verse 16, *"And the earth was reaped."*

While the church awaits the rapture, there is a good harvest before us even now. Jesus said, *"Lift up your eyes, and look on the fields, for they are white already to harvest."* Our business as Christians is to be witnesses of Christ and His gospel. The world must hear His message of salvation, and we are responsible to tell it to the uttermost part of the earth. (L. Strauss)

Secondly we focus our attention upon:

B: THE COMING JUDGMENT IN THE HARVEST! Verses 17-20 This judgment is often referred to as the *"grape judgment."* These verses combined with the sixth vision may well be a preview in brief of Armageddon. We are presented with one of the most devastating pictures of time. There is much that we cannot fully understand in these verses but there are two truths that confront us. **First**, verses 17-18, present the *cause of judgment* in the words, *"For her grapes are fully ripe."* This is announced by another angel (verse 18). The interesting point is this angel came from the alter. Do you recall the events of chapter 6: 9-11? There the tribulation saints are crying, "How long?" They are asking for God to judge the earth. This is a part of the answer to their prayer. It is in God's time. We should be encouraged in knowing that prayer activates heaven.

The *"Vine"* of verse 18 is the earth. The grapes being ripe are a picture of the world. The word *"ripe"* is not the same as in verse 15. Here it means "overripe," the juice is bursting the grape. It is the juice of corruption; mankind is ready for judgment. The cause of this judgment is the corruption of the earth.

Secondly we note the *consequence of this judgment* in verses 19-20. Verse 19, *"And gathered the vine of the earth and cast it into the great winepress of the wrath of God."* Crushing the grapes produces wine. The people would walk on the grapes in large vats to crush them. The world is going to be crushed under the wrath of God. (Isaiah 63:1-3; Joel 3:13-14)

The words, *"Without the city"* in verse 20 speaks of the unbelieving world. This is a graphic description. From Dan to Beersheba was 1600 furlongs, that is, about 200 miles. This is outside the city where He was crucified, in the valley of

The Apocalypse: The Revelation of the Redeemer

Jehoshaphat, the valley of judgment; the Lord will complete the trampling on of His foes. Flowing from Armageddon, a deep crimson tide of human blood is seen (Phillips). This is the end of man's glory and Satan's rule in the earth. It will be the worst slaughter of human life in history. Ezekiel describes it by relating that 7 years will be required to rid the earth of weapons of warfare amassed by nations, and seven months to bury the dead (Ezekiel 39: 8-16). So great will be the slaughter that in some places the blood will be more than two feet deep (L. Strauss).

Conclusion:
Let the lost turn to Christ and escape the wrath of the God's judgment that is coming. Today mercy is extended to all. Come to Jesus today!

The Next Step is Judgment
Revelation 15:1-8

The world has experienced five major crises; the first was the fall in Eden; the second was the flood, the third was the tower of Babel; the forth was the Egyptian bondage, and the wanderings of Israel. The fifth was the cross of Calvary. Each of these was the consequence of sin. In each crises God became involved. We are now awaiting the sixth crises. The Bible calls it the *"Great and terrible Day of the Lord,"* the tribulation. It will also occur in relationship to sin, especially as it pertains to God's judgment of sin. It will see Gods intervention by His coming to earth to involve Himself in this particular crisis. This time He will put and end to sin and Satan. Even now the stage is being set for that closing time in mans history.

The Scriptures contain three major signs of the end time. There are lawlessness, the propagation of the doctrine of demons and the rise of apostasy. These will reach their height during the tribulation period. These are signs of the revelation of Christ and not the rapture of the church. We are not looking for signs but the Savior. The Lord Jesus taught that the world will wax worse and worse as His coming approaches. Therefore, we should not be shocked at events that are transpiring. He also said that He would come to judge sin. He does judge sin now but the full extent of His judgment upon sin will not occur until the tribulation period on earth. During this period God will bring judgment on the devil, on his demons and on his dupes. Dupes are lost people that he uses for his own schemes and purposes.

Make a mental note of a glorious fact; God's plan of salvation is designed to save man from His own wrath. The same One that will bring wrath has provided salvation that man might be delivered from that wrath.

The Apocalypse: The Revelation of the Redeemer

Revelation 15 is an introduction to the final trumpet judgment. This trumpet will complete God's judgment on earth as it relates to the tribulation period. This final trumpet contains 7 vials or bowls of wrath.

There are three thoughts for us to consider. First, note:

I: WHAT THE SERVANT SAW! Verses 1-2 There is something unusual revealed to our hearts; the full and final judgment of God is about to be poured out but we observe God is in no hurry! (He never is!) With a calm majestic poise He invited us to join this servant and gaze upon this scene. This servant, John, has seen sights that could not be placed in words. I believe that he probably would have preferred not to see this particular coming event.

The servant saw three things that we, too, can see. First, the servant saw:

A: A MARVELOUS SIGN! Verse 1, *"And I saw another sign."* The word "another" informs us that there have already been signs given. This is the third sign. The others are in chapter 12. They are "the woman," Israel and "the dragon" that is the devil. The sign here is *"seven angels having the last plagues."* Here we witness the completeness of God's wrath; seven being the number of completeness and the number is used eight times in these verses, thus we are witnessing the completeness of God's judgment on earth. These are the *"last plagues."* The Greek word last is *escatos*. We get our word eschatology or the study of last things from it. These plagues are so overwhelming that we cannot begin to conceive their destruction. That is why this sign is called *"great and marvelous"* in verse one.

When the last plague is poured out in chapter 16, Jesus will immediately return to earth in His Revelation with His saints.

The picture shared in verse 7 allows us to witness the contents of God's wrath. This is a picture of a bowl filled to absolute capacity, verse 1, *"For in them filled up the wrath of God."* That bowl is being poured out upon the earth. It is not in a small slow stream but as if it was turned, all at once, upside down. This is indicated somewhat by the meaning of the world *"wrath"* in verse one. The word literally means "rage." God is seen in a rage of fury. This is a balanced view of Sovereign God. He is seen dealing with sin in proportion to the sin.

The second thing the servant saw was:

B: A MIXED SEA! Verse 2, *"And I saw as it were a sea of glass mingled with fire."* As we gaze with the servant upon this awesome scene let us seek to identify the sea. The words, *"as it were"* inform us that this is not a literal sea. Therefore, to identify this sea we will look at the Scripture. In chapter 4:6 John saw a *"sea of glass."* In Exodus 24:9-10 Moses saw (verse 10) under His (God's) feet as it were *"A paved work of sapphire stone, and as it were the body of heaven in his clearness."* In Revelation 21:21 referring to the streets of heaven John saw *"the street of the city was pure gold, as it were transparent glass."* Each of these references confirms that this sea the servant saw is in heaven. Please keep the identification of the sea in mind as we seek to identify the symbol. The sea is *"mixed with fire."* The symbol is one of judgment. 11 Peter 3:7 and 10 testify to this truth as well as Hebrews 12:29

What is the point? The judgment that is about to be experienced throughout the earth comes from the very presences of God. He is its source and sender! This will be especially important when we observe the severity of the judgment.

Our concept of God is rather limited. In this day of grace we are prone to believe that grace is all there is or will be. This, however, is not the case now nor will it be when He deals with this earth during the tribulation period, especially the last three and one-half years. Now an individual can choose what he will receive from the hand of God. He may choose grace and be saved or judgment and be damned. In this day he has already chosen and his choice is one of judgment.

The servant saw a third thing; namely:

C: THE MARTYRED SAINTS! Verse 2 The servant sees these saints standing on the sea of glass. We can gather from their location that they are in the presence of God. Further, their location seems to indicate that what is forthcoming is in response to their request in chapter 6:9-11.

I would mention *their conquering*. The words of verse two are inspiring, "And them that had gotten the victory." To experience victory indicates that a battle has been fought. In any battle there are several possibilities; the first is victory; the second is defeat and the third is a draw. These were engaged in a struggle with the powers of hell and they conquered. They are in heaven so we know that it was not a victory without a price. The price was exceeding but they willingly paid all that was asked. Their conquering involved victory over the beast. He is the world ruler in the tribulation period but he lost the spiritual battle to them. They were victorious over the image of the beast; they refused to worship the image of chapter 13. This is somewhat reminiscent of Daniel's companions. Their conquest was over his mark. That mark was needed to buy and sell; to eat and survive. In our day one grows weary of the puny excuses given for not being committed to Christ and His church. In light of the conquering of these martyred saints and knowing that in that day individuals will pay with their lives how grateful we should be for the freedom and opportunity to worship, witness and work on behalf of Christ, His church and His cause.

In addition I will mention *their cheer* in the words *"having the harps of God"* reveals their cheer. Remember that harps are related to joy in the Bible. When Israel was captive in Babylon they hung their harps on the willow tree. There was nothing to cheer. These martyred saints are experiencing and expressing great joy. Their joy is possible because they refused to compromise even in the face of death. Now they are rejoicing in their eternal rest with God.

Secondly we consider,

II: WHAT THE SAINTS SING! Verses 3-4 there are two songs stated in verse 3. They are *"The song of Moses,"* and *"The song of the Lamb."* We really do not know what the song of Moses is; many believe it is the song of triumph over the Egyptians in Exodus 15. The point is it was the faithfulness of God to Moses that made the song of the Lamb possible. It is possible that the song of Moses deals with how God brought them out of bondage and the song of the Lamb might declare how he brought them into His presence.

The song the saints sing has three stanzas. First,

A: THEY SING OF THE GREATNESS OF GOD MANIFESTED IN HIS WORKS! Verse 3, *"Great and marvelous are Thy works Lord God Almighty."* As one the host will join and sing, "How Great Thou Art," and everyone will be on key. How often do we sing or speak of the greatness of God in our lives? As we face life with all its perplexities are our eyes focused on the greatness of God or the greatness of our problems? When we focus on the greatness of God everything else seems to be indeed small.

How great is God? He is great enough to purge our sin and provide salvation. He is great enough to provide security and produce satisfaction. Learn to sing, or in cases like mine, to hum those songs that magnify the greatness of God.

Secondly,

B: THEY SING OF THE GOODNESS OF GOD MANIFESTED IN HIS WAYS! Verse 3 states this in the words *"Just and true are Thy ways, Thou King of saints* (nations).*"* The goodness of God is manifested in His justice and righteousness. If He is not just with sin maybe He will not be just with those that have trusted Christ. If He does not punish sin maybe He will not reward faith; if sin is not punished how different will heaven be from the earth. The reality is that justice plus love equals Calvary and that saves man from the wrath of God.

Is God good? What flows from goodness? Only that which is good can flow from goodness. We are the people of God; our lives should be characterized by truth and goodness.

Thirdly,

C: THEY SING OF THE GLORY OF GOD MANIFESTED IN HIS WARS! Verse 4 shares this in the words *"Who shall not fear Thee, O Lord, and glorify Thy name."* All that we do should have as its goal to glorify God. Surely we seek to do this when we gather together in worship, praise and celebration but do we do this in our homes and on our jobs? Redeemed people are a singing people and our song should seek to glorify Christ as these sing of the glory of God they mention three aspects of His glory. They sing of His virtue, *"For Thou alone art holy."* They sing of His victory, "For all nations will come and worship before Thee." And thirdly they sing of His vengeance, *"For Thy judgments are made manifest."*

In light of what these saints sing how scriptural and spiritual are our songs? Does the song of my soul glorify the Savior or self?

Thirdly we observe:

III: WHAT THE SCRIPTURES SHARE! Verses 5-8 The word *"testimony"* in verse 5 is a reference to the law or the Scriptures of God. His word is unchanging and unchangeable; men may try but it stands as sure today as it did when God gave it by His Spirit.

First,

A: THE MESSENGERS OF WRATH! Verse 6 We are not seeking to identify the angelic messenger of wrath merely to notice two of their characteristics. They are characterized by *divine righteousness*; this is revealed in the fact that they are clothed *"in pure and white linen."* They proceed from where God dwells; they do not act with impatience nor are they motivated by a spirit of independence. Their actions are in keeping with the will of God. Further they are characterized by *divine restraint*; this is shared in the words, *"girded around their breast with a golden girdle."* There is no hot passion of their own mingled with their acts. They are calm, like the surgeon that uses his knife on quivering flesh. He does so without passion. False piety does not hold him back from what he knows must be done.

Secondly,

B: THE MEDIATOR OF WRATH! Verse 7 One of the living creatures gives one bowl to each angel; these living ones are found in chapter 4; their faces were like a lion, calf, eagle and man. I think the one here is the one with the face of a man because the judgments will have a tremendous affect upon man.

Thirdly,

C: THE MANIFESTATION OF WRATH! Verse 8 The smoke reveals that God is now dealing in judgment. There is a sobering truth presented in verse 8; that is the inability of anyone to enter the temple until the last plague was finished. God's wrath, once poured out upon His Son on man's behalf, is to be outpoured again, this time however; it will be upon the world. There is a truth that must not be missed; that is that during this awesome judgment period the way into the holiest is barred by the Shekinah fire of God's own burning glory.

Conclusion:
The terrifying reality is that there is a judgment and the inhabitants of this earth that have rejected Jesus Christ are going to experience the fierceness of the wrath of God. We must do what we can while we can.

God's Final Fury
Revelation 16:1-21

There are texts that I delight in preaching; this is not one of them. Just reading this chapter rips and tears your heart; this is a terrifying passage because it is the culmination of all the judgment of God...it is His full and final wrath! A reasonable inquiry could be, if it strikes such a terror why preach it? For me there are three reasons, first, it is in the Word and I must be faithful in declaring the whole council of God. Second, I preach it with the earnest hope that the Spirit of God will awaken our hearts to the reality of the lostness of mankind and thirdly, to awaken Christians to the fact that the Christian life is not something to be postponed; that evangelism, missions, personal witnessing and worship are to be done now because there may not be a tomorrow.

Chapter 16 prophetically reveals God's final sweep of judgment; up to this point His judgment has been partial, not now. These judgments are so severe that they are almost unbelievable. They are as severe as sins demand. At the time of the bowl judgments the world will be openly and deeply involved in Satan worship. There are now temples to Satan, but what we witness now, as dark, depraved and destructive as it is, is only a token of what will be in that day. It is difficult to conceive of the entire world, except for a small minority of believers that are martyred, openly engaged in Satan worship. We think the commands of God are blatantly broken now, that day they will not even be regarded as the commandments of God.

God has demonstrated throughout history that His desire for man was to spend eternity with Him in joy and peace and not experience judgment and wrath. This shared in the Old Testament by the prophets He raised to tell of His love. Later, He sent His

Son to die on the cross and raised Him from the dead to reveal that He approved of the work of Christ for the sins of man. In the tribulation He is still seeking to convince man that he is loved and if he will come to Him he will have eternal, abundant life with Him. In addition there are the two witnesses and the 144,000 dedicated missionaries to preach the everlasting gospel and tell them there is a God that does love them and they can be forgiven by coming to Christ. When man continues to say "no thank you, I will not come to Christ" every gracious deed is turned to fury. When men do not respond to God's grace they must face His judgment. Just as it was true in Noah's day it will be true in the days preceding Jesus return in revelation to the earth.

Chapter 16 is the end for man. This is God's final fury before Christ returns as King of kings and Lord of lords. The challenge before us is to reach men with the message of salvation while there is time and their hearts are sensitive to the Spirit of God. I could never exhaust the depth of this passage; at best we will only deal with surface matters. There are three thoughts that I would like for us to seriously consider. First we have:

I: THE FINAL PLAGUES! Verses 1-4; 8-14; 17-21 These final plagues are similar to those experienced in Egypt and those already considered in the trumpets. While they are similar they surpass anything this earth has ever witnessed. As we seek to understand as much as we possibly can we acknowledge how limited we are in understanding what our minds can not conceive. There are two major thoughts for us to contemplate. First we will notice:

A: THE FEATURES OF THE FINAL PLAGUES! Verses 1-2 and the overall context will present some of those features. It is imperative that we note the similarities but more that we see the features, traits or characteristic that set these final plagues apart from all that have preceded them. The **first** feature, shared in verse 1, is *their source*. The servant is hearing *"a great voice."* The speaker is deity; the location of the voice is *"out of the temple."* The instructions are then given to the seven angels *"go your ways.'* They have been waiting to hear this command, *"and pour out your vials upon the earth."* God is sovereign and

The Apocalypse: The Revelation of the Redeemer

He is the source of these final plagues that the earth will experience. This reveals that He was, is and will continue to be totally in charge of all the events that transpire in the earth during the tribulation. Heaven, hell and the earth are under His authority. The source of these final plagues is a holy, righteous, just and true God that knows exactly what He is doing; He makes no mistakes. This is true in our lives; we may not desire to acknowledge it but He is working according to His own will in our lives.

A **second** feature of these final plagues is *their scope*; this is shared in verses 1-2. The earth and those that do not know Jesus as Savior will be the recipients of these final plagues. The plagues were localized in Egypt; the surrounding countries were not affected. During the trumpet judgments one-half of the earth, trees, grass, fresh water, sun, moon and stars were affected. The scope of this final fury is worldwide. There will not be a single spot on earth that will not experience these final plagues. One of the old songs said, "There is not hiding place down here," and it is true.

A **third** feature of these final plagues is *their speed*. The words "*and the second, third and forth etc angel went*" are not in the Greek. The preceding judgments have been rather slow and give the outward appearance of being more deliberate; these come in rapid succession. They are not like a single shot rifle rather they are like a rapid-fire machine gun. The speed of these plagues will add to the confusion of the world.

A **fourth** feature of these final plagues is *their severity*. When these bowls of wrath are poured forth they are not progressive; that is one does not end before the other beings. Except for the sun these are cumulative. They are on top of each other adding to what has already been experienced. Note an example; men still have the sores of he first plague when the sun scorched them in the fourth plague. The severity of these final plagues is seen when we realize that they affect the physical, mental, emotional and spiritual life of every unsaved person in the earth. They are unparallel. The mind can not fully comprehend the severity of the final fury of God when these final plagues are poured forth upon the earth.

Secondly we consider,

B: THE FOCUS OF THE FINAL PLAGUES! Verses 1-4; 8-9; 18-20 We must give our attention to the target and content of these final plagues. The focus in general is everything that is in existence at the time of judgment. We do desire to be somewhat more specific in our focus if possible; in so doing we will note the focus **first** upon *the earth* in verses 1-2 and 18-20. Verse 2 says it this way, *"And poured out the vials of the wrath of God upon the earth."* Yes, this physical earth will undergo this horrendous final plague. Even in this area of focusing upon the earth there are some specific areas for us to note. **One**, *the rebellious in the earth* is shared in verse 2. The rebellious are those individuals that have received the mark of the beast and that worship the image. The reward of their rebellion is stated, *"And there fell a noisome and grievous sore upon them."* *"Noisome"* means "painfully bad." These sores are ulcerous open sores; the word literally means "malignant." Think of a cancerous world infected with cancerous sores. This word is used in Luke 16 to describe the sores of Lazarus. The boils in Egypt, as bad as they were, are nothing to be compared with this. It is imperative that we understand that this will be the experience of rich, poor, young, old, educated and ignorant throughout the entire earth. **Two**, there is *the rearranging of the earth* as shared in verses 17-21. This is the seventh plague. It is the final act of God preceding the coming of Christ. Verse 17 shares with us the *beginning* of this plague. This verse also presents the place of *commencing* in the words, *"in the air."* This is significant in that this is the present headquarters of Satan. We know at this point in time his domain includes the earth as well, but he must be defeated and removed from every location. There is a present day lesson for each of us in this great truth. We can be tolerant of any area in our lives that will allow the enemy the opportunity to defeat or discourage us. Further, verse 17 reveals the pronouncement of Christ in the words, *"it is done."* Think of it all the prophecies of centuries past are completed. Jesus said this once before when He hung on the cross for man's redemption in this day His pronouncement results in the ruin of man. Each person stands at one of these pronouncements of Christ; at the cross he can be redeemed, at the plagues he will receive retribution.

The Apocalypse: The Revelation of the Redeemer

In addition, verses 18-20, present to us *the body* of this final plague on the earth. There is an earthquake so great that it surpasses anything the earth has every experienced. It tears the earth apart. In verse 19 Jerusalem is torn into three parts. It is not destroyed because there will be a throne there. Verse 19 also informs us that the system that has been in charge of the earth is literally ripped apart. (Babylon will be considered in chapters 17 and 18) Verse 20 reveals something of the tremendous impact of this earthquake.

Next, in verse 21, we have *the burden* of this final plague, *"And there fell upon men a great hail out of heaven every stone about the weight of a talent;"* that is a weight of from 100 to 125 pounds each. Do you remember the "ice man," of yesteryear; he delivered blocks of ice to the home. Now imagine a 25 pound block of ice being dropped from 50 feet and hitting a man. These are five times that size and they are falling like rain all over the earth. This is indeed the judgment of God; it is beyond comprehension.

Finally there is *the blasphemy* of the final plagues in verse 21. After all that has transpired man only looks at God to blaspheme Him for this plague of hail. This reveals how hard the human heart can become when it continually refuses to repent.

We will now move from the earth in our focus of this final plague to *the elements* in verses 3-4 and 8-9. While the entirety of these plagues, to some degree, focus on the elements there are two specific arrears presented to us in these verses. **First** in verses 3-4 we have *the water*. The water is divided into two specific parts; *the sea* in verse 3, *"everything in every salt water body across the earth dies,"* and floats to the top. Try as we may we can not imagine the pollution that the second plagues causes (most of us have had the pleasure of smelling the aroma of one spoiled fish, think of the stench of millions of rotten fish!) It is described as being like blood. It does not say it was blood but like blood, to say the least this will have a definite effect upon the food supply. The second part shared in verse 4 is *the springs*; this is pollution of all fresh water. It becomes undrinkable it is like blood. How long can a person maintain life without liquid intake;

it is a matter of days. I am told that to die of thirst is a horrible, agonizing death.

The **second** element in verses 8-9 is *the weather*, *"And the fourth angel poured out his bowl upon the sun,"* Luke 21:25 declares *"And there shall be signs in the sun and moon and stars..."* The result of this plague is that men are scorched with a fierce heart. In the trumpet judgments God had darkened the sun by one-third; now He increases its heat. We are located in exactly the right position, with regard to the sun, to live. If we were further away we would freeze, if we were closer we would burn up. The reality is that God can do what He pleases with the sun; it is His creation. There is an interesting note in all of this, everything God gave to man to demonstrate that He was there, is now used against man to demonstrate that He is there. We must not forget that while the sun is scorching, there is no water; grass or trees and they still have the sores!

There is a reaction to this plague stated in the words, *"Men refused to give God glory."* This is almost beyond belief. How is such a thing possible? This demonstrates the reaction of individuals that are sold out to Satan. They have hardened their hearts against God; this reveals a tremendous truth: if man rejects the love of God he can reject the judgment of God as a means of leading him to repentance. When man hardens his heart is like the sun on clay or too much sun on a flower. A little fellow heard that some of his mother's plants needed sun so he got a magnifying glass and burned the plants. This is what happens to the heart that rejects the love of God that flows from the cross of Calvary.

Thirdly, in verses 10-12, the focus of this final plague is upon *the enemy*. The enemy of God is the enemy of the people of God. There are two important facts that should be observed. The **first** is *the seat of wickedness* in verse 10. God centers His wrath upon the source of wickedness, the seat or throne of the beast. He is the one men will be worshipping on earth at that time and men will see their leader helpless in the face of the judgment of God. God now turns the sun completely out and men gnaw their tongues because of the pain. Each of us knows what it is like to accidentally bite either our tongue or lip. In the face of all this

The Apocalypse: The Revelation of the Redeemer

man does not repent because he is so deeply involved in Satan and demon worship.

We should not be surprised at this. In our time there are Christians that refuse to hear and heed God's call to repent. There are those that say, "I know this is wrong but I am willing to take my chances with God" as though the Christian became the exception to the principle of the judgment of God. He does not! When we meet Jesus it will not be in reference to sin, He, in my opinion does that while we are here. The Bible declares that if one continues that God will *"destroy the flesh that the spirit might be saved in the day of the Lord."*

Secondly there is *the surprising way* in verse 12. The river Euphrates is dried up. This has always been a protection for Israel. There is only one place to cross it and that is in the northern part. Therefore, when Babylon, from the east, came they were called the enemy from the north. The water is dried up to make way for the armies of the east. The army of China now has in excess of 200 million soldiers. The Bible uses that number about the army that will be brought to this place. The stage is being set for this event to take place.

The focus of these final plagues is upon all things that have to do with the creation of God being defiled by man or the devil.

The second major thought is:

II: THE FACINATING PARENTHESIS! Verses 5-7 and 13-16 These verses are set in the midst of the most horrendous judgment this earth has/will every experience. Verses 5-7 are not really a parenthesis they are actually a part of the third vial or bowl that is being poured forth upon the springs of fresh drinking water. Verses 13-16 follow the pattern established early in the book. There is a parenthesis between 6th and 7th seal and between the 6th and 7th trumpet. This one is between the 6th and 7th bowl of God's final wrath visited upon this rebellious world.

Note first,

A: THE DECLARATION OF THE RIGHTEOUSNESS OF JUDGMENT! Verses 5-7 This is stated clearly by the angel of the water in verse 5 and a voice from the altar in verse 7. This really isn't a matter that we give much attention to but it is something that we should consider, especially in light of the severity of God's final fury. The **first** thing declared is *the righteousness of God* in verses 5 and 7. Why would this angel of the waters say, *"Thou are righteous?"* The water has been turned to blood and there could be those that would think/say that God has gone too far. Before this happens the angel declares "God is right, therefore, do not question God by asking, 'aren't You overdoing it?'" God has dealt with those that have been responsible for persecuting His people. (Compare Deuteronomy 32:40-43) His righteousness is further attested to in verse 7 in the words, *"true and righteous are Thy judgments."* It is understood that this is from the perspective of heaven and it is not the opinion of the inhabitants of the earth that are experiencing His judgment. Something of a proper respect is shared in how God is *addressed* in verse 5, *"Which art and wert, and shall be."* He is the permanent, unchanging God that sovereignty rules the world. This respect is also witnessed in their *acknowledgement* in verse 7. He is *"true and righteous."* He is true because He is truth and He can not be anything less. His righteousness is based upon His truth. In light of this, the next time you are tempted to criticize how the Lord is managing His world remember, He knows the end from the beginning and He is true and righteous in all His deeds.

A **second** thing declared, shared in verse 6 is *the reaping of the godless*. These shed the blood of His saints and servants now they are given blood to drink, *"for they are worthy,"* can be translated as "for they deserve it." This is not a new principle; it is you reap what you sow or what goes around comes around. When I do something to you I am in reality saying this is the way I want you to treat me. The judgment may appear to be harsh to us but it is merely in keeping with the principle that God established when He created this world. That is law of sowing and reaping; it has not nor will it change as long as time endures.

God is declared righteous in His judgments. He is unchanging in His person, unchanging in His principle and unchanging in His purity.

Secondly we have:

B: THE DECLARATION OF THE RETURN OF JESUS! Verses 13-16 After the 7th bowl is poured forth on the

The Apocalypse: The Revelation of the Redeemer

earth; Jesus comes in power and glory with His saints. This is recorded in chapter 19:11. This is the last parenthesis and it is significant that it declares the coming of Jesus. There are some interesting facts that we should note. **First**, in verses 13-14 we have *the picture of demonic activity*. The *description* informs us that these are from the unholy trinity. They are associated with the slime, mire and filth of hell. These demons, which are spread out by satanic trinity are like frogs, swift-aced, cold-blooded, creatures of two worlds, full of venom and poison for mankind. Their deception is clearly presented in verse 14. Why are these kings of the earth here? These demonic spirits deceive them. They work miracles and through trickery and satanic magic they persuade these kings to proceed to Armageddon. If you are wondering how this could possibly transpire simply read the account in 1 Kings 22 which shares the account of Ahab and his going up to Ramoth-Gilead. A lying testimony was put in the mouths of the prophets and they persuaded him to go up. This or something similar will happen again in the last days. These verses reveal that God is God and that He is in control; He can use the demons of hell to accomplish His purpose.

Secondly, verses 14-16 share *the plan of divine action*. We are not to be overwhelmed by these things because this God is our God. In this plan of divine action we have three interesting facts. **First** *the Warrior* expressed by the word *"almighty"* in verse 14. The word is El Shaddai; the Warrior. It is this holy warrior that all the powers of darkness will confront in that day. In this picture of divine action we have **secondly** *the warning*; this is presented in verse 15. The warning is to tribulation saints. He is saying, "be ready." Remember it is dark for them as well. Their water, food and supplies have been affected also. This is not like Egypt where their forefathers were protected from the plagues. The warning is stay dressed, be prepared. I heard about a man that decided to trick his neighbor. He pounded on his door at 3 a.m. and cried "your house is on fire; your house is on fire." The man jumped out of bed, ran outside naked. The other man had gathered the neighbors; the naked man was so shamed that he went back inside and killed himself. God is saying "be ready, keep your clothes on, I'm coming." In the plan of divine action **thirdly** there is *the war* in verse 16. Note the words, *"And He* (God) *gathered them* (the armies of the antichrist) *together into a place called in the Hebrew tongue Armageddon."* (Compare Revelation 19: 11-21) Napoleon said this was the most natural battlefield on the face of the earth. Some have questioned if this is possible in the day of atomic and nuclear weapons. Will the foot soldier be outdated? No, for at least two specific reasons; first you must have an army to occupy the land you are conquering; and second no weapon will do any good unless you have a concentrated target. Armies will be needed to push enemies into a concentrated area. This is a war that is talked about but in reality it is not fought between men, nor is it fought between men and God. The fact is God by His word defeats the armies of darkness alone!

Conclusion:
Now may I bring back to our hearts the reality that in the midst of God's final fury men blasphemed the God of heaven no less than three times in these verses? They knew what was happening yet; they refused to acknowledge His power and worth.

If you are saved remember time is short; place your eyes not only upon Jesus but a lost world as well.

Mystery, Babylon
Revelation 17:1-18

Religion will flourish during the first portion of the tribulation period in the false system called Babylon, the harlot. This system will be unchallenged until the middle of the tribulation, then the beast (antichrist) will see this as a challenge to his own power and program; therefore, with his league of 10 nations he will destroy the harlot and set himself up to be worshipped.

In the midst of the judgment being experienced in the earth the Holy Spirit reveals the nature of the crime that has caused such judgment to be experienced. The time for this event is in the middle of the tribulation period.

Babylon is referred to in revelation 14:8 and 16:9. There we are informed *"Babylon is fallen"* and *"great Babylon came in remembrance before God to give unto her the cup of the wine of the fierceness of His wrath."* Chapters 17 and 18 reveal the details of Babylon's fall and the cup of God's wrath poured out upon her. Who or what is Babylon? In chapter 17 Babylon is a worldwide religious system. In chapter 18 it is a system of commerce and government.

Chapter 17 shares some of these shocking truths. First we have:

I: THE HARLOT! Verses 1-6 Remember the great harlot called Babylon the great, mystery Babylon is a worldwide false system of religion headed by the false prophet during the tribulation period.

One of the angels said to John, *"Come hither."* Three times this expression is used in the book, 4:1, the vision in heaven; 17:1, the judgment of the great whore; 21:9, the bride, the Lamb's wife. Before we witness the Lamb's bride in her perfection we see the harlot in all her corruption. The goal is to gain as much insight into this harlot as possible, to assist in doing this observe first,

A: HER UNIVERSAL POWER! Verses 1-2 This is a new vision that John is witnessing and its theme is judgment. It is a vision of the false harlot church in illegitimate union with the world. The false church cannot commit adultery because she was never married to Jesus. She is a harlot; she could not be unfaithful to Him because she was never faithful to Him. There are two interesting facts for us to consider. **First**, verse 1 shares *her authority* in the words that she sits *"upon many waters."* These waters according to verse 15 *"are peoples and multitudes, and nations, and tongues."* She has authority over these people and nations. She is a massive, worldwide ecumenical religious system. **Secondly**, verse 2, shares *her associations*. The harlot church, the apostate religious system of the last days, forms an unholy intrigue with the political leaders of the earth. These are drunk with the wine of her fornication or immorality. Her sensual doctrines and views have an intoxicating influence over the minds of the people. Secondly we have:

B: HER UNIQUE POSITION! Verse 3, *"Sitting upon a scarlet beast."* John is transported by the Spirit into the wilderness, when the Lord showed him the bride of Christ, He took him to a great high mountain; but to show him the course and development of religion in this world He carries him into the wilderness. Wherever there is spiritual harlotry there is desolation and a desert of dreary, weary waste.

John sees the woman *"sitting on a scarlet colored beast."* That scarlet colored beast is (Revelation 13) the antichrist. The religious system is sitting upon the political system. Who seems to be in control? The religious system! She is riding and controlling the beast, the political aspect of Babylon. It will be worth remembering that at the outset of the tribulation period that the false harlot religious system headed by the false prophet will be more powerful than the antichrist in the political system. Later the antichrist will devour the religious system.

"A smiling young lady from Nigar
Took a ride on the back of a tiger

The Apocalypse: The Revelation of the Redeemer

They came back from the ride
With the lady inside and
A smile on the face of the tiger."

The beast is scarlet colored; in scripture this is the color for the imperial thus indicating that the beast is the revived Roman Empire headed by the antichrist. When he is presented in chapter 13:1 he has the name of blasphemy upon his heads; in 17:3 we are informed that this scarlet colored beast is *"full of names of blasphemy."* The entire system is one of blasphemy. Of all the unions this is the most unholy; a blasphemer is supporting the false church. The seven heads and ten horns will be the federated states of Europe. Thirdly we witness:

C: HER UNLIMITED PROSPERITY! Verse 4 *"And the woman* (the harlot church) *was arrayed in purple and scarlet color and decked with gold and precious stones and pearls..."* Everyone wants a name for this harlot church of the tribulation; while this system is broader than the Roman system, it does involve the Roman church. Even now purple and scarlet are reserved for the pope and cardinals; pope Paul 11 made it illegal for anyone else to wear these colors. The present estimated wealth of this system in America is about 34.2 billion dollars. It isn't any wonder that John marveled for the only church he knew was despised, poor, hunted, hounded and hated. For one to name the person of Christ was to be brought before a Roman provincial judge and there be sentenced to be burned at the stake, beheaded or crucified.

This organization is rich, she controls governments, she crowns and uncrowns kings, and she says "yea" and "nay" to legislation.

The fourth truth is:

D: HER UNHOLY PASSION! Verses 4-5 we witness the false religions of the work drunk from one cup of the wickedness of Satan himself.

We have witnessed that one of the chief characteristics of the woman is harlotry. Harlotry is the standing symbol in the Word of God for a debauched worship and false devotion. When people worship for God what is not God, or give their hearts to idols, or institute systems, doctrines, rites, or administrations, to take the place of what God has revealed and appointed, the Scriptures call it whoredom, adultery and fornication.

This one is named *"the mother of harlots and the abomination of the earth,"* she must be the great embodiment, source, and representative of all idolatry, false worship and perversion of the word and institutes of God. The record is that she is the great original of all harlotries and abominations of the earth, of which many have sprung from, and that all the harlotries of time have her for their mother. The imagery goes back to the beginnings, out of which all-false systems, and false worships and abominations of the earth have come.

The background of the development of this religious idolatry is seen in the very name written on her forehead, *"And upon her forehead was a name written, mystery, Babylon the Great, the mother of harlots and the abominations of the earth."* In John's day prostitutes were often identified by a name on their forehead. If the false church of the tribulation period is call "mystery" what does this cause one to think of the true church? In Ephesians 5 the true church is called a mystery.

The false religious system goes back to Genesis 10 and 11. Turning to these chapters we learn the beginnings of the kingdom of Nimrod, the grandson of Ham, was Babel or Babylon. The inhabitants of the earth, it is implied, came there under the leadership for Nimrod, whose name means rebellious panther, and that under him began the first great work of rebellion against God, which brought the confusion of tongues and inaugurated the original of all the subsequent harlotries and abominations of mankind against the command and know intent of the Almighty, it was there undertaken to "build a city and a tower whose top might reach unto heaven." It appears, also, that from slaying of wild beast, and with the armed forces grouped around him that Nimrod betook the enslavement of men. The Arab record informs us he was the first king. It is said of him that he professed have seen a golden crown in the sky, that he made one like it, put it on his head and thus claimed to rule in the name and as the earthly impersonation of the power of the sky, either as Orion or the Sun.

The Apocalypse: The Revelation of the Redeemer

Nimrods' wife's name was Semiramis. She is called in ancient history the first high priestess of idolatry. When the people were scattered from Babylon they carried with them their system of idolatry. In answer to the promise made to Eve that the seed of the woman would deliver the race, Semiramis, when she gave birth to a son, said he miraculously conceived by a sunbeam, and she offered her son as the promised deliverer of the earth. His name was Tammuz. When he was grown a wild boar slew him, but after 40 days of the mother's weeping, he was raised from the dead. In this story Semiramis and Tammus began the cult worship of the mother and child that spread through out the world. In Assyria she is called Ishtar and her son is Tammus. I Phoenicia she is called Isis and her son is called Osiris. In Greece she was called Aphrodite, and her son was called Eros. In Rome she was called Venus and her son was called Cupid.

When Babylon was destroyed the high priest gathered up all the idols and images and moved to Pergamos. Attalus 111 bequeathed Pergamos to Rome when he died in 133 B.C. and the Babylonian mysteries eventually found their way to Rome. Here in Rome the high priest of Babylon religion took the title of pontifex maximus. This title was imprinted on his miter; this title represented dragon the fish god. From that time on every emperor in Rome bore the title Pontifex Maximus because the first high priest of Babylon idolatry bore that name. That title is now given to the pope. Thus, the light of this, the pope is not the successor of Peter the fisherman but dragon, the fish god.

When Constantine became a professing Christian the ancient Babylonian mysteries were simply transferred bodily into the church. Pagan temples became Christian churches, pagan gods became Christian saints, pagan festivals became Christian feast, and pagan customs became the customs of the church. The virgin Mary became the queen of heaven. Little by little all the trappings of paganism became an established part of the religion of Christendom.

The cult of the worship of mother and child spread throughout the whole earth. She was worshipped by the offering of a wafer (a little cake) to her as the queen of heaven. There was always forty days of lent, of weeping over the destruction of Tammus before the feast of Tammuz, prior to the feast of Ishtar, at which time his resurrection was celebrated. The sign of Tammuz was an Ishtar egg, a symbol of his resurrection.

In a study of archaeology where anthropologist have gone where they have never heard of God, heaven, hell, Jesus or Mary or the prophets, in every group of people is their story concerning a virgin birth, mother, child relationship and a flood. This is a part of the strategy of Satan. He spread that which was not true however; it is based upon the truth. We can seen in these things a satanic corruption and confusion.

In the Babylonian religion there was the priestly ablutions, sacramental rites and rituals, the dedication of virgins to the gods and purgatorial fires and in a thousand other things that are familiar to us today.

The prophets cried bitterly against that mother and child cult. In Jeremiah 44 he describes the idol worshippers among the children of Israel that burn incense to the queen of heaven and who offer wafers in her name. In Ezekiel 8 God takes the prophet and shows him the inner life of the people of the Lord that are idolatrous: "He said also to me, turn thee yet again, and thou shalt see greater abominations than these. Then He brought me to the door of the gate of the Lords' house which was toward the north; and, behold there sat women weeping for Tammuz." Ezekiel was beholding the forty days of Lent in which they afflicted themselves and wept for Tammuz. But after those forty days the end of weeping was celebrated with the feast of Ishtar, in which the peplum exchanged Ishtar eggs.

As we have observed that cult of the worship of mother and child spread throughout the whole world, from Babylon to Assyria, to Phoenicia, to Pergamos, and finally to Rome. There the Roman emperor was elected Pontifex Maximus, the high priest of all the idolatrous systems of the Roman Empire. When the Roman Empire passed away that title of high priest of the rites and mysteries of the cult of mother and child was assumed by the bishop of Rome.

The fifth truth about the harlot is:

E: HER UNNUMBERED PERSECUTIONS! Verse 6 *"And I saw the woman* (the Babylonian false system of idolatry)

The Apocalypse: The Revelation of the Redeemer

drunken with the blood of the saints and with the blood of the martyrs of Jesus." The word *"drunken"* indicates being continually drunk, it was not that she just made a single mistake and slew Gods' servants. John said, *"I saw that drunken whore drunken with the blood of saints…"*

Who invented the Inquisition where thousands of the people of God were brutally burned at the stake and 10's of thousands tortured; who invented the torture rack; and burned at the stake millions of Gods' servants; the scarlet harlot. Sir Robert Anderson of Scotland Yard fame estimated that 50,000,000 Christians were killed by Rome.

This system has not changed. She continues as she commenced in Genesis. The one of the tribulation period will be more intense, more hate filled and horrible than anyone can possibly imagine.

The challenge for us is to be busy about our Father's business; to make Jesus known with every available means to every available person at every available time.

We now want to focus upon:

II: THE HOPE! Verses 7-18 The word "hope" is not used in the normal since of "well I hope he will come to church;" rather it is used with the meaning of "our sure hope of salvation in Jesus Christ." It is a term of certainty, trust, reliance and not doubt.

The hope is not for the evil system that will be filling the earth but for the defeat of the system that has dominated, deluded, destroyed and damned the souls of sinners.

In these verses there are three truths presented to us. First,

A: THE PERPLEXITY IS EXPLAINED! Verses 7-12 the angel asked John in verse 7 why he is marveling; then he informed him that he would remove his perplexities by explaining the mystery to him. I confess that even with the explanations there is enough in these verses to confuse even the best Bible students. Therefore, as much as we can, we will keep it simple.

We have already identified the woman; she is the false harlot church of the tribulation period; she is corrupt as well as corrupting. The beast is the same one we introduced in chapter 13. These verses tell us that *"was, and is not, and shall ascend out of the bottomless pit, and go into perdition"* Verse 11 *"And the beast that was, and is not, even he is the eight, and is of the seventh..."* This is the antichrist, the political system, the revived Roman Empire. The Roman Empire was, and then was not and it will be again.

The seven heads (verse3) are said to (verse 9) seven mountains on which the woman sits; this is a reference to Rome. In one translation of the Catholic bible it says in a footnote that this is a reference to Rome; Rome becomes the center of the final evil system.

There is also the fact that these seven heads (verse 10) "are seven kings." This is a reference to the world governments. The beast is the embodiment of all past world governments. John is told five of these are fallen; that is, five of the world powers are no longer world powers. These were Greece, Babylon, Egypt, Persia and Assyria. When John wrote, Rome was in power. The one to come, the ten horn federation of European states, the eight is of the seventh. That is the revived Roman Empire under eh control of the antichrist.

Verse 8 informs us that the people of the earth will wonder after the beast. They will be deceived and believe the lie.

The second aspect of the hope is:

B: THE PURPOSE EXAMINED! Verses 12-13 We have already discussed much of this therefore, we will give a brief word concerning their purpose. The ten horns are ten kings that do not have, as yet, a kingdom. They are the federated states of Europe. They receive their power from the antichrist. Their one purpose is to help the beast, antichrist, overthrow the harlot and then the Lamb.

Note that these have one mind and neither do they think for themselves. They, with the beast, will make war with the Lamb of God. A simple surface truth for the true church is that if the enemy can get his helpers to have one mind how much more should the body of Christ seek to have His mind!

Daniel 7:24 indicates that three of these kings will rebel. The antichrist will use force to subdue them. Their purpose here is to support the beast in all he does.

The third area of hope is:

The Apocalypse: The Revelation of the Redeemer

C: THE PROSTITUTE IS EXTINGUISHED! Verses 14-18 Verse 16 is very descriptive; the forces of the antichrist devour her. There are two interesting aspects of this; **first**, they are *defeated by the Savior*, verse 14. The antichrist and his federation make war with the Lamb; this is a picture of Revelation 19:11. We are told that the Lamb overcame them; this He did because of Who He is. It was not more military, money or men. What a day that will be!

Observe that there is a company coming with the Lamb. They are *"called, chosen and faithful."* Who are they? They are the blood-washed, spotless redeemed; His church. **Secondly**, verse 17 shares that they are *directed by Sovereignty*. The antichrist is ready to make his move; this transpires in the middle of the tribulation period, he cannot tolerate the system of the harlot anymore. He sets up an image in Jerusalem that the world might worship him. He does away with the harlot false religion; he becomes god. This is referred to as the abomination of desolation spoken about by Daniel and the Lord Jesus.

Verse 17 is one of the most assuring verses in the Bible. It informs us that God is in total charge of all the events that are transpiring. It is He and not the antichrist, false prophet nor the false religious system but God that is in Sovereign control; *"For God has put in their hearts to fulfill His will, and to agree, and to give their kingdom unto the beast, until the words of God shall be fulfilled."* This verse reminds me of Jeremiah 18:7 "…to pluck up, and to pull down, and to destroy it."

Conclusion:
The stage is being set; the foundation is being laid; the world church and the system that replaces the Lord Jesus Christ and His salvation is gaining ground in what was considered at one time to be solid churches and denominations. We need to stand firm and fast for our Lord and His Word.

The Destruction of Babylon
Revelation 18:1-24

Ours is the age of luxury; we are a people preoccupied with and by possessions. Mankind is mark by madness for the material, yet; this day does not begin to rival the lustful appetite for the material just prior to the coming of Jesus in glory. The Bible teaches that Jesus Christ will return to this earth; He will establish His glorious kingdom and He will reign on this earth a thousand years and then He will create a new heaven and a new earth over which He will reign and we shall reign with Him!

He came once and He said He would come again. The first time He was crowned with mockery; the next time He will be crowned with majesty. The time He came He reigned from a tree; the next time He will reign from a throne. The time He ruled with a reed; the next time He will rule with a rod. Make no mistake; this world is destined to climax in the return of Jesus Christ to this earth in power and glory. This great event is described in Chapter 19. Chapters 6-18 provide the details leading up to that coming. Chapters 20-22 are a record of the events following that coming.

The chapters are not in chronology order. Chapter 19 follows in sequence chapter 16; chapters 17 and 18 are an overview of the entire tribulation period.

We are considering the basic world system that will be in operation during the seven-year period covered in chapters 6-18 known as the tribulation. This will be an atheistic ecclesiastical system that will control the economy of the world. It will be headed by the antichrist. There are several thoughts in theses verses that we want to address. First, note:

I: THE PREDICTION! Verses 1-3 The prediction has its foundation in the Old Testament. Does that surprise you?

The Apocalypse: The Revelation of the Redeemer

Prophecy often has a near and far interpretation; the immediate and the future. The prophet Jeremiah had a mind-boggling prophecy for Babylon in chapter 51 of his book. They had captured Jerusalem and God rose up Jeremiah to share a prophecy of destruction for Babylon. Imagine telling people that the greatest empire in the world is going to fall in one day! Yet it happened in 520 B.C. what Jeremiah predicted about Babylon in chapter 51:36-37; 41-44 is applied to the one in Revelation.

There are four truths for us to consider about this prediction in these verses. First:

A: THE RELATOR OF THE PREDICTION! Verse 1 This is another angle. Some have said that this is Jesus but it is not. The word *"another"* is *alos*. There are two Greek words for another. One is *heterious*; it means "another of a different sort or kind." The second, *alos* means "just exactly like the other, another of the same kind." If I said bring me herterious bibilious you could bring me any old book you desired, however; if I said bring me alos bibilious you would have to bring me one just exactly like this one with its marks and notes. This angel is *alos*; just like the one referred to in chapter 17. There is only one Jesus! The relator of this message indicates that this is an extremely important message.

He comes from heaven with power and things that come from heaven usually have abundant power. Here the earth was lighted by his presence. The relator of the prediction is a heavenly messenger. This relates to the dark days tribulation, however, we, as the people of God are to be relators of a heavenly message. We are to be, according to Jesus in Matthew 5:14 *"The light of the world."* We are to be as John the Baptist a reflector of the light of the Lord that lives in us.

One can not be a relator of a heavenly message apart from possessing that message and the source of that message is Jesus. We can not imagine all that would transpire if the people of God were to become serious about relating the prediction of doom of this world and the deliverance that is available through Jesus Christ. Secondly we have:

B: THE RECIPIENT OF THE PREDICTION! In verse 2 the recipient is clearly identified; it is Babylon. Is this a literal city? There are those that consider this to be the case. However, Isaiah 13: 19-22 indicates that Babylon, the city, would never again be inhabited. It is my opinion that this is a reference to the corrupted ecclesiastical system that controlled the economy; it is called Babylon because this system will be like the one of old.

Babylon has always been the word used to describe godlessness; Babel has long been the by word for rebellion, confusion and false religion. It was the first independent political government uniting all the people in rebellion against God (up to this point they had accepted the rule of God). The systems of the world found their organization in the unity aspect of Babel. This does not mean that there must be a worldwide organization or that the whole world is united into one organization. It is not so much an official unity as it is the world or the peoples of the world having the same common disdain of the Person of God and rebellion against all that is of God. Thirdly we have:

C: THE RESULTS FOR THIS PREDICTION! Verse 2 shares that the royal messenger predicts the results before there is any sing of Babylon being destroyed. He cried with *"a strong voice"* indicating the authority with which he spoke. He declared, *"Babylon, the great is fallen, is fallen"* informing us of the assurance with which he spoke. There are some powerful results shared with us in this single verse. There are three such results shared in this verse. The **first** result of her fall is that she became *a habitation of demons*. In verse 2 the word *"devils"* is more accurately translated as *demons*. There is but one devil and he is nothing like the picture presented by Hollywood. Demonic activity is growing in this day and it will become more intense the nearer we get to the coming of Christ. There is at this time a restraint imposed by the Person of the Holy Spirit; this will not be the case during these days. The system of that day will be a demonized one; the demons will be at home in the system of Babylon and will use the system for the purpose of hell.

A **second** result is she will become *the headquarters of deception*; in verse 2 the word *"hold"* is translated incorrect in NAS. There it is translated *"prison;"* it is better understood as a stronghold, fortress or headquarters.

The Apocalypse: The Revelation of the Redeemer

It is important that we observe what is headquartered here; "every foul spirit." What else could be expected in the habitation of demons? There are several spirits referred to in Scripture that we need to be aware of even in our day. There is the spirit of the world (1 Cor. 2:12); the spirit of disobedience (Eph. 2:2); a spirit of error (1 John 4:6); there is a spirit of fear (1Tim. 1:7); and a spirit of bondage (Rom. 8:15). These deceiving sprits are working like maggots in a garbage heap in the system of ecclesiastical and economic control.

We desperately need the Spirit of discernment to know what is of God. This is needed in the area of Christian living. The enemy and his emissaries are constantly at work seeking to deceive the people of God.

The **third** result is that she will become *the home of defilement*; shared with us in verse 2 in the words, *"And a cage of every unclean and hateful bird."* What do these strange words mean? A portion of the answer is given by noting the parables of Jesus in Matthew 13. There a mustard seed is sown, the tree grows to unnatural proportions. The tree symbolizes the kingdom that is under the control of the enemy during these days. The birds of the air lodge in the branches of this tree. The birds in the parables were stealing the gospel seed; now their home is in the tree.

They are *"caged"* that is a home of birds. They are *"unclean"* that is their defiling nature. They are *"hateful"* that is their actions. The system that will be in charge of the world is one that is demonic, deceptive and defiling. If it is going to be true in that day be assured that the enemy is already at work in our day using the same strategy.

The fourth truth about the prediction is:

D: THE REASONS FOR THE PREDICTION! Verse 3 One might wonder why God judges Babylon so harshly. There are at least three reasons given in verse 3. **First**, we have *the extent of her seductive influence*; *"For all nations."* This is worldwide in its scope; this is not some localized issue. It reaches the entire world with its corruption. **Secondly** there is *the explanation of the seductive influence; "have drunk the wine of the wrath of her fornication."* They (the nations of the world) are intoxicated (controlled and thrilled) by the wrath (her fury upon those that were not in her system) of her fornication. The word fornication helps us understand a portion of what was/ will be transpiring. It means sexual immorality; spiritually it is mixing with ungodliness. It is associated with idolatry and the occult. The **third** reason for the prediction is *the effect of her seductive influence*. Riches abound; this system provides ways for sensuality to be joined with the sacred and for those doing so to be made wealthy. There is little wonder that the judgment of God will fall on those in that day that are responsible for such heinous, flagrant sins against all that is Godly.

The prediction of this angel will come to pass just as it did when Jeremiah said Babylon would fall.

The second thought is:

II: THE PLEA! Verses 4-5 The plea, like the prediction is recorded in Jeremiah 51: 45 *"My people, go ye out of the midst of her, and deliver ye every man his soul from the fierce anger of the Lord."* Verse 47 states *"...the days come, that I will do judgment upon the graven images of Babylon: and her whole land shall be confounded."* There are some noteworthy facts that are shared with us in these verses. First, observe:

A: THE SOURCE OF THE PLEA! Verse 4 *"And I heard another voice from heaven;"* this is not the voice of the angel that gave the prediction. This is another voice. The source of the plea is *"from heaven;"* the voice could but does not command. It is in my opinion, the voice of the Father that is pleading. Does this strike you as being strange? It may but this is the same pattern that Jesus used when He ministered among men. His call was for volunteers. The response was not one of compulsion but one of commitment.

The voice is the voice of authority yet it issues a plea. In this day of grace He pleads for the sinner to come in repentance. In that day the sinner is not called to repentance but to retribution.

Secondly consider,

B: THE SUBJECTS OF THE PLEA! Verse 4 *"...My people;"* these are tribulation saints; those that have come to know Jesus through the ministry of those sealed Jewish missionaries.

The Apocalypse: The Revelation of the Redeemer

These will refuse to take the mark of the beast. These saints will be pressured by family and friends, as well as their finances to become a part of the system that is controlling the world.

It is easy for us to say what another should or should not do but consider a hypothetical case. Here is a man that, because of his commitment to Christ, cannot buy food for his family, he can not receive medical attention and is loosing his job. All of this will be corrected if he will "adjust his position" and get with the program. What would you recommend that this man do? What form of logic would you use to persuade him to either become a part of the system or to remain faithful to Christ? How many of us would suggest that he go through the form but inwardly be faithful to Christ? Is that not the compromise that has crippled Christianity in this day?

Thirdly we have:

C: THE SUBJECT OF THE PLEA! Verse 4 This is a pleas for separation; *"come out of her."* In Jeremiah's prophecy the Lord said for His people to come out of Babylon and deliver every man his soul. I do not believe it is possible for us to fully understand the price that these tribulation saints will be called upon to pay for their separation. These verses are literal and will be literally fulfilled during those days. However, I believe there is a present application because the sprit of antichrist is already at work in this world. The subject of this plea is not a new subject for the people of God; He called Abraham, Lot, Moses, Israel and His church to be separated from the vile and vexing elements of this worldly system. God is calling His people to separation; we are to be in the world and yet, not a part of its system. I heard about a congregational meeting to discuss the kind of pastor the church needed. One man said, "We want a good mixer." That is what a lot of folks think they need but the real need is for a good separator.

The world has the idea that it will be the most wonderful thing when all religions get together. If you want recognition from a civic club or a medal from the mayor simply be the promoter of a national brotherhood day where all religions embrace and says your faith is just as good as mine. The world says, "Isn't it nice, those religious fellows are finally getting together! That's just wonderful." This is the sort of thing that makes sense to the world and it should not surprise us because this is the system of the antichrist. When we speak of separation it is called arrogance and bigotry. Some even call it un-American. God says in 11 Corinthians 6:14-18 that His people are to be separated.

There are a number of reasons people criticize public speakers. The easiest way I know for one to be the recipient of a verbal public attack is to share that a church that does not preach and teach the word of God is not worthy of their support. When one says something like that among the responses he will hear is, "My mother and grandmother were in that church." That really is not the issue; if they do not preach and teach the Bible, get out!

A lady asked a preacher what she should do because her church no longer preached the gospel of Christ. He responded, "Get out!" She then said, "Could you explain what you mean by that?" He said; Watch my lips...Get Out." She got mad, got out...of the meeting that is.

A pastor asked at another meeting "What if your denomination no longer holds to the inspiration of the Bible or preaches the gospel?" The reply was "Get out!" "What will I do?" He got mad left the meeting and worked against the preacher and the meeting. A year or so later the two men met. The one that had been mad...got out...got saved and started a Bible church.

Dr. Adrian Rogers shared this true experience. He was new in an area and decided he would attend a ministerial meeting. At that meeting they were voting on receiving into their membership a man that was a member of a false cult. They did not believe in the deity of Christ, salvation by grace, hell and they have another book they say is as inspired as the Bible. Dr. Rogers asked, "Why are you voting on this, this is supposed to be an organization of Christian ministers?" This man has missionaries trying to win your members from the faith you proclaim. One said, "O, Adrian, if we don't cooperate we will never bring in the kingdoms." He did not know that the kingdom is not going to be brought in by a homogenization of unbelief but when Jesus Christ comes to rule in righteousness. Dr. Rogers simply said, "When you vote him in, you are voting me out." They voted the false religion in!

The Apocalypse: The Revelation of the Redeemer

I am not suggesting that there are not civic projects that we ought not be involved in, we should. Further, this is not saying that Christians should not be involved in politics. We should!

There are those that say, "I know they do not believe the Bible, but I'm going to stay in it as a missionary." God says get out as quickly as you can. Those that deny the faith and the Bible do not deserve your support. It will be a great day when believers put their tithes, time and talent in churches that preach the gospel of Jesus Christ. One preacher heard a message on the importance of preaching the gospel. He was impressed and said to the speaker "I think I'll have a gospel Sunday each year and preach the gospel."

From my heart I want to say two important things to each of our hearts. First, if your membership is in a church that you can not support with your presence, prayers and participation through your time, tithes and talents you should move that membership to a church you can support. Second, if you have the privilege of being in a church that preaches and teaches the word of God renew your commitment and determine in your own mind and heart that you will support her and her pastor and teachers with your prayers, presence and participation.

Forth, we have:

D: THE SERIOUSNESS OF THE PLEA! Verses 4-5 Why is this plea so serious? Note the words of verse 4, *"That ye be not partakers of her sins, and that ye receive not of her plagues."* It will be and is now possible for God's people to allow themselves, whether directly or through deception, to become involved in a system of satanic sacrilege. If this is done the word makes it clear that those that do the partaking will experience the plagues.

Verse 5 gives further insight into the seriousness of the plea to come out of Babylon, *"For her sins have reached unto heaven."* There is, I think, a play on words. It was Nimrod that decided he would build a tower to heaven. Well, he or his idolatrous system has succeeded but they reach heaven by laying sin upon sin. God declares, *"Your tower of iniquity has reached to heaven."*

The last part of the verse is significant, *"...and God hath remembered her iniquities."* God has a perfect memory if you do not get forgiveness and a perfect forgetter if you do. There are some things God cannot remember. For example, suppose you say, "Lord, do You remember that time I did such and such?" The Lord responds, "No, it is in the sea of My forgetfulness." But there is not one sin He has forgotten that has not been confessed and placed under the blood of Jesus. They are written with a pen of iron and ink of lead and letters of flame. We are to confess our sins and then He forgives and forgets them.

The third truth is:

III: THE PAYMENT! Verses 6-8 and 21-24 This is one of the most sobering sections of Scripture in the Bible. The final check will one day be drawn; payment will be made in full. The world is now "enjoying the fruits of her labor and she rejoices in her wealth and wickedness," but as one of the songs states, "There will be a pay day at the end of life's road." It is better stated by Paul in Galatians 6:7-8, all that is sown will eventually come up and will be reaped. For those that *sow to the Spirit* this will be a time of glory, for those that *sow to the flesh* it will be a time of groaning. There are two disturbing truths that desperately need to be observed about this payment. First,

A: THE RETRIBUTION IS DOUBLE! Verses 6-7 How many of us have reaped a double dividend on an investment? Would you value the opportunity to do it again? Not many of us would shun a proven (absolutely no risk) investment that would double our initial investment in a three year period. Not many of us would refuse such an offer in the area of finance. What we are dealing with in these verses of Revelation 18 is not merely finance. There are two elements of this retribution; **first**, note *that the fact is apparent* as verse 6 clearly states in that the word *"double"* is used three times in this single verse. A person would have to deliberately close his mind not to see that the retribution upon this hellish system will be doubled. *"Double upon her double"* is a principle written in the Mosaic Law (Ex. 22: 4, 7 and 9). Its purpose was to deter crime. If a man knew he had to pay back double he might hesitate before involving himself in criminal activity. **Secondly**, verse 7 shares that *the foundation is arrogance*. This entire verse flows with arrogance, pride and presumption. *"She has glorified herself and lived in luxury."* She says of herself, *"I sit as a queen and am no widow and shall see no sorrow."* She is so filled with arrogance that she refuses to see reality. She believes that her prosperity, power and pleasure will be hers forever. She cannot even imagine anything that would or could disturb her domain. The phrase, *"Sit as queen"* enables us to see her feeling of superiority and at least in her mind she is sovereignty independent. She is her own god. She is like the rich fool that declared in Luke 12 that his possessions were all he needed. This is also the arrogance displayed by the Laodiceian church in Revelation 3.

The words *"So much torment and sorrow give her"* inform us that she has been judged in proportion to her sin. This is the foundation of her double retribution. She is judged according to the character of her sin.

A thought for our day is that one reaps not only what he sows but he reaps more than he sows because the seed will eventually produce and the one sewing will receive either the benefit or the burden of the sown seed; if not in this life surely in the one to come.

The second aspect of the payment is:

B: THE RUIN IS DEVASTATING! Verses 8 and 21-24
Before we address the devastation it is proper that we consider the source of the devastation. Verse 8 concludes, *"For strong is the Lord God who judgeth her."* This is God Himself and not an angel or agent sent from Him. The sin of Babylon (the system of ecclesiastical corruption that controls the economy) is so vile and vexing that God will execute this judgment Himself. It will be learned, albeit to late, that *"It is a fearful thing to fall into the hands of the living God"* (Heb. 19:31). There are four things to note about this devastating ruin in these verses. **First**, verse 8 reveals *the vindication of the ruin*; *"therefore shall her plagues come."* *"Therefore"* informs us that this devastating ruin is coming because of the previous actions of Babylon. To vindicate is to inflict punishment by way of repayment. God is repaying Babylon. This is not based upon emotions but upon and according to the sins of Babylon. God is not a capricious Being that is not stable. His actions are according to His word. The actions and

attitude of Babylon are not the result of ignorance but they we committed with full intelligence. **Second**, verse 21 shares *the violence of the ruin*. I will not speculate as to what the *"Stone"* may or may not be. The verse indicates by the use of the words *"Like a great millstone"* that it may not be a literal stone in the sea. The main thing is that at one moment Babylon is strong and arrogant and is sought by the world. The next moment she is gone, forever gone. This is done with such violence that it can not be missed that the One behind the devastating ruin is the Lord God Almighty. **Thirdly**, verses 22-23 share *the vastness of the ruin*. In these verses there are six "no mores." There will be *no more music*. This is a symbol of joy and mirth. Music does have charm and in this day of devastating ruin all entertainers and entertainment will disappear. However, this was not the kind of music that honored God. Dr. Ironside said, "Music charmed the weary sons of Cain as they sought to make themselves happy in this world apart from God;" our world seeks to escape the reality of life through this media. The Beatles were paid, I'm told, a hundred thousand dollars a word for "I love you, ya, ya, ya." There will be *no more mechanics* that is no trade. The tools of the craftsmen will be silent. This means the wheels of industry will cease. There will not be one building being built. There will be *no more mills*, that is, food production for mankind will no longer be in operation. There will be no more marriages. There will not be heard the sounds of rejoicing as heard at the wedding feast, for even love will die. Compare Jeremiah's words in 25:9-11!

There is an additional "no more" that is not stated in those words but is nonetheless a reality. There is *no more mercy*. When the devastating ruin begins mercy will be no more.

The **fourth** truth about the devastating ruin in verses 23-24 is *the validity of the ruin*. Just in case anyone thinks God is being to severe we are given three reasons for this action. First, she will experience this wrath because she worshipped wealth and luxury, playing the harlot to the merchants of the world (verse 23). Second, she will be judged because of her witchcraft and doctrine of demons that led many astray (verse 23). Third she will be judged because of the blood of the "prophets and saints that was

The Apocalypse: The Revelation of the Redeemer

found in her (verse 24). She must pay for her murders and persecutions inflicted upon god's people.

The fourth major truth is:

IV: THE PRODUCT! Verses 9-20 With all that is transpiring what would be the most natural product of this devastating experience? A mere reading of these verses will reveal that what is actually produced is a far cry form what one might hope to be produced. There are two diametrically opposite products in these verses. These reveal in a fresh way the importance of perspective. The first product we will observe is:

A: THE DISTRESS OF HUMANITY! Verses 9-19 The word "distress" means "the state of being in serious trouble or in mental or physical anguish." Now note these words *"bewail, lament, weep, mourn, fear, weeping, waling, cried and cast dust on their heads."* This is indeed a picture of distress. Who is experiencing this distress? These verses reveal that humankind is divided into three groups. All of these have profited from the cities influence, trade, and power, from its wickedness and from its wealth. In each of these groups the expression, *"Alas, alas"* is used (10, 16 and 19). It means disappointment, consternation and at times expected disaster, an exclamation of sorrow or regret. The **first** group experiencing this distress (verses 9-10) is *the monarchs*. These are probably allied with the beast. Their power is centered in the city. They have been close, *"Committed fornication and lived deliciously with her"* but now they stand afar off, watching, wringing their hands over their losses. These seem to recognize that this fall of Babylon is a visitation of the judgment of God. In spite of their power, armies and resources of science and technology, they are impotent to save their city. The **second** group experiencing this distress (verses 11-17a) is *the merchants*. There are twenty-eight categories of merchandise, including the *"souls of men"* listed. This is the world's great vanity fair. It offers articles of adornment and display, beautiful things to grace the mansions of the world's millionaires. It deals in spices and perfumes, in delicacies for the table, in provisions for banquets, in slaves and in the souls of men. The merchants harnessed these industries, the wealth of the world passed through her clearinghouse. Now nothing is left of the city. Her giant warehouses have gone up in smoke; the shopping centers are reduced to rubble. The world is falling apart and these are crying because sales are down. The fact is that neither power nor possessions can stay the hand of God. The **third** group experiencing this distress (verses 17b-19) is *the mariners*. This is the greatest seaport city of the world; all the transporters of merchandise must shut down because the world's commercial center has been destroyed. Those that have made their money and expanded their operations by means of Babylon's influence and needs are shut down because all business comes to a standstill.

The second product is:

B: THE DELIGHT OF HEAVEN! Verse 20 These words are strange to our ears; *"Rejoice over her."* This accomplished because justice is being served. This is natural. It is a principle of human nature, but with God there is never a wrong spirit but He does deal justly with sin.

The cause of heaven's delight must be noted. It is due to God avenging His people. The delight is in heaven. Earth has no joy during these days of darkness. The world now rejoices in its wealth and wickedness but the day is soon coming when the earth will be silent. The songs of mirth will be songs of misery.

In God's grace your songs of misery can be transformed into a song of majesty. You can be redeemed by the blood of His Son and escape the destruction of this earth.

Christ Coming for His Church
Revelation 19:1-8

The greatest experiences of the church are still in the future. That is not to imply that she has not or that she is not now being blessed or that she is not a blessing. It simply says that there are greater things in store for her.

We can read of these grand events that are shortly to be experienced by the church. A part of what is to be experienced is recorded in Revelation chapter 19. There are two exciting events presented to us that should be a source of joy and jubilation for all the saints of God.

In the first 10 verses we read of that time when Christ crowns the church. This is indeed a beautiful scene of joy. The church has been anxiously waiting that time when she shall become the bride of Christ Jesus.

We have this illustrated for us in any of the parables given by Jesus. For example, consider the parable in Matthew 22: "the kingdom of heaven is like unto a certain king, who made a marriage for his son." In addition, the parable of the ten virgins in Matthew 25 should also be carefully considered.

This event, of course, follows Christ coming for His church and the time of tribulation on earth and the judgment seat of Christ in heaven.

We will consider two thoughts in these verses. First observe the:

I: UNUSUAL REJOICING! Verses 1-6 Heaven is a place of joy and celebration. It is a place that is really quite emotional. This rejoicing is unusual only if we consider it from our present perspective. In order to properly understand this rejoicing we must view this scene from heavens perspective. Before we address the rejoicing it is imperative that we understand that all the praise is given to God. Verse 1 concludes, "Unto the Lord our God." He is the only one worthy of worship. Further the words *"Alleluia"* and *"amen"* are significant. *"Alleluia"* means, "Praise the Lord;" it is used four times in these verses and this is the only time it is used in the bible. It is translated "Praise the Lord" in many of the Psalms. The word *"amen"* is the highest word of praise that human speech can utter. It is a heavenly word of avowal, of committal to truth. These are heavenly words; they are rendered in praise to Him that sets on the throne. If I am going to be a part of that rejoicing multitude, I want to live a life that praises Him now.

The first aspect of this unusual rejoicing is over His:

A: DELIVERANCE! Verse 1 Our deliverance is witnessed in that beautiful word "Salvation." The host of heaven is rejoicing over their deliverance. Christ is about to appear with His church to complete the deliverance He began at Calvary. The great day of deliverance for all creation will surely come to pass. It is wonderful to know that we do not have to wait to know that deliverance is presently ours in Christ. Can you rejoice with the host of heaven over your deliverance?

Secondly, they were rejoicing over His:

B: DESTRUCTION! Verse 2-3 Verse 2 begins by saying *"for true and righteous are His judgments;"* all of His judgments whether upon good or evil are true and righteous. If that could only be said of man our world would indeed be a better place.

Now we see His destruction, *"He hath judged the great whore...her smoke rose up for ever and ever."* The harlot has received a just retribution for her evil, and her destruction is an everlasting witness to the righteous judgment of God. The destruction of the great whore is given in chapter 17 and 18 of Revelation. Who is this harlot? She is the false religious system in chapter 17. In chapter 18 she is the economic system of man. Both of theses are judged and destroyed by the God of heaven. The permanence of His destruction is seen in verse 3, *"And her smoke rose up for ever and ever."*

The third thing that brings rejoicing is a:

The Apocalypse: The Revelation of the Redeemer

C: DECLARATION! Verses 4-5 All the redeemed now join in rejoicing. They say *"Amen, alleluia."* Then a voice from out of the throne says, *"Praise our God, all ye His servants."* Does this include you? I believe this third *"alleluia"* is a declaration of the greatness of God. Have you by your life declared God's greatness?

The fourth item for which they rejoice is His:

D: DOMINION! Verse 6 the final shout comes from the whole host of heaven. They say, *"Alleluia; for the Lord God omnipotent reigneth."* The Psalmist declared, "The Lord reigneth, let the earth rejoice." The prayer of the saints of all ages is about to be answered. We have prayed, "Thy kingdom come..." and now that prayer is about to be answered. The hallelujah time for heaven and earth is at hand. This is that time when His enemies shall be His footstool; the time when every knee shall bow and every tongue confess. When He comes again it shall be a time of dominion by Christ, all men regardless of power, position, and prestige will bow at His feet! If He is to, and He shall, have dominion and if all men shall bow in that day, and they shall; doesn't it make sense to bow before Him now as Lord and Savior.

The second thought is:

II: THE UNIQUE RELATIONSHIP! Verses 7-8 This is not to infer that we do not presently possess a wonderful relationship with Christ; however, our present relationship will fade away in comparison to that unique relationship that we shall experience. Verse 7 shares this unique relationship in the words, *"For the marriage of the Lamb is come."*

During the time of Christ the marriage was in three parts. First there was the betrothal stage this was usually arranged by the parents when the children were very young. This was much stronger than our present day engagement period. This provided the children the opportunity to grow in their relationship. Second there was the step of maturity. The groom would go to the house of the bride and escort her to the house he had prepared for them. They exchanged gifts, the bride gave her dowry, and the bridegroom gave gifts to the bride. The third step was the consummating event; the wedding feast. To this gala event would be invited many guest to share in this time of joy. This is what has and will happen with the church.

There are two persons that I would like for us to notice in this unique relationship. First note the:

A: BRIDEGROOM! Verse 7 We are not standing while the music plays here comes the bride, but here comes the bridegroom. He is the central figure of attraction.

Verse 7 indicates that He is entitled to two things from the entire heavenly host. **First** He is the cause of our *rejoicing*, *"Let us be glad and rejoice."* This is true because the waiting is over. It seems as if He has also been anxious for this event. We are to be glad and rejoice because He is glad and rejoicing. Secondly we are to give Him *reverence*, *"And give honor to Him."* This is done because His marriage is come. It is He that has made it all possible. It is totally because of Him that these events are taking place.

The second person that we are introduced to is the:

B: BRIDE! Verses 7-8 Who is the bride? Many would try to convince us that the bride is Israel. No! Israel is the wife of Jehovah. The bride is none other than His church. There are two important things for us to closely consider as we look at the bride, His church. **First**, observe, in verse 7, her *preparation*; *"And His wife hath made herself ready."* Carefully note that it is the wife that is engaged in the preparation; not the Bridegroom. He has always been prepared. If she had to make herself ready that tells us that she was not ready prior to this time. Please keep in mind that the church is going to be presented to Christ as a pure virgin; without spot or blemish. That surely cannot be said of the church as she presently exists. It is my opinion that this preparation takes place at the judgment seat of Christ. It is sad but true that all saints will not be prepared to meet Christ when He comes for His church.

Before we reign with Him, there must be a reckoning with Him. The judgment seat for many will not be a happy event; for many it will be sorrow and shame because of our failure to build upon the foundation of Christ with gold, silver and precious stones.

The Apocalypse: The Revelation of the Redeemer

Secondly, verse 8, shares her *performance*. Her performance can best be illustrated by referring to the clothing of Jesus' day. The people wore two pieces of clothes and they are illustrated in verse 8. **First** there was the *tunic*, *"And to her was granted that she should be arrayed in fine linen, clean and white."* This is the garment given to the Christian and the church by Christ. It is the tunic, the garment worn under the outer garment. This is the imputed righteousness of Christ; that which seals us; that which saves us. It is a free gift to us from Christ. This is our positional righteousness that is ours when He washed our sins away. **Second** there was the *toga*, *"For the fine linen is the righteousness of the saints."* This is the toga, the outer garment that is made up of our works and service rendered to Christ. This is our practical righteousness. This is the garment that we are weaving by our own hands. This is why Paul said in 1 Corinthians 15:58 *"Always abounding in the work of the Lord."* The toga that you and I are weaving for ourselves will belong to us for eternity.

Conclusion:
This is an awesome day. We are making our wedding garment. Do you like what you are weaving? There is something missing in these verses. There is no mention of the ceremony. It is my opinion that this union of Christ and His church will be a private matter, a time of love unknown to man up to this point. The good news is that if you do not know Him, you can receive His imputed righteousness by coming to the foot of the cross in repentance and faith. If you do not like the garment you are weaving now is the time to surrender to His Lordship and allow Him to use you in any manner that will bring glory to Him.

The Marriage Supper
Revelation 19:7-10

Think of the most beautiful wedding you ever attended. What we have presented to us in this passage is an event that the Lord Jesus has been waiting for.

This is sufficient to inform us that the greatest experiences of the church are before her; her marriage to her Beloved.

In revelation 19:7-10 there are two thoughts, first we have:

I: THE COUPLE! Verses 7-8 Verse 7 declares, *"For the marriage of the Lamb is come and His wife hath made herself ready."* In order for this couple to be where they are there has been a betrothal and a presentation. What waits is the consummation. As we observe this couple we will note first,

A: THE BRIDEGROOM! Verse 7 *"For the marriage of the Lamb is come."* This is an "odd" statement to us. He is the central figure. The music plays "Here comes the Bridegroom." Consider two things about Him. **First**, His *designation is important*; He is *"The Lamb."* One of my favorite songs states, "Precious Lamb of glory... loves most wondrous story, heart of God redemption of man, worship the Lamb of glory." He is designated as a Lamb and not a lion. He is the Lamb rejected and crucified; He is the Lamb raised and crowned. It is appropriate that we join our hearts in singing "O, hallelujah praise the Lamb." **Second** their *delight is inspiring*, *"Let us be glad and rejoice."* Who is "us?" and why is there rejoicing? The ones rejoicing are those that know Him. Their delight is also observed in their reverence, *"And gives honor to Him."* This is done because He has made it all possible. This will be a time of sweet submission to Him.

Secondly we have:

The Apocalypse: The Revelation of the Redeemer

B: THE BRIDE! Verses 7-8 Who is the bride? The Bridegroom is Christ; the bride is the church. There are three figures used to present the church. She is a building (shows usefulness), a body (show unity), and a bride (shows union). She is not Israel; Israel is the wife of Jehovah. There are two things to consider. **First**, verse 7, *the bride is ready*, *"And His wife hath made herself ready."* The expression "hath made" surely indicates that she was not always ready. It is my opinion that she made herself ready at the judgment seat of Christ. Remember, only saved people are at the judgment seat of Christ. Before we reign with Him there is a reckoning with Him. All the dross and impurities are burned. The bride is then presented without spot and blemish. **Second**, verse 8 informs us that *the bride is robed.* The robe is symbolic of righteousness. This righteousness is positional (verse 8a); that which is imputed by Christ at salvation. This righteousness is also practical (8b). Here the word actually means *"righteous deeds."* We are weaving our wedding garment.

The second thought is:

II: THE CELEBRATION! Verses 9-19 There is no mention of the ceremony. I believe the union of Christ and His church is a private matter. However, there will be what we would call a public celebration. In Jesus day this was an indication of the Fathers wealth. Could the thousand years be the marriage supper???

Note first,

A: THE CALLED TO THE SUPPER! Verse 9 *"Blessed are they which are called."* It is my opinion that the called are the Old Testament saints, and the tribulation saints. Matthew 11:11 states, "He that is least in the Kingdom of heaven is greater than he (John)." All the saved that were/are not a part of the church will be the invited guest at the marriage supper.

Secondly we have:

B: THE CORRECTION OF THE SERVANT! Verse 10 John is so overcome with all that is happening that he falls before the wrong one. This happens a lot in this day. The correction is *"Worship God."*

Note: the use of the name of Jesus. It is before this name that everything will bow (Ph. 2: 5-11). It is little wonder that we sing, "Precious name, o how sweet."

Conclusion:
The primary question is "Do I know Jesus? Is He my Savior, and am I a part of His church?"

The Revelation of the Redeemer
Revelation 19:11-21

Biblical history reveals that Satan used every possible devise to prevent the initial coming of Christ. It is my conviction that the words of Jesus in John 8:44 reveal a portion of the strategy of Satan to accomplish all his plans. It reveals his motive is to murder and his message is a life. From the murder of Abel by Cain to the plot of Haman all the way to Herod's murdering the innocent children was the hellish plot of Satan to prevent the coming of Christ to redeem mankind.

Just so he will do everything in the realm of his power to prevent His coming the second time...not in the rapture but in His revelation. This is because when the Lord Jesus comes in His revelation it will not be as a Savior but as Sovereign; not as a redeemer but as ruler. He will not be on a tree but on a throne. Therefore, the closer we get to His coming the more intense will be the demonic hostility. It must be understood that Satan's main objective is to destroy Christ. People are pawns in his hands to help him achieve his purpose.

He was not successful in preventing the incarnation neither will he succeed in keeping Jesus from the throne of this earth.

There are two challenging truths presented to us in these verses from Revelation 19 that should inspire us in our daily walk with the Lord Jesus Christ. First we will consider:

I: THE COMING OF THE LORD! Verses 11-16 Chronically verse 11 of chapter 19 follows the sixth vial or bowl being poured out in chapter 16: 12-16. There are four things we want to notice about the coming of the Lord in these verses. First,

A: HIS AIM! Verse 11 His aim is two-fold. **First** there is the *revelation of Christ*, *"And I saw heaven open."* It opened in

4:1 for the church to be raptured; it opens now for Him to come with His church. This is seven years later. There are no signs that precede the rapture. There are signs that precede His revelation. His coming in rapture is not visible to the earth. His coming in revelation is visible to the earth. The **second** aim is the *retribution of Christ*, "And in righteousness He doth judge and make war." Observe that He is on a white horse. Zechariah had prophesied that He would enter on the donkey and that has happened. This is a picture of a triumphant procession, yet; this was only after victory. The victory is already won.

His title *"Faithful and True"* make it essential that He come. He said He would and if He is faithful and true He must. He is now the judge. He was judged by men now He is the judge. All that He does is in *"righteousness"* for He is The Righteous One!

In the coming of the Lord we also witness:

B: HIS APPEARANCE! Verses 12-13 His appearance in His revelation is drastically different from His appearance as the redeemer. There are two special features of His appearance that we want to note. **First** we have *His nature* is shared in the words *"His eyes were a flame of fire"* in verse 12. Those are piercing, penetrating eyes that see all. These are different eyes from those that looked at Peter after his denial; those were filled with compassion. The time of compassion has ended. His nature is also seen in the words, *"And on His head were many crowns."* This is symbolic of His sovereignty. In 11 Samuel 12:30 David took the crown from off the king of Rabbah and put it on his head. This was the custom in Eastern orient settings. When you removed a king you took his crown. Kings collected crowns. It was a demonstration of their power and position. The beast in 13:1 had seven crowns for seven kingdoms. The second beast had 10 crowns showing dominion and power.

We are told, *"On His (Christ) head were many crowns."* How many is many? He had all of them. This is shared in verse 15 "Smite the nations and rule them with a rod of iron." He will have the sovereign rule over all. That is a fair exchange for one crown of thorns isn't it?

In His appearance we note **secondly** *His name* in verses 12-13 and 16. There are three separate aspects of His name. **First** it

The Apocalypse: The Revelation of the Redeemer

is a name of *mystery*, "*That no man knew.*" It is strange that commentators spend pages telling what the name is. That is ridicules. Do I know this name? No! Nor will I speculate. I like those things in the Bible I do not know. If I knew all that I would know as much as God and God would be in trouble. It is not taught that the Bible reveals the mind of God on everything. The world has scorned and cursed the name of the Lord Jesus now they cannot know Him even if they want to know Him. **Second** it is a name of *ministry*; verse 13, "*His name is called The Word of God.*" His ministry is different at this coming. Now (in that day) it is a ministry of battle and blood. He is heavens minister of war. He is wearing a wardrobe of war. They are blood spattered. A portion of this may be from Calvary but also from the defeat of the armies at Armageddon. **Third** it is a name of *majesty*; verse 16, "*King of kings and Lord of lords.*" Pilate called Him "Jesus of Nazareth, King of the Jews." He was close. The difference is here He is not King of the Jews but the King of kings.

The name we do not know speaks of His deity, His eternal Being. The second reveals His first coming as God's revelation to man. The third speaks of His coming to rule the entire earth.

The third truth about the coming of the Lord is:

C: HIS ARMIES! Verse 14 Who are the armies of heaven. Colossians 3:4 states, "*When Christ who is our life shall appear, then shall ye also appear with Him glory.*" This is at His revelation not the rapture. Is this army made up of Angels? Is it Old Testament saints? This army is, at least in my opinion, the church of Christ.

Try to imagine this scene. The world is in darkness; tragedy after tragedy has occurred for seven years; they look up and see the sky parting like a scroll and the Holy One rides forth followed by the redeemed clothed in a brilliant white linen and glory filling the sky. Indeed, "What a day that will be…!"

The forth truth is:

D: HIS AUTHORITY! Verses 15-16 It is Christ and not we that do the fighting. We are coming to rule with Him in His kingdom by grace. It is the Lords battle. That is the principle that is in operation today. It is the Lord that does the work through us and not our effort or energies; when we use human strength and wisdom we are defeated; when we are humble vessels His power is unleashed and He wins all the battles. The Lord said to Jehoshaphat in 11 Chronicles 20:15, *"The battle is not yours, but Gods."* The battle we face in life and as a church are not ours, but His. We should desire to be instruments that are useable for Him to use without hindrance to accomplish His work.

Verse 16 shares with us His weapon in the words, *"A sharp sword;"* however, this sharp sword is proceeding from His mouth. This is not a dagger but a full sword. He is prepared to put down the rebellion of man. This sword that proceeds out of His mouth is His word. His word is so powerful that He spoke to a fig tree and it withered. Try it! He spoke to the wind and it ceased. He spoke to demons and they fled. Here He speaks and war is over. He spoke and the world was created; He will speak and it will be cremated.

We do not need any carnal weapons; our defense is Christ. His word was so patent that soldiers fell to the ground when He said, *"I am He."* We have that very word; we are to be faithful in giving the word. His word is its own defense. We need to share it without embarrassment.

The expression *"rod of iron"* helps us understand His awesome authority. He will be a perfect dictator. He will crash outward rebellion the instant it raises its head.

Secondly we have:

II: THE CONQUEST OF THE LORD! Verses 17-21 From chapter 16:14 we learn that those gathered for this battle at Armageddon are here because of demonic drawing. Demon possessed leaders from all over the world will be persuaded to come here. It is not that God needs them there but to reveal His power and His control.

Those in verse 19 are drawn to Armageddon. Many battles throughout history have been fought here. It was here that Deborah and Barak defeated Sisera. Gideon defeated the Medianites; Josiah was slain here. But nothing will be like the last battle.

The place was for years a swamp. One of the first things the Israelites did was to drain it; they admitted they did not know why. Napoleon commented that it was the most natural battlefield in the entire world.

There are two thoughts about the conquest of the Lord that we will consider. First,

A: THE BANQUET OF THE FOUL! Verses 17-18 An angel makes a special announcement. He is calling to the birds. Those that have refused to be guest at the marriage supper of the Lamb are going to be supper. Those that reject the invitation will be a banquet for the foul of heaven. It is not a small thing to refuse any invitation from the lips of God.

Secondly,

B: THE BANISHMENT OF FOES! Verses 20-21 Here the beast and false prophet are cast alive into the lake of fire. The Greek word for *"cast"* is hurled. Like one would hurl a javelin at a target. Remember chapter 13:4 *"Who is like the beast and who is able to make war with him?"* They thought he was invincible. He is no match for Christ. They are herald alive. They are still here after one thousand years; then the devil is cast into the lake of fire. Then all the lost of all time will be there tormented day and night forever.

Conclusion:

Jesus is coming for His church and with His church. The issue at hand is for those of us that know Him to be engaged in sharing the good news of salvation so that those that do not know Him will have the opportunity to experience His salvation.

Reigning with the Redeemer
Revelation 20:1-10

The order of events for the last days is, as I understand them, the rapture of the church; this is an event that can occur at any moment. This is followed by the tribulation on earth; unbelievers are left here to experience what Jesus called the "Great Tribulation." It is called in the Old Testament "A time of trouble such as was not." This is when the antichrist will appear; he will offer peace and enter into a covenant with Israel. This will be broken when he reveals his purpose to be God by the "Abomination of desolation" when he sets himself up as God. Then will follow the battle of Armageddon when the antichrist and his forces are seized against Jerusalem and have gathered to make war with God. He will be defeated. Then the Lord Jesus will return to this earth, not for but with His saints and we will enter the time called the millennium.

There are three basic schools of thought concerning the millennium. The word "millennium" means a thousand years. It is the age of perfect peace and righteousness in which the Lord Jesus will rule this earth. The three schools of thought deal with this section of Scripture. These are: a) the *A-millenniumal*. These believe in the literal second coming of Christ but they do not believe in a millennial reign. These say God is through with Israel as a nation, that there are no more prophecies concerning Israel to be fulfilled. These believe the promises to Abraham are spiritually fulfilled in the church. These believe that the church and the preaching of the Gospel is the millennium and we should not look for a literal thousand-year reign; second, b) the *Post-millenniumal*. These believe (their ranks have decreased considerably) that Jesus is coming back after the millennium. These believe that through the preaching of the Gospel and the work of the church that a

The Apocalypse: The Revelation of the Redeemer

golden age of peace will be accomplished. They believe that things are going to get better and better in spite of the clear word that there will be "perilous times" and that "men shall depart from the faith." Third, c) the *Pre-millenniumal* (I personally do not consider this a theory rather it is my conviction that this is what the Bible teaches). These believe in the rapture of the church before the tribulation and the events in prophecy, unless stated, are literal. These believe in a literal reign of Christ on this earth, for there cannot be any lasting peace apart from the prince of peace.

In the verse under consideration there are two thoughts that should bless and burden our hearts. First we have:

I: THE DEFEAT OF SATAN! Verses 1-6 Just reading these verses should produce a shout from the saved; we know that the enemy was defeated at Calvary, there his head was given the wound that bruised (Genesis 3:15); yet, we realize that he is still free and defeating the majority of the people of God. He does, however, know that his time is limited. We will observe two exciting truths about the defeat of Satan. First,

A: THE REMOVAL OF SATAN! Verses 1-3 It is difficult if not impossible for finite minds to comprehend a society free from the attacks of an aggressive adversary. These verses have some thrilling truths. **First** we have *the channel* of his removal in verse 1, *"And I saw an angel come down from heaven."* This angel is not specified. It is not Michael or Gabriel. God, who alone has the power, turns to an angel and instructs it to take care of Satan. This is rather amazing. In 1 Chronicles 19:35 one angel slew one hundred eighty five thousand Assyrians. When Jesus was on the cross He could have called legions of angels and any one of them at the proper time could bind Satan. We must realize that Satan has limited power and that God allows him to have that power but everything is under God's control. The fall of Satan is recorded in Isaiah 14; it is summed up in two words that are used five times in verses 13-14 those words are, "I will." The cross is an "I" cancelled out. When Satan was saying, "I will ascend," Jesus was saying, "I will descend. It is good to know that is still the Father's world. The **second** thought about the removal of

Satan, shared in verses 1-2 is *the chaining*. The "key" is a symbol of control. The angel controls the key; this is delegated control. Now the question is "What kind of chain is this?" It is not what we think of but it is whatever God chooses to bind Satan. Jude 6 informs us that some of the angels that followed Satan are "Reserved in everlasting chains under darkness unto the judgment of the great day." The A-millenniumal says that Satan is already chained and he was chained at the cross. If he is chained it is the longest, loosest chain of all time because he has climbed clear out of the pit. 1 Peter 5:8 declare, "Your adversary the devil walks about as a roaring lion." He is not now but he will be chained by the power of God. The **third** thing we note in verses 2-3 about the removal of Satan is *the casting* in the words, *"And cast him into the bottomless pit."* Note *who is cast*; verse 2 reveals four titles of the enemy. There are *"dragon, old serpent, devil and Satan."* Make no mistake the one cast is the archenemy of God. Also note *where he is cast*; verse 3 states that it is the *"bottomless pit."* The word is "abyss" and it is used 7 times in Revelation. This is not like a pit we are familiar with; this is a prison house for evil spirits. This is not hell, not the lake of liquid fire. Recall that in chapter 9 that some of these are loosed; there is an invasion of demonic forces from the bottomless pit. Then observe *why he is cast*, verse 3, *"That he should deceive the nations no more."* He is a deceiver. If it were not for the Person of the Holy Spirit he would deceive the elect. He can make you think that black is white and white is black. He can make you sell your mother, prostitute your daughter and curse your God. He has tremendous power and it is the power of deception but he is limited. There are two dangers that the Christian faces; one, he can overestimate him and two, he can underestimate him. We need to realize how much bigger he is than we and how much smaller he is than God.

Our second thought is:

B: THE REIGN OF THE SAINTS! Verses 4-6 These verses are at the center of controversy. Those that actually believe these verses are often called fanatics. This is due to the fact that the natural mind can not understand them therefore, the easiest thing for them to do is explain them away; but they will not go away. While a great deal of time could be invested in a debate of

The Apocalypse: The Revelation of the Redeemer

these verses that is not my purpose. I am merely going to call your attention to two truths. **First** in verses 4 and 6 we *have a portrait of those that reign.* These are seen seated on "thrones" literally seats. They are presented in verse 6 as "Priest of God and of Christ." It is my studied opinion that these reigning priests are the saints of God. You, if you know Jesus, are destined to rule with Christ during the millennium. Paul declared in 1 Corinthians 6:2 *"That the saints would judge the world."* We have this illustrated for us in the parable of the returning ruler in Luke 19:11-17. This portrait enables us to see that those that reign with Him are that have been (1) faithful in their witness; (2) followers of the word and (2) fearless in their worship. These, during the antichrist rule, will be beheaded but they will be faithful unto death. **Secondly** in verses 5-6 we have *a portion of the resurrection,* "But the rest of the dead lived not;" verse 6, *"Blessed and holy is he that hath part in the first resurrection."* Therefore we can easily conclude that there are two resurrections. The first is for the saved; the second, a thousand years later, is for the sinner. There is not a general resurrection. The first resurrection, of the saints, is itself in three parts. Note 1 Corinthians 15:20. The first-fruit is Christ. The first-fruit was a hand full of whatever the crop was waved heavenward. It anticipated more to come. Some others in Matthew 27:52-53, an example of what was in store for all believers. The second part of the first resurrection is the harvest. This is presented in 1 Thess. 4:16. This is the saint's resurrection. The third part of the first resurrection is the gleanings. This is before the millennium; it is the tribulation saints.

The words *"second death"* are a reference to a second kind of death; in the lake of fire (verse 14). If one is born twice he dies once, it he is born once he dies twice. If one is born twice he is in the first resurrection and if he is born once he is in the second resurrection.

The second thought is:

II: THE DECAY OF SOCIETY! Verses 7-10 These verses cause great concern for many. They cannot understand how or why such an experience e would be possible. It is not my purpose

255

to argue or provide all the answers (I could not, I do not have them). There are, however, two truths presented to us. First we have:

A: THE RELEASE OF SATAN! Verse 7 In light of all the havoc and harm he has inflicted on humanity if it were up to me he would be there now. A reasonable inquiry is why is he released? During the millennium the earth is experiencing the answer to a prayer prayed by the people of God for ages, *"Thy kingdom come."* It has come, so why mess it up? The devil has not changed after a thousand years of the abyss. If a man were released from hell would be the same. Those in hell are not pleading for mercy they are gnashing their teeth and cursing God. What happens here reveals human nature for what it is. We are not having the problems we are as a result of slums, parents, education or environment. Those that advocate a social gospel tell us "Change the conditions and your will change the man." This verse reveals, at least to my limited understanding, that this is not the case.

Secondly we have:

B: THE REVOLT OF SOCIETY! Verses 8-10 The devil will do what he does best, *"Go out to deceive."* Who are these that are deceived? Aren't they all Christians? No! There will be those that enter the millennium in physical bodies and those with bodies like the one Jesus had after the resurrection. Those with natural bodies will reproduce. The off springs will be the ones that revolt. Before man had a rotten sin nature he fell in a perfect environment in Eden. We know that children that come out Christian homes, attend church,; often go the way of the world. When Jesus performed miracles the Pharisees said, "You did that in the power of the devil." They chose to hate Jesus. We should never think that all a person needs to change is to come face to face with Jesus or suffer in hell. No! The depth of depravity is beyond comprehension.

This is not the event of Ezekiel 38-39. The time frame does not fit. Why does Jesus rule in the Millennium with a *"rod of iron?"* These will give open reverence but at the first opportunity they will rebel.

The Apocalypse: The Revelation of the Redeemer

In verse 10 the devil is taken out of the frying pan and put in the fire. Hell is forever a place of conscious existence. The beast and false prophet are there after a thousand years. These, beast and false prophet, are humans. Hell is not annihilation. It is a lake of fire; if this were a figure of speech whatever fire is to you now hell will be to you then. The figure is always weaker. If you doubt this merely look at a beautiful sunset and then look at a painting. Which is more beautiful?

Conclusion:

Is He reigning over you now or are you living in spiritual rebellion?

The Great White Throne Judgment
Revelation 20:11-15

This section of Scripture is, without doubt, the most awesome in the Word of God. There are passages that challenge our hearts to love the Lord, and passages that challenge our hands to labor for the Lord, but this one of the judgment of the damned does both because of the tremendous loss that is involved. This Scripture answers Jesus question of *"What shall it profit a man if he gain the whole world and lose his soul?"* The Bible declares *"It is appointed unto man once to die;"* this will be the experience of all if Jesus tarries His coming. Few of us would argue this in light of the overwhelming evidence that confronts us daily. However, the verse does not end there it states, *"And after this the judgment."* It is this part that man refuses to believers. Satan has been successful in persuading mankind that there is no future accounting to God. He has persuaded man to adopt the philosophy of "eat, drink, and be merry" for there is not future beyond death. This lie is exposed in the Word.

The Word shares with us the details of this judgment. It is imperative that we have a clear understanding of this vital truth; all men are not judged at the same time or for the same thing. The saints shall appear before the *"Bema,"* the judgment seat of Christ. This is not a judgment for sin, but service. Paul shares the details of this judgment in 1 Corinthians 3; Romans 14, and 11 Corinthians 5. The sinners shall appear before the Great White Throne. This is the record before us. This is not a judgment to determine if one is saved or lost, this is determined while one lives. At the Great White Throne judgment, there are no saved people.

There shall be a day of accounting to God. The Bible says it like this, *"Be not deceived God is not mocked for whatsoever a*

The Apocalypse: The Revelation of the Redeemer

man soweth that shall he also reap." Each person, saint or sinner, shall reap the full harvest on that day, nothing less but so much more.

Should your life end right now at which of these judgments would you appear? You will be at one, it is now your decision and it must be made while you live in the earth because after death it is too late.

There are two thoughts presented for our consideration. First,

I: THE SECENE AT THE GREAT WHITE THRONE! Verses 11-13 John is the observer of this scene. He states four times in this chapter *"I saw."* He is reporting fact not fantasies. What John saw is a scene too terrible for the mind of man to fully comprehend. There are three interesting things for us to note. First,

A: THE DESCRIPTION OF THE THRONE! Verse 11, *"And I saw a great white throne."* This may be the same throne that he saw in chapter 4 but what proceeds from it are exact opposites. In chapter 4 it is a thrones from which comes mercy; judgment proceed from this one. It is called *"Great,"* at this speaks of the *power of this throne.* There is not a throne with which to compare it. This is the throne of the great courtroom of God; here there are neither pardons nor paroles. It is described as being *"White,"* and this speaks of the *purity of the throne.* It is unmixed with human emotions. The judgment that proceeds from this throne will be in righteousness; it will be just and fair, unlike the treatment our Lord received in Pilate's court.

Secondly we have:

B: THE DEITY ON THE THRONE! Verse 11, *"And Him that sat on it."* Who is the occupant upon this throne? We know that it is deity, and John 5:22 tells us that the *"Father has committed all judgment unto the Son."* The person, in my studied opinion, is Jesus. Men for centuries have ignored Him, denied Him, cursed Him, crucified Him, disbelieved Him, sold Him; but now, they must face Him. You may choose to do the same; if you do, you will be a part of the crowd that faces Him as He sits in judgment on the great white throne.

Carefully not the phrase, *"From whose face the earth and the heaven fled away."* This is not because for the horror of the face but the holiness of the face. What a face! The ungodly spat in it, slapped it, plucked the beard form it and now they must gaze into it. To look upon the face of Jesus for the lost will be the first agonizing stab of hell. When Peter looked upon that face it led to repentance; that will not be the case here.

Thirdly we have:

C: THE DAMNED AT THE THRONE! Verses 12-13 The phrase, *"Stand before God,"* is literally "standing before the throne." There are things that one may or may not do in this life, but there is one thing all will do in eternity…stand before the throne of God. Each of us must decide if we will stand with Him or before Him. There are two questions I want to ask and hopefully answer. **First,** *who are these people before the great white throne?* Verse 12 provides the answer in the words, *"And I saw the dead."* When there is a reference to the Christian it is "dead in Christ;" not so here. These are the dead outside of Christ. They are the lost of all time. John says, "Small and great," but they are all lost. Cain and his followers will be there with the works of their hands trying to convince God with their ability to do good. The wicked in Noah's day with their contempt and ridicule will be there, Pilate washing his hands in compromise; but not clean. Small and great, the known and the unknown, rich and poor, learned and ignorant all will be there. The people before the great white throne are people just like you and me! You will be there if you do not know Jesus as your personal Savior. What a fellowship to be a part of, you and Hitler, Herod and all the Christ rejecters of the world. **Secondly,** *where do these people come from that are before the great White throne?* This is the second resurrection; these come from the grave that is what "death" refers to in verse 13; and from Hades, that is what hell means in this verse. Just as the *"just"* are raised bodily, so shall the *"unjust"* be raised bodily. The grave yields up the body, Hades the soul. Hades is the place of conscious suffering of the lost (Luke 16), but it is not the eternal "lake of fire." The question of questions is will you be numbered among the lost that appear at the great white throne?

The Apocalypse: The Revelation of the Redeemer

The second truth is:

II: THE SENTENCE AT THE GREAT WHITE THRONE! Verses 12-15 John does not waste words; there is no attempt to conceal the truth of this matter from any seeking soul. There are two truths that should disturb our very souls, and if they do not may God awaken our hearts to the need. First we should be aware of:

A: THE BASIS OF THE SENTENCE AT THE GREAT WHITE THRONE. Verses 12-13 share that the basis of the sentence is the works of man; both use the same words, *"according to their works."* One might ask how this is possible. The Lord has a perfect record of every man's work recorded in His books. Verse 12 states, *"...And the books* (plural) *were opened."* What are these books? The book of words (Matthew 12:36-37), "Every idle word shall be accounted for." The book of thoughts; probably a book of messages that one has heard that presented the gospel of Jesus will be opened.

It is the nature of the lost man to want to stand on his record, in that day he will. The sinner can either ask God for a free pardon or a fair trial. If he chooses the fair trial, it will land him in the lake of fire for he will be judged according to his works and there are not any works acceptable to God (Cain was the first to try and failed), none that can replace the atoning blood of Jesus.

The books are not opened to determine if a person goes to heaven or hell. There will not be a giant pair of scales on which the works of man are placed; all present will go to hell. The great white throne judgment concerns the degree of punishment of the lost and is not a test to determine if they are lost. It is my studied opinion that there will be degrees of punishment in hell (Read Matthew 11:21-24 and Luke 12:48). Do you suppose that the heathen that has never heard of Jesus and the man that has heard of Jesus, been witnessed to, prayed for, and wept over are going to experience the same punishment in hell? It is my opinion that God will take into account the opportunities to accept Christ, the amount of light one has received, the environment in which he lived and the degree and amount of sin, and then judge accordingly.

And to insure that there will be not one protest heard in any part of the universe against the justice of God, the Book of Life is also opened. There all men will be confronted with the fact that even though their names may have appeared in a lot of places, it never appeared where it counted; in the Book of Life.

Secondly we have:

B: THE BANISHMENT OF THE SENTENCE AT THE GREAT WHITE THRONE! Verses 14-15 Verse 14 says, *"death* (the grave) *and hell* (Hades) *were cast into the lake of fire."* Both of these came into existence because of man sinned, now they are cast into the place where all belong that are contrary to the holiness and righteousness of God. Then John states, *"This is the second death."* This is not a blotting out of existence, but endless separation from God.

The banishment is stated in verse 15, *"Whosoever,"* that is the same word that is used in John 3:16 and Revelation 22:17, *"Whosoever will let him come."* Here it says, *"Whosoever was not found written in the Book of Life was cast into the lake of fire."* This is the eternal state of the wicked. Think of it, spending eternity with the devil, the beast and the false prophet (verse 10).

This is the literal hell, the place that Jesus described as, *"Where the worm dieth not, the fire is not quenched, where there is weeping and wailing and gnashing of teeth."* Notice please how verse 10 ends, *"...And shall be tormented day and night for ever and ever."* Did you hear it? Endless torment, endless separation from the loving Savior, endless fellowship with the devil. No rational person could want this.

Conclusion:
Jesus came to provide a way for us not to be among those at the great white throne. He bled freely for our salvation. If you do not come to Him now for salvation, you will face Him at this day and be sentenced to eternity in the lake of fire.

What is New
Revelation 21:1-22:5

"When we all get to heaven, what a day of rejoicing that will be..." "O that will be glory for me, when by His grace I shall look on His face that will be glory for me." The Bible refers to heaven no less than 700 times. Every religion has a heaven and I have never had anyone tell me that they did not want to go to heaven.

This is the most difficult part of the book because no one is adequate to explain it nor has anyone witnessed heaven, except with the eyes of faith, other than perhaps Paul and he could not tell of it. How can we talk about something as grand and glorious as a eternity yet to come? All we can do is get God's revelation of it. This is what the last two chapters of the book of Revelation presents to us.

There is a difference in speculation and revelation. The Mormons believe there are three heavens; the celestial, terrestrial, and telestial. Only those married in their temple go to the celestial heaven. The Jehovah's Witness are more concerned with the number of people in heaven. According to them only 144,000 will be and the rest will have the left over. The Moslems believe heaven is going to be a place of endless sensuous pleasure there they can drink all they want and it will not affect the mind. There, according to them, will be beautiful maidens to be enjoyed for eternity. All of this is speculation. We have the revelation of God about heaven in His Word.

I am going to divide this chapter into two major divisions. First we will consider:

I: THE NEW CREATION! Verses 1-8 It is not my purpose to deal in the area of speculation but to present as simple as I can what these verses reveal to us about the new creation. These will not be deep or profound thoughts but more surface because there is a limit to the mind of man in dealing with the glorious events of the future. There are a number of truths yielded from these verses. First,

A: THE RADIANT PLACE! Verses 1-2 The observer is John. He relates what he sees as an eyewitness. It is difficult for us to comprehend the reality of what he is seeing. Notice two important things about this radiant place. **First**, in verse 1, we have *the elimination of the temporal*, *"A new heaven and a new earth."* There are three heavens. The first is in Genesis 1, the firmament, the space surrounding the earth, the atmosphere. The second is the galaxy. The third is the abode of God. There are two words for *"new."* One has to do with time. That is not the word used here. The other, used here; is for a kind or quality or substance; new as not the same as now. (Read Isaiah 65:17; 2 Peter 3:13)

"Earth" means a new kind of earth. There will always be a planet but it will be purged. *"And there was no more sea."* They will not be needed. The surface of the earth is 75% water; it will be eliminated because it is a part of the old order. Chapter 22:1 informs us of the water supply, *"A river of life."* These may be symbolic meaning or application of this fact. The *"seas"* have represented the Gentiles nations and these will no longer exist as we know them. They also represent boundaries and turmoil as well as separation. All of these will be eliminated because they are temporal. **Second**, verse 2 shares with us *the entrance of the timeless*; *"The holy city."* This is the title of Jerusalem now but it is as wicked as any city in the earth. It is a city of rebellion and sin. It was to have been a city of peace but it is one of pollution. This will change.

Note the *descent* in verse 2, *"Coming down from God out of heaven."* This represents both a place and people. If I say "Fayetteville is a beautiful city in the spring" I am talking about a place. If I say "Fayetteville is a wicked city" I am referring to the people or portion of the people. Note also the *dress*, *"Prepared as a bride adorned for her husband."* Who did the preparing? John 14:3 "I go to prepare a place for you." The city is "adorned as a bride for her husband." I have seen some brides that were not

The Apocalypse: The Revelation of the Redeemer

exactly pretty. To be truthful some have been homely, but I have never saw a bride on her wedding day that was not beautiful.

Secondly we witness:

B: A RENOUN PRESENCE! Verse 3 This *"great voice"* is heard 21 times in Revelation. This is the last time. This is securing attention. This verse is beyond my ability to begin to express. God who created us will dwell with us in the New Jerusalem. He is dwelling everywhere now but then we enter into a new level of understanding. Then it is more intimate. It exceeds anything ever experienced by man with the exception of Adam in the Garden of Eden. It is personal; we will get to know Him. If someone says to you that they would like to get to know you they are implying that they would like to spend some time in conversation with you. Do you desire a more personal intimate, personal fellowship? That need not wait until you are in glory. That is available to you and me now.

In the new creation we notice thirdly:

C: THE REMOVAL OF THE PAST! Verse 4 I am glad that the blood of Jesus does this for me now with regard to my sin but I still have a memory and connections with the past because of my nature. This thankfully will be removed in the city of God.

"And God shall wipe away all tears from their eyes," is literally "every single tear will be wiped away." Why will there be tears? I will offer this bit of speculation. It is possible that up to this point one might know that someone was not there or it might be known that one has experienced the judgment of God. The fact is we do not actually know. What we do know is that God will be our comfort. It is good to know that even now He cares about the little things that confront us.

"There shall be no more death." Death has been called "the graffiti of mankind." It is no respecter of persons. It stalks all. We spend a major portion of our time trying to avoid death. That's why we wear seat belts. If you have lost a loved one or friend you know how precious it is to hear God say, *"No more death."* There will be no obituaries, no cemeteries, no one with the job of undertaker (I did not say no undertakers). This is reality; eighty-three people die every minute here but not there because *"there is no more death."*

The words, *"Neither sorrow"* are literally *"mourning."* This is the cry of the broken heart. It is the vocalizing of inner pain. There are those things that break the heart. A wife with an alcoholic husband cries over the abuse. The husband that has been told "I don't love you any more" and his wife walk away. All of this will be removed.

The words *"Nor crying"* is the quite response of a broken heart. There are times when you cannot say it but you can weep it and god bottles those tears. There will be *"no pain."* There will no longer be a need for medication. The old order of things has passed away. How could any person with average intelligence want to miss heaven?

The forth truth is:

D: THE REMARKABLE PROVISIONS! Verses 5-6 John must have been so absorbed that he was just sitting in worship and wonder. The voice of God instructs him to *"Write, for these words are true and faithful."* Observe *the source* is shared in verse 6, *"I am Alpha;"* the first letter of the Greek alphabet; *"the Omega;"* the last letter of the Greek alphabet. *"It is done,"* and when God says it is done, it is done. He is the consummator of all things. What He originates He consummates. *The supply* is given in the words, *"I will give to him that is athirst of the fountain of the water of life freely."* If one is really thirsty only water can quench his thirst. It is good to know that in the measure of any need He has the water that is needed. I do not have to go from day to day with unsatisfied thirst in my heart. He supplies it now!

The fifth truth we observe about the new creation is:

E: THE REWARDING PROMISE! Verse 7 *"He that overcomes."* Who is the overcomer? 1 John 5:4 declare, *"For whosoever is born of God overcomes the world."* The overcomer is the child of God that walks in the power of His Spirit by faith.

What is the inheritance? Note 2:7, 11, 17, 26-28; 3:5, 12 and 21. Notice we are told, *"I will be his God."* He is now but then in a new more meaningful manner. *"And he shall be my son."* 1 John 3; 2 *"...doth not yet appear what we shall be..."* This is a relationship that exceeds anything we can imagine at this time.

The sixth aspect of this new creation is:

F: THE RIGHTEOUS PUNISHMENT! Verse 8 *"But"* there is a contrast. The *"fearful"* this is cowardly; those that deny Jesus to save their own flesh; those that lacked courage or for some temporal god. The verse shares more in the following words: *"unbelieving;"* the rejecters of grace and Jesus as God's only way of salvation; the *"abominable;"* the vile or polluted; the *"murders;"* those responsible for taking innocent lives. Next we have the *"whoremonger"* the sexual perverted and spiritually unclean. We are told that 1 person in 5 has a sexual transmitted disease. This is followed by *"sorcerers;"* this drugs and drug users or sellers. The Greek word is the one from which we get our word pharmacy. *"Idolaters"* are next; these are worshippers of anything other than the living God. *"Liars"* is next; this refers to those that believe and practice lying as a way of life. These will be excluded from the new creation. They will experience forever the second death.

Secondly we now observe:

II: THE NEW CITY! Verses 9-22:5 The older hymn books were sprinkled with songs about heaven; do you remember this one "There's a land that is fairer than day and by faith we can see it afar for the Father waits over the way to prepare us a dwelling place there. In the sweet by and by we shall meet on that beautiful shore; In the sweet by and by we shall meet on that beautiful shore." Perhaps you remember, "Beyond the sunset, O blissful morning, when with our Savior heaven is begun, earths toiling ended, O glorious dawning, beyond the sunset, when day is done."

What do we know about the place called heaven? We know from the words of Jesus in John 14 that it is a real place. There Jesus called it "My Fathers house." We know it is a roomy place for He said "Are many dwelling rooms." We further know it is a ready place for He said He is "preparing it for us."

But what will this new city really be like? I wish I could show you a picture but I cannot. There are those that want to know if this is a literal record of the new city in Revelation 21. I can only say that the figure is always less than the fact. If it is not, and I tend to believe it is, there is something waiting that neither the mouth can convey nor the mind comprehend.

There are several thoughts for our hearts to ponder in these verses about this new city. First, we have:

A: THE DESCRIPTION! Verses 9-11 An announcement is made by an angel but he is designated as *"One of the seven which had the seven vials full of the seven last plagues."* This is intriguing, on one hand he is pouring out judgment and on the other he is introducing John to the glories of heaven. Verse 9 states that this angel *"talked with* (him) *me."* How many conversations have you had with angels? He not only talked with him in but in verse 10 he transported him, *"And he carried me in the spirit."* This is not a reference to the Holy Spirit but rather it refers to not being in the flesh. This is what he was referring to in chapter 1:10 as the "Day of the Lord;" and in 4:1 where he is transported into heaven. When he is transported "He saw that great city." There are 44 separate visions given to John in this book. He says *"I saw"* no less than 60 times. What he is seeing now surpasses everything he has witnessed. It is the new city and he seeks to describe it for the believers that will be residing there.

He describes, in verse 9, the city **first** *as the bride,* *"I will show thee the bride, the Lamb's wife."* This speaks of a relationship of love that must be experienced rather than explained. This is the relationship that the saint enjoys now with the Savior but it is limited by our inability to let go of the physical.

This new city that John describes as a bride is **secondly** described *as brilliant* in verse 11, *"Have the glory of God."* Psalms 19:1 declares *"The heaven declare the glory of God..."* *"And her light was like unto a stone most precious, even like jasper, clear as crystal."* There are those that say this is a diamond but there is nothing in the original to warrant this being a diamond. It is crystal and the light shines brilliantly through it. If a lost person could go to this new city in his old unregenerate condition he would not want to remain there. God is light and man in his fallen state prefers darkness. The brilliant light exposes all because it shines through it all.

The second truth for our consideration is:

The Apocalypse: The Revelation of the Redeemer

B: THE DIMENSIONS! Verses 12-21 This could be a rather humorous study if one sought to read all the rather ridicules theories about this new city. There are those things that cannot be understood by man as yet. He can speculate but speculation should be a private matter and not a pulpit message. Therefore, I will share only what I can with some degree of conviction. There are three aspects of the dimensions that I want us to observe. **First** in verses 12-14 notice *the structure*, *"And had a wall great and high;"* verse 17, *"And he measured the wall thereof, an hundred and forty and four cubits."* There is much discussion as to whether this refers to height or to its thickness. It is my opinion that the wall surrounds the entire new city and that it is 216 feet thick. The wall has a *purpose*; it is for exclusion. There will be no sinners or sinful activity in the new city. The wall has its *protections*; *"And at the 12 gates, 12 angels."* This is security. Remember that only one angel was needed to defeat armies of the earth. I think of these as the honor guard. The wall has a *passage*, *"And had 12 gates."* This is an entrance. The names of the 12 tribes indicate that all believers have passed through the same passage. There are 3 gates on the east; someone has suggested that this represents those that come to Jesus at an early age or those that never developed mentally. The north 3 gates suggest those that entered through difficult circumstances. There are some cold churches and we usually think of the cold north wind. The south 3 gates suggest to them those that entered in middle age and the west indicated those that entered in late life. I will leave this with you for your own thought process.

Verse 14 shares the fact that there are 12 foundations and in them are the names of the apostles. This is a picture of the unity of believers. The foundations are laid one upon the other. Ephesians 2:20, "And are built upon the foundation of the apostles." That is the church of the Lord Jesus is built upon this foundation.

The **second** aspect of the dimensions is, in verses 15-17, *the size*. The angel that talked with John now measures the new city. It is foursquare, that is, a perfect cube. It is as wide and high as it is long. The angel measured 12 thousand furlongs; that is 1500 miles. The size of the new city is 1500 miles wide; 1500 miles long and 1500 miles high. That figures to a circumference of 6000 miles across. Someone has figured that this is over 2 million 225 thousand square miles. If you had stories 10 feet high you could house over 100 billion people and every person would have a ranch of 37 and 1/2 miles. The size of this city would be as large as 49 Pennsylvania's, 14 Delaware's; 2 Districts of Columbia and 1 Rhode Island; all of these could fit in it.

Will there be a 100 billion people in this city? No, not if you use the standard of man, yes if you use the grace of God. There is at this time room for you but you must make a decision to repent and receive Jesus as your Lord and Savior.

The **third** aspect of the dimensions in verses 18-21 is *the splendor*. This is beyond man's ability to describe. I am merely going too point out a little of the splendor of this new city. **First** the *gold is pure* and light shines from and through it. I am told that the purest gold has been shaved to examine a portion of it. The light shines through it as clear as crystal. I am not even going to comment on the fact that the foundations are "garnished with all manner of precious stones;" except to say that the value of the new city is so vast that it can not be calculated. A word of caution must be shared; be extremely careful in giving our names and meanings to the stones listed. They may not be the same. **Second** the *gates are pearl*. Verse 21 shares that each gate was made of a single pearl. An oyster makes the pearl. It makes the pearl because something has penetrated and is causing it pain and suffering. It produces a milky substance to go around whatever is causing the irritation. These gauges are made of a single pearl. All the other gems are metal or stone, the pearl is the only one formed by living flesh. The pearl is the oyster's answer to what injured it. What have we made of the bitter experiences of life, a pearl or more pain? The new city is God's answer, in Christ, to the world that crucified the Son of God. The saints will be eternally reminded that they have access to God's home because of Calvary. The size of those gates symbolizes the gigantic suffering of the Savior for our sins.

The third thing we observe about the new city is:

C: THE DELETIONS! Verses 22-27 With all the splendor of the new city one might think that it would contain everything

The Apocalypse: The Revelation of the Redeemer

know to man. However, we discover that there are some things not present in the new city. There are at least three deletions. **First**, as verses 22-24 share there is *no temple*; *"And I saw no temple therein."* The architects of our world have exhausted their greatest skill in designing and building of shrines. The tabernacle in the wilderness and the temple in Jerusalem served a purpose in their day. The temples men build are not without value. Earthly temples are supposed to symbolize the presence of God but in the new city the Lord Jesus Christ is the temple. The temples on earth suggest a localized presence that is not the case in heaven. In the temple there is no light (verse 23) for *"the Lamb is the light."* There is no lack (verse 24) for the kings and *"nations that are saved walk in the light of it."* **Secondly**, verse 25, there is *no terror*, *"The gates of it shall not be shut at all by day: for there shall be no night there."* There is no darkness. Everything is open; this suggests the lack of fear and free open communication with heaven. **Third**, verse 27, there is *no tainting*. This new city is not only free from sinners but from all that would taint it with sin. This is a place where only the saved will abide. Even if a sinner could approach it he would detest it and flee from it because there is nothing there that draws his fallen nature.

The forth truth presented is:

D: THE DELIGHTS! 22:1-5 With all that has been indicated in this new city what else could there possibly be to delight the redeemed that will dwell there? There are some special delights that we want to note. **First**, verses 1-2, we have *the provisions of the Lord*, *"And He showed me a pure river of water of life proceeding out of the throne of god and of the Lamb."* Ezekiel saw reviving water proceeding from the altar in the temple, the place of sacrifice (Ezekiel 47:1), but in the new city it issues from the throne, the place of sovereignty, for in that day there will be no need of sacrifice. (Strauss)

Most of earth's ancient cities were built around the banks of important rivers which soon became polluted. Here, however, is a river whose streams make glad the city of God. This river flowing from the throne, a source of terror to evildoers is the source of life to those that know and love the Lord. A river in scripture is used to symbolize both pleasure (Psalms 36:8) and prosperity (Psalms

1:3). These are the very things Satan uses to draw men away from God.

In verse 2 he mentions *"The tree of life;"* which reminds us of the Garden of Eden where the fruit was forbidden to man. The tree of life now flourishes in glory. We are not told what the fruit is, the full delights of glory are not revealed. The expression "Healing of the nations" is a mystery and I with you will wait for the revelation of its meaning in the new city. If one desires to he can eat and drink in the new city.

The **second** delight in verses 3-4 is *the presence of the Lord*. There will be *"no more curse."* This is true because God is present. There will be no night but we shall see His face. John had learned from his Master; He keeps the best wine until last! This is the delight of delights. This is heaven's crowning joy. Will heaven be all that we expect it to be? Words are totally inadequate to describe it but it is enough to know that He will be there and we will be identified as His, *"And His name shall be in their foreheads."*

The **third** provision, verse 5, is *the purpose of the Lord*, *"and they shall reign with Him forever and ever."* We will not sit in rocking chairs but we will be busy in glory serving Him. We should be getting practice now. How long shall we serve? The millennium comes and goes, He endures, and we endure sharing His position and power as we serve Him.

Truly joy unspeakable and full of glory awaits us in glory, in the new city of our God. Are you prepared to meet the King?

What to do Till Jesus Comes
Revelation 22:6-21

Three times in these verses Jesus declares, "I am coming!" In each case (verses 7, 12 and 20) He adds the word "quickly." Yet, we know it has been over 2000 years and still we wait. What did He mean by His statement? The book opened (1:7) with His promised coming in the clouds. This is to be understood as sudden rather than soon in our terms. When He comes these events recorded in this book will unfold quickly.

An important matter for the Christian is what do we do until He comes? Are we to gaze heavenward and look for Him? I believe these verses have a powerful message for us as to what we are to do until Jesus comes. The Christian should be engaged in:

I: PONDERING THE WORD! Verses 6-7 and 10-16 The word ponder means "to give serious thought to, to consider or examine attentively or deliberately." It is to contemplate, to think over and study. If this is true there is not much mental pondering done, especially with regard to the word of God. We should ponder the word first because:

A: THE SCRIPTURES ARE FAITHFUL! Verse 6 *"And he* (the messenger) *said unto me, 'these sayings are...faithful.'"* That is, it possesses those qualities that merit confidence and trust. We know these words are faithful because we are told in verse 16, *"I Jesus have sent mine angel to testify unto you these things in the churches."* Heaven and earth shall pass away, but My words shall not pass away (Matthew 24:25). We also see the reminder in verse 6, *"The Lord God...sent His angel to show unto His servants the things that must shortly come to pass."* This is a reminder of how the book commenced. He has been consistent all the way through.

This word is faithful. I am challenged to hide it in my heart; to meditate upon it and to consume it. If the word was not faithful in any respect it may not be faithful in the area of my need.

Secondly we note,

B: THE SCRIPTURES ARE FACTUAL! Verse 6 *"These sayings are...true."* What sayings are factual? Is he referring to those just in the Revelation or is he informing us that the scriptures are factual? I believe the Bible is God's God breathed word; that it is without error. Jesus said in John 14:6 "I am...the truth." We have His word in The Word and I am more comfortable believing Him than I am some "scholar" that cast aspersions on anything he cannot explain. I believe every believer has the right to interpret the scriptures for himself but no one has the right to disregard any scripture.

Thirdly we are to ponder the word because;

C: THE SAVIOR IS FORTHCOMING! Verses 7, 12 and 20, "Behold I come quickly." Jesus Christ is coming again. He said He would in John 14:3, "I will come again." How many lies did Jesus tell as He ministered among men? If there was one we would have cause to doubt His coming but there was not one word that was not factual. It is a part of the enemy's strategy to discourage and defeat the people of God by casting doubt upon His coming again. Remember Peter declared that in his day there were those that scoffed saying *"Where is the promise of His coming for since the fathers fell asleep, all things continue as they were from the beginning of the creation"* (11 Peter 3:4).

Verse 7 shares the sixth beatitude of the book in the words, *"Blessed is he that keepeth the sayings of this book."* The word *"keeps"* means one is to live in purity and faithfulness in light of Jesus coming. It is not a reference to the sequence of forthcoming events but to challenge us to walk in obedience and for Him to be projected in our lives in such a way that others will be challenged by the awareness of His presence and power in our lives.

We should ponder the word for a fourth reason,

D: THE SIGNIFICANCES OF THE FUTURE! Verses 10-16 The Word of God is not a crystal ball that reveals the secrets of the future to some strange acting person. However, if one is committed to pondering the word he will be enlightened as

The Apocalypse: The Revelation of the Redeemer

to the events that are coming in the future. The awesome weight of those future events makes them all the more significant. In these verses we want to observe a number of truths that should greatly bless and burden our hearts. These are factual, faithful sayings of our Lord. We are not observing foolish fantasies. **First** in verse 10 we note that *the prophecies are not sealed.* We are not dealing with a closed book; albeit, it is closed to the majority of people. I mean literally it is on a shelf collecting dust and keep sakes!

There was a man named Daniel that received an awesome word from God but he was told in chapter 8:26; 12:4 and 12:8 to "seal up the vision" and "I heard but understood not." John is informed that he is not to *"seal the sayings of the prophecy of this book for the time is at hand."* This is to be shared. Does this refer to only the visions of John? In the proper sense it does. However, we are part of the age of the ministry of the Holy Spirit; He that inspired the word can and will illuminate our minds and instruct us in the word as well as interpret the word to our hearts. I shall never forget being a young preacher; on my face before God I said, "Father, I want to receive from You for myself...I thank You for the blessing You have been to these great men of the faith but I desire to receive fresh manna from You as well."

This wonderful book of God is not to be hid away in a trunk but it is to be herald as the truth that sets men free. In light of the statement in verse 10, *"For the time is at hand,"* we should be seeking to share the message of salvation, service and stewardship of life with the entire world. **Secondly**, verse 11, *the positions are settled.* The meaning and message of this verse is one that should reach out and grab our hearts. It informs us of a future event that is so significant that we should be tearful in the present. There is absolutely no possibility of change in the future eternal state. The key word is *"still."* When any person goes into eternity if he is unjust or filthy when he leaves he will be unjust and filthy in eternity. I do not believe that individuals in hell will be pleading for mercy but cursing God.

The fact for us to write in our heart is not all are going to respond to the message of Jesus the same. Those that reject Him in his life will be rejected by Him in eternity. We are challenged to give them the opportunity to either receive Him or reject Him because in the eternal state the position of sinner and saint is settled.

Thirdly, verse 12, we note that *the promise is sure*. The promise that is sure is two-fold. It is a promise of His return. This should serve as a reminder to each of us to be constantly taking advantage of our opportunities to share His love. The second aspect of this sure promise is His reward *"and My reward is with Me."* This should be an incentive to serve. The Greek word for "reward" is *mis-thos* and it means "wages." The expression *"to give"* is "to recompense." This is done on an individual bases. Therefore, every man will receive a just recompense for what he has done. This sure promise informs us that there is a day of reckoning.

What kind of day will this be for us? This is not a day to determine one's destiny. It is a reckoning of one's stewardship to God.

A **fourth** truth in verse 13 and 16 is *the person is the same*. Why make an issue of the person? Because there are places where the Person of Christ is not preached as the only way of eternal salvation. There is no gospel, good news, without Him. I have dealt with these titles somewhat and will not belabor the point. I will mention the titles in verse 16, *"I am the root and offspring of David."* He is both the Root and Shoot of David's family. *"The bright and morning star,"* informs us that Christ is the Star of the Dawn. To the Christian, Christ is the promise of a new day. "The morning star of the church shines today as brightly as in the day of John; He does not fall or set." (Swete)

Fifth we have in verse 14 *the participation of the saints*. This is the seventh beatitude of the book and it involved the participation of the saints. Note the words, *"That do His commandments."* I hurriedly point out that they are "His commandments" and not mans. This prompts the question of what commandments is He referring too? I believe *"His commandments"* are summed up in 1 John 3:23, *"And this is His commandment, that we should believe on the name of His Son Jesus Christ, and love one another, as He gave us commandment."* This is not legalism but love. It is not passive but positive. It is not merely the not doing what is evil; it

The Apocalypse: The Revelation of the Redeemer

is the doing of what is good. Those that participate have the right to the tree of life and free access to the city of God.

The future is significant for a **sixth** reason in verse 15 and that is *the prohibition of sinners.* This verse seems to be a summary of chapter 20:11-15. Do not think that these are walking around outside with a mere restriction placed upon them not to enter the city. The term *"dog"* is used to describe those that were defiled by long contact with the foul vices of pagan society. Our day has witnessed an alarming recurrence of the kid of pagan living that characterized the first century. These people along with sorcerers, those that move in the drug traffic, whoremongers (fornicators) impure or perverted sexual activity, those that take the life of the innocent; those that elevate anything to the position demanded by God and those that practice lying as a life-style will be already in hell. They will not have access to the city of God.

What are we to do till Jesus comes? We are to be engaged in pondering the word and in;

II: PROPER WORSHIP! Verses 8-9 Worship is one of those terms that is almost indefinable. This is true because we hear it used in so many improper ways. To one it is a "deep, ardent, and often excessive attachment or love." To another it means, "to honor and admire profoundly and respectfully." Another says it is "to feel a passion, devotion or tenderness for." None of those constitutes Biblical worship. While worship does involve reverence, devotion and adoration these do not express the entire concept of worship. "The worship of God is nowhere defined in Scripture. It is not confined to praise only. It may be regarded as the direct acknowledgement to God, of His nature, attributes, ways and claims, whether by outgoing of heart in praise and thanksgiving or by deed done in such acknowledgement" (vine).

Everyman is a worshipper of someone or something. We all bow before what we consider to be worthy! Worthship is closely connected to worship. Because there is so much apparent misunderstanding of worship we are challenged to know who as well as why we worship what we do. There are two thoughts for us to consider about proper worship. First we note,

A: THE MISTAKES OF THE MAN! Verse 8 The man making the mistake is clearly identified. He is not a novice. He has been an eyewitness of the rapture and revelation of Christ. This man is John.

It is indicated in verse 8 that what John saw and heard had a tremendous impact upon him. How long has it been since anything you saw or heard caused you to respond in bowing in worship? The mistake was in the object not in his action of bowing or falling prostrate. Ours is a part of a sophisticated society. We have reached the point that we no longer kneel to pray rather we approach God as our equal. This mistake is as bad as not approaching Him at all. The mistake of the man is one that is common in our day. He was offering worship to a created being. It would be easy for us to excuse John because of who he is. This is all the more reason for him not to offer worship to anyone but God.

One of the reasons the cults flourish is they practice a perverted worship. The fallen nature of man is more open to the polluted than the pure. That is worship to another other than God Himself. Paul admonished the church at Colosse in chapter 2:18 not to be deceived in the matter of worshipping angels. The cults seek to show the individual anything he wants to see. The payment is worship of a false god. We are not to worship anyone or anything but God and God only. That means those idols I have allowed to continue in my life must be destroyed if I am to walk with God. The mistake of this man was not in the offering of worship but the object of the worship. If the apostle John, who leaned on His breast, watched Him die; saw Him raised, beheld Him ascend; witnessed the vision of the Revelation could make this mistake we surely must take care and allow His Holy Spirit to direct our worship or we will find ourselves making the same mistake. Am I presently worshipping self, substance or the Savior?

The second truth about proper worship is,

B: THE MESSAGE TO THE MAN! Verse 9 The angel did not allow the worship to continue; *"Then said he unto me."* He had a message that John and Christians of all time need to hear. Note **first** *the injunction of the message,* *"See thou do it* *not."* This injunction is evidence that this messenger is no ordinary man of the earth, if so he would have delighted in this worship. The Caesars killed thousands because they refused to acknowledge then as "Lord and God."

This angel must have known that such actions grieved the heart of God. How His heart must be grieved today. What are some of the things that this messenger would say to us *"See thou do it not"* that we are worshipping? I will not yield to the temptation to share a list of "things." I will simply say the problem of the (every) church is a "love" problem. By that I mean we do not love Jesus as we should. When we do the "things" of this world will loose their attraction.

Secondly verse 9 reveals *the identification of the messenger.* This messenger is identified as a *"fellow-servant"* and of *"Thy brethren the prophets."* This is not an "angel" in the proper sense. Chapter 1:20 helps us understand that this is a messenger of the Lord. The wondrous thing is that we can be in this day of grace messengers of the good news of God to all men.

Verse 9 concludes the identification of the messenger by stating that he was one *"that kept the sayings of this book."* I am fully aware that there are those things that we may not be able to understand or explain, yet, we are to obedient to the light we have and walk faithfully with the word when it appears to us that darkness is in control.

Thirdly verse 9 shares *the instruction to the man, "Worship God."* Worship is loving Him for who He is! The more one knows Him the more he will desire to worship Him. How long has it been since you told the Father that you loved Him? Worship can and should be both private and public. However, what transpires from 11 a.m. to 12 noon on Sundays, the majority of the time, is not real worship. It is dead ritual and dull routine. To worship is to meet with someone you love and give Him your individual, undivided attention and unadulterated affection. What occupies your mind right now; is it Jesus or junk? Someone will object to anyone having the audacity to question if junk is on their mind…what is everything else when compared to Jesus? What are we to do till Jesus comes; we are to ponder the word, properly worship and thirdly, we are to:

III: PROCLAIM THE WORD! Verses 17-21 As wonderful as pondering the word and properly worshipping are they are not all we are to be doing till Jesus comes. The fact is that proclaiming the word is the natural outcome of the others. That is, if we are doing them, this will be automatic. There are two powerful reasons that we should be proclaiming the word. First,

A: BECAUSE OF THE INVITATION TO COME! Verse 17 There are countless invitations in the word and none of them is without significance. Yet, in the order of priority the invitation to come must be first. We cannot go, do say or be anything He instructs us to until we come to Him. The importance of the invitation to come is set forth in two ways. **First,** we have *the extenders of the invitation* in the words, *"The Spirit and the bride, and he hearth say come."* This expression has been interpreted in various ways. When is this invitation extended? Is it a chronological table? If so the latter part of the verse does not fit. It is my opinion that it expresses the desire of the Spirit and saints since the church began to see individuals come to Christ in salvation. The issue is are we engaged in extending the invitation to come to Christ while the door of grace is open; if we do not who will share His love with a dying world of lost humanity? **Secondly**, we have *the extent of the invitation* in the concluding phrase of verse 17, *"And whosoever will."* There is a prerequisite however, that is shared in the words, *"And let him that is athirst come."* He is coming to partake of the Water of Life but he will not be a partaker if he is not thirsty.

Here is one of the major reasons so many people that have their name on a church roll somewhere are not involved in the things of Christ. They do not have a thirst for them. Jesus said, *"If any man thirst let him come to Me and drink."* These need to ask Jesus for a thirst for Him.

The invitation to come is issued to you and me. It is extended to sinner and saint. The sinner can come for salvation and the saint can come for spiritual sustenance. What is your present need? It can be ministered to only if you accept the invitation to come to Christ for yourself. That *"Whosoever"* that is now extended for you will become the *"Whosoever"* of chapter 20:15

The Apocalypse: The Revelation of the Redeemer

if you refuse His invitation to come and receive His mercy and grace.

Secondly we should be engaged in proclaiming the word **B: BECAUSE OF THE INFORMATION IT CONTAINS!** Verses 18-21 The information I am referring to is stated in the text and it deals with four arrears. **First**, it deals with *the prophecy* in verses 18-19. Does the word prophecy in these verses refer to only those John received or does it refer to the larger body of the word of God? In the proper sense it refers to the Revelation given to John. In the lesser application it refers to the word given by God.

In these verses we have a strong warning not to tamper with these prophecies by adding or subtracting anything. This does not refer to comparing manuscripts for the best reading of the text. It is a solemn protest against the spirit which handles rashly or deceitfully the word of God which adds it sown thoughts, or deletes its warning, or impoverishes the fullness of its promises.

Secondly the information deals with *the promise* in verse 20 in the words, "*He which testifieth these things saith, 'surely I come quickly.'*" The "*He*" is Jesus. It literally reads, "*I am coming quickly.*" In light of the passage in 11 Peter 3:8-9 it has not been two days. The passage declares, "That one day is with the Lord a thousand years, and a thousand years as one day. The Lord is not slack concerning His promise…"

The last promise of the Bible is as sure to come to pass, in God's time, as the first promise that the Messiah would come of the seed of woman. Remember His word is both faithful and factual. He will come to receive us unto Himself and then we shall ever be with the Lord. The promise is a challenge as well as comfort to all our hearts.

Thirdly the information contains *a prayer* in verse 20 in the words, "*Amen come, Lord Jesus.*" This was the prayer of John who represents the church in response to what he had seen and heard. This is the prayer saints have prayed for generations. It is a prayer that is close to being answered by the Father. Are you praying for His return? Are you prepared for His return? Those that are prepared join John in praying "Come, Lord Jesus come."

Fourthly the information contains *the provisions* in verse 21 in the words, *"The grace of our Lord Jesus Christ be with you all."* Our Lord Jesus has provided the provision for our living a life of victory and that is "His grace." What do I need that His grace has not already provided for me? I must in faith appropriate His grace. We have sung it a thousand times but its words are still true, "Amazing grace how sweet the sound that saved a wretch like me, I once was lost but now am found, was blind but now I see."

Conclusion:
What are we to do till Jesus comes? We are to be engaged in pondering the word, in properly worshipping and in proclaiming the word. What are you presently doing with your love, life and labor? You will probably be doing the same thing when He comes. Is that the way you desire to meet Jesus? If not His grace is sufficient to impart to you the courage to trust Him to change you.

Bibliography

Anderson, Robert, Sir; *Forgotten Truths*
Bloomfield, Arthur E.; *Before The Last Battle*
Bloomfield, Arthur E.; *How To Recognize the Antichrist*
Chappell, Clovis G.; *Sermons From Revelation*
Criswell, W. A.; *Expository Sermons on Revelation*
De Haan, M. R.; *Revelation*
Gaebelein, C. Arno; *The Revelation*
Greene, Oliver B.; *The Revelation*
Halsey, Laura A.; *Notes on the Revelation*
Ironside, H. A.; *Lectures on The Revelation*
James, Edgar O.; *Day of the Lamb*
Jeffrey, Grant R.; *Armageddon Appointment With Destiny*
Kirban, Salem; *The Day Israel Dies*
LaHaye, Tim; *The Beginning of the End*
Larkin, Clarence; *The Book of Revelation*
Levitt, Zola; *The Cairo Connection*
Lindsey, Hal; *The Late Great Planet Earth*
Lindsey, Hal; *There's A New World Coming*
McGee, J. Vernon; *Revealing Through Revelation*
Nee, Watchman; *Come, Lord Jesus*
Odle, Joe, T.; *Is Christ Coming Soon?*
Pache, Rene; *The Return of Jesus Christ*
Phillips, John; *Exploring Revelation*
Richards, E. H. *The Revelation Letters*
Rivers, William; *Revelation: A Study Guide*
Ryrie, Charles Caldwell; *The Living End*
Ryrie, Charles Caldwell; *Revelation*
Seiss, J. A.; *The Apocalypse*
Stedman, Ray, C.; *What On Earth's Going to Happen*
Strauss, Lehman; *The Book of the Revelation*
Strauss, Lehman; *The End of this Present World*

Strauss, Lehman; *God's Plan for the Future*
Van Gorder, John S.; *A.B.C.'s of the Revelation*
Vines, Jerry; *I Shall Return...Jesus*
Willimington, H. L.; *The King is Coming*
White, Wesley, John; *The Coming World Dictator*

Commentaries

In addition to the books the sources and references used are:
Clarke, Adam Commentary
Barnes Notes Volume 14
Beacon Bible Commentary Volume 10
Ellicott's Commentary on the Whole Bible
Maclaren, Alexander; Exposition of Holy Scripture
MacArthur, John; New Testament Commentary
Meyer, F.B.; Bible Commentary
Erdman, Charles R.; Commentaries on the New Testament Volume 17
Expositor's Bible Volume 5
Henry, Carl F.; The Biblical Expositor
Henry, Matthew Volume 6
Jamieson, Fausset, Brown Commentary
Layman's Bible Book Commentary Volume 24
The Preacher's Homiletic Commentary Volume 31
The Pulpit Commentary
Simeon, Charles; Expository Outlines on the Whole Bible Volume 21
Wycliffe Bible Commentary

Bibles, Word Studies, Dictionaries

The Kirban Reference Bible, King James
The MacArthur Study Bible, New King James
The Ryrie Study Bible, New American Standard
The Zodhiates Study Bible, King James

The Apocalypse: The Revelation of the Redeemer

Robertson, A. T.; *Word Pictures in the New Testament*
Vincent, M. R.; *Word Studies in the New Testament*
Zodhiates, Spiros; *The Complete Word Study, New Testament*

The Englishman's Greek Concordance of The New Testament
Vine, W.E.; *Expository Dictionary of New Testament Words*
Brown, Colin; Editor: *Dictionary of New Testament Theology*

Printed in the United States
77171LV00001B/88-129